Quilting school

Quilting school

Ann Poe

Contributing Editor

Angela Besley

THE READER'S DIGEST ASSOCIATION, INC.
Pleasantville, New York
Montreal

QUILTING SCHOOL

A READER'S DIGEST BOOK

Designed and edited by Quarto Publishing plc

The acknowledgments that appear on page 176 are hereby made a part of this copyright page.

Library of Congress Cataloging in Publication Data

Poe, Ann.
Quilting school / Ann Poe.
p. cm. – (Reader's Digest learn-as-you-go guides)
Includes index.
ISBN 0-89577-471-2
1. Quilting–Handbooks, manuals, etc.
I. Title. II. Series.
TT835.P63 1993
746.46–dc20 92-43792

Senior Editor: *Honor Head*
Editor: *Maggi McCormick*
Publishing Director: *Janet Slingsby*
Art Director: *Moira Clinch*
Senior Art Editor: *Amanda Bakhtiar*
Designer: *Sheila Volpe*
Illustrator: *Sally Launder*
Photographer: *Paul Forrester, Chas Wilder*
Picture Researcher: *Carmen Jones*
Picture Manager: *Rebecca Horsewood*

Printed in Singapore by Star Standard Industries Pte. Ltd.

CONTENTS

SECTION 4

EXTENDING YOUR SKILLS

SECTION 5

PATTERN LIBRARY

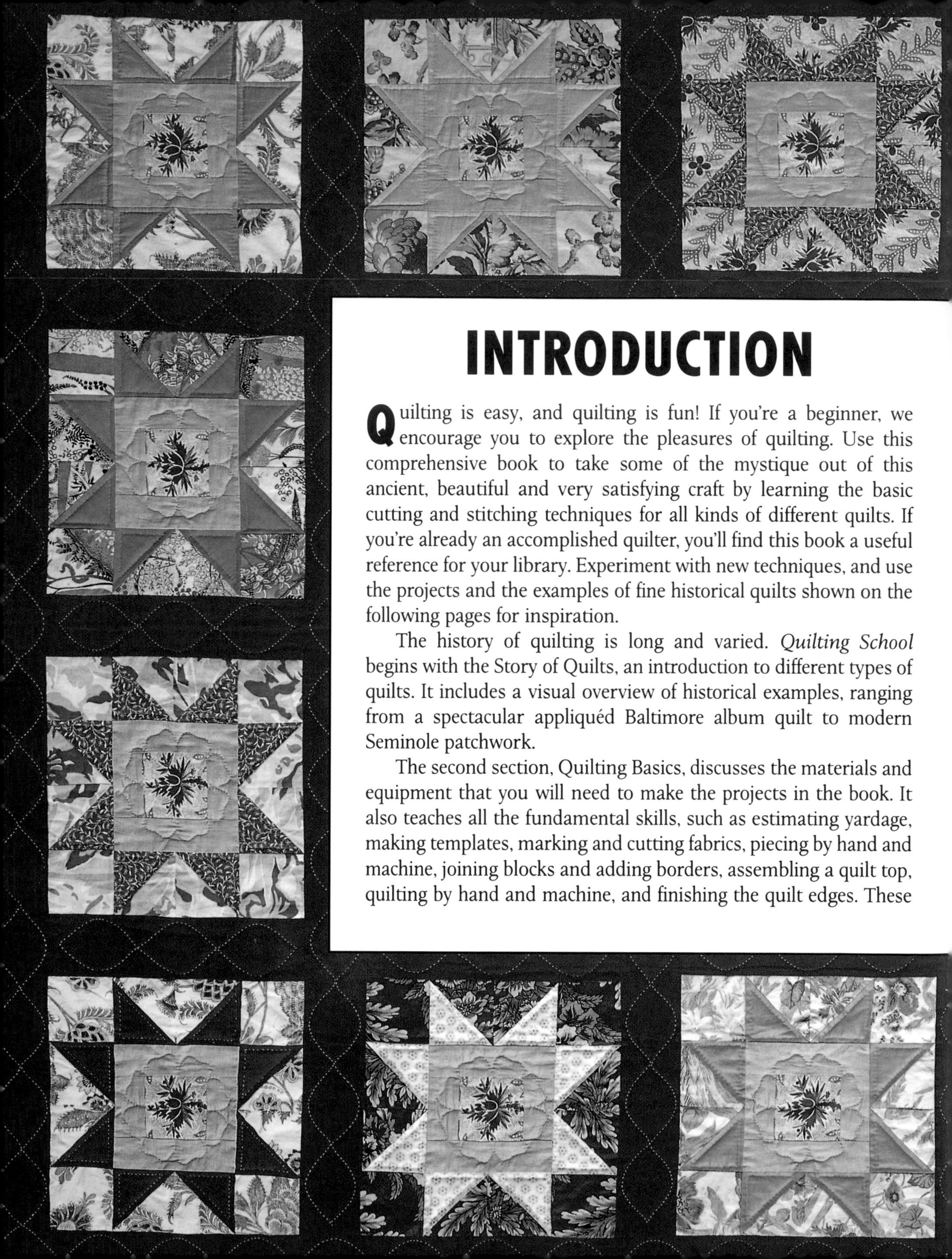

INTRODUCTION

Quilting is easy, and quilting is fun! If you're a beginner, we encourage you to explore the pleasures of quilting. Use this comprehensive book to take some of the mystique out of this ancient, beautiful and very satisfying craft by learning the basic cutting and stitching techniques for all kinds of different quilts. If you're already an accomplished quilter, you'll find this book a useful reference for your library. Experiment with new techniques, and use the projects and the examples of fine historical quilts shown on the following pages for inspiration.

The history of quilting is long and varied. *Quilting School* begins with the Story of Quilts, an introduction to different types of quilts. It includes a visual overview of historical examples, ranging from a spectacular appliquéd Baltimore album quilt to modern Seminole patchwork.

The second section, Quilting Basics, discusses the materials and equipment that you will need to make the projects in the book. It also teaches all the fundamental skills, such as estimating yardage, making templates, marking and cutting fabrics, piecing by hand and machine, joining blocks and adding borders, assembling a quilt top, quilting by hand and machine, and finishing the quilt edges. These

are techniques you will need for making the sampler quilt in the next section, and they will help you stitch many more patchwork and quilting designs, traditional and modern.

The next section, the Sampler Quilt, takes you step-by-step through the stages of making a quilt, from creating nine different blocks to the final binding. Every stage is clearly shown, so that you learn how to make the various blocks, add sashing, make and add a checkered border, and finally mark, quilt, and finish your quilt. If you do the lessons in this section, you will end up with a beautiful sampler quilt in traditional colors.

Extending Your Skills introduces some of the more unusual types of piecing and quilting, including sashiko, trapunto, Italian cording, wholecloth quilting, and English patchwork. Each new skill features full instructions for a simple project.

The Pattern Library illustrates a wide range of the most popular quilting and piecing designs. Use these for your own projects or substitute them for some of the designs used in the sampler quilt.

The final section gives you advice on restoring, caring for, and displaying quilts. A glossary of common patchwork and quilting terms is in the back of the book.

1

The story of quilts

The story of patchwork and quilting is extensive and intriguing. Techniques are rooted in the practical details of everyday life in times before most people had the leisure to pursue arts and crafts for their own sake. Piecing was a necessary skill, so that leftover dressmaking scraps or the best parts of worn clothing could be used and re-used for economy when fabric was still a precious commodity. People kept

The story of quilts

warm with quilting in clothes and bedcovers; soldiers wore quilted armor and padded jackets for protection.

But human beings are naturally creative and as patchwork and quilting developed, designs began to appear. Rather than piece or stitch haphazardly, sewers began to use particular patterns, which were refined and developed while being handed down from generation to generation. Craftspeople, itinerant workers, and patternmakers spread new ideas to different areas; certain places and peoples developed their own specialized techniques, a process which continues today.

To give you an overview of some of the main types of quilting, we have put together a gallery of fine historical examples, showing the skill and versatility of our ancestors.

Shells, flowers, and interlocking chains have been combined in this wholecloth quilt dating from 1935; the main motifs have been set off by the contrasting checkerboard background texture, worked both straight and diagonally.

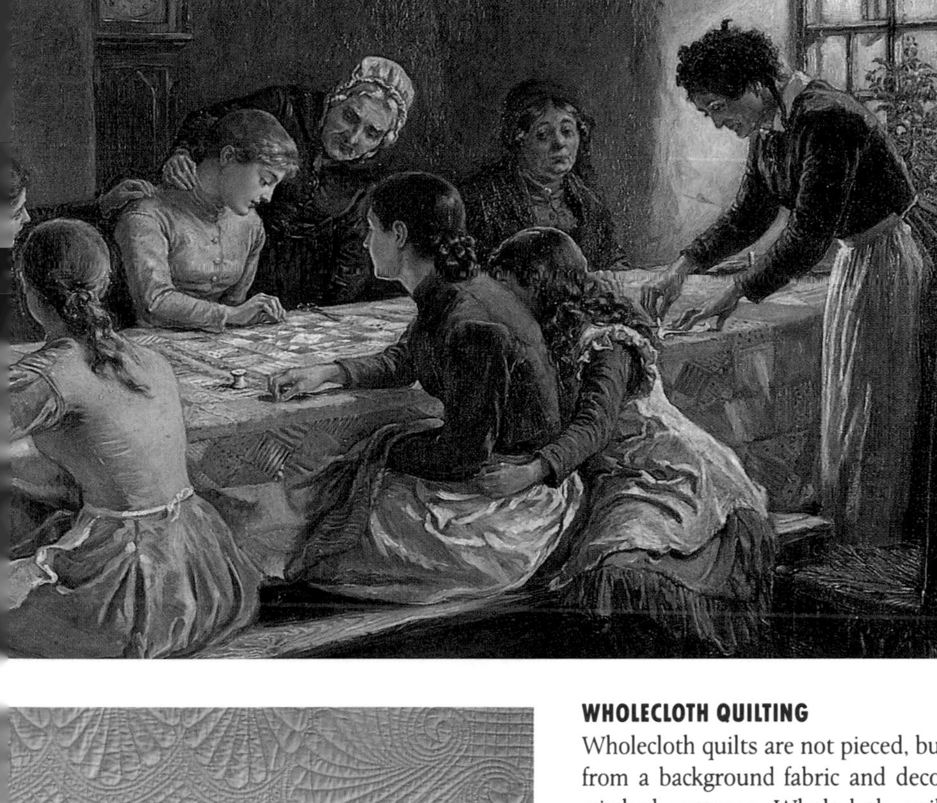

This 19th century painting called The Wedding Quilt *by Ralph Hedley, shows women and girls sewing at a quilting bee.*

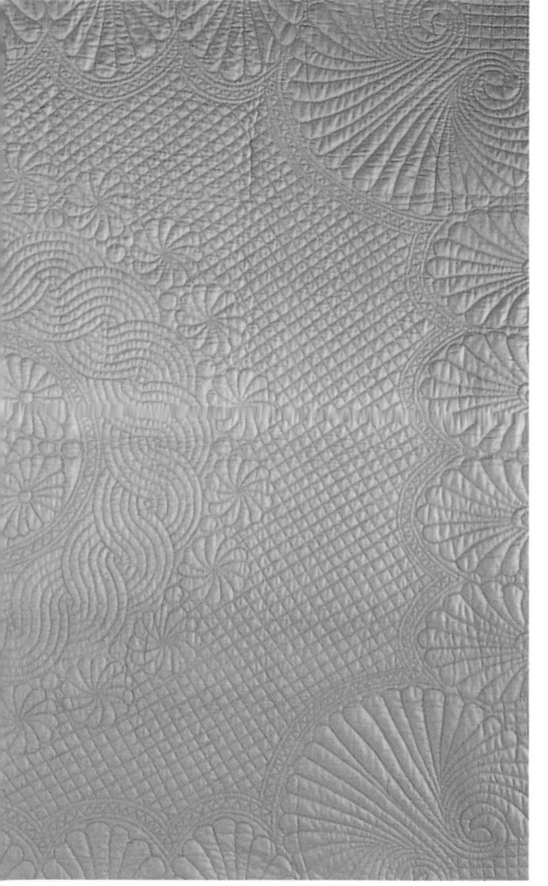

WHOLECLOTH QUILTING

Wholecloth quilts are not pieced, but are made from a background fabric and decorated with stitched patterns. Wholecloth quilting dates back several hundred years in many traditions, especially in the North of England, Wales, and North America. The fabrics and battings used depended on the materials most easily available in the area. The quilting is often worked in the same color thread as the background fabric, although occasionally a contrast color is used. The traditional quilting stitch is a running stitch, worked through all three layers of top fabric, batting, and backing fabric; the stitch holds the batting in place.

The designs of wholecloth quilts were usually inspired by everyday objects – leaves, flowers, feathers, goose tails and wings, cords, fans, shells. Leaf shapes were often created by drawing using a flat-iron as a template; one side of the iron would be traced, then turned around for the other half of the leaf shape. Because quilting was usually done in groups, it is difficult to know where the traditional designs originated; individual quilters would add their own touches to the chosen patterns.

AMERICAN BLOCK QUILTS

Traditional American quilts were often pieced in square blocks. Stitching one block made the work easily portable, and blocks could be stockpiled until there were enough for a whole quilt top. In the earliest quilts from colonial days, the seams were stitched by hand. With the advent of the sewing machine, the stitching became much quicker, but many quilts are still pieced by hand in blocks.

The range of block designs is phenomenal, many of them with evocative names like Oh Susannah, Goose in the Pond, Rising Star, and Steps to the Altar.

It was customary for an unmarried girl to piece quilt tops and store them in her Hope Chest. When she became engaged, her friends and relatives would join in, add remaining layers of batting and backing, then stretch, stitch, and finish the quilts, helping her get ready for her new life as a married woman.

Despite the wandering appearance of the overall pattern, this quilt is actually made in blocks; pieced blocks of 25 squares alternate with plain white blocks that have had small squares appliquéd in the corners. The design is known as Irish Chain.

The vivid colors, multiple borders, and central diamond of this quilt are all typical features of Amish quilts – finished with exquisite quilting in every section.

AMISH QUILTS

The Amish people take their name from Joseph Amman, a Swiss who was a model of conservatism. When William Penn invited persecuted people to join him in his new land, the Amish went from Switzerland, Germany, and the Alsace to America. Still clinging tenaciously to their clothing styles, traditions, and religious observances from centuries past, the Amish people today live apart from their fellow countrymen and follow a simple way of life.

With this stress on simplicity, it is easy to appreciate the stark beauty of the Amish quilts. Many of them are made from the plain hand-dyed fabrics also used in the traditional Amish clothing. Sometimes large sections of solid-color cloth are used in the quilts instead of pieced blocks. The quilts may have one or more borders and are always quilted with exquisite and intricate designs, sometimes stitched in a contrasting color such as orange or purple. Often the large areas of pure colors are offset by black borders or binding.

ENGLISH PATCHWORK

English patchwork differs dramatically in technique from American patchwork but possesses an equally noble history. The earliest known example dates from 1708. In English patchwork, the fabric pieces are basted over paper shapes, then sewn together to form a simple or complex pattern. As with many other techniques, English patchwork from different eras varies in appearance with the kind of fabrics that were fashionable at the time. When exotic prints were imported in large quantities from the Middle East in the 19th century, patchwork was made from those; when Britain began producing inexpensive cotton print fabrics later on, the appearance of the patchwork changed accordingly.

During Queen Victoria's long reign, patchwork made from pieces of solid colored silk became extremely popular; certain patterns, such as diamonds and hexagons, were especially in vogue. English patchwork has been very useful for social historians because it was often worked in scrap fabrics such as pattern samples from mills. Also, the papers used in the inner templates were often cut from old letters, ledgers, and books, and provide fascinating information when pieced together from unfinished bits of patchwork.

The bright solid colors and geometric design of this quilt, dating from the end of last century, are typical of English patchwork at its height.

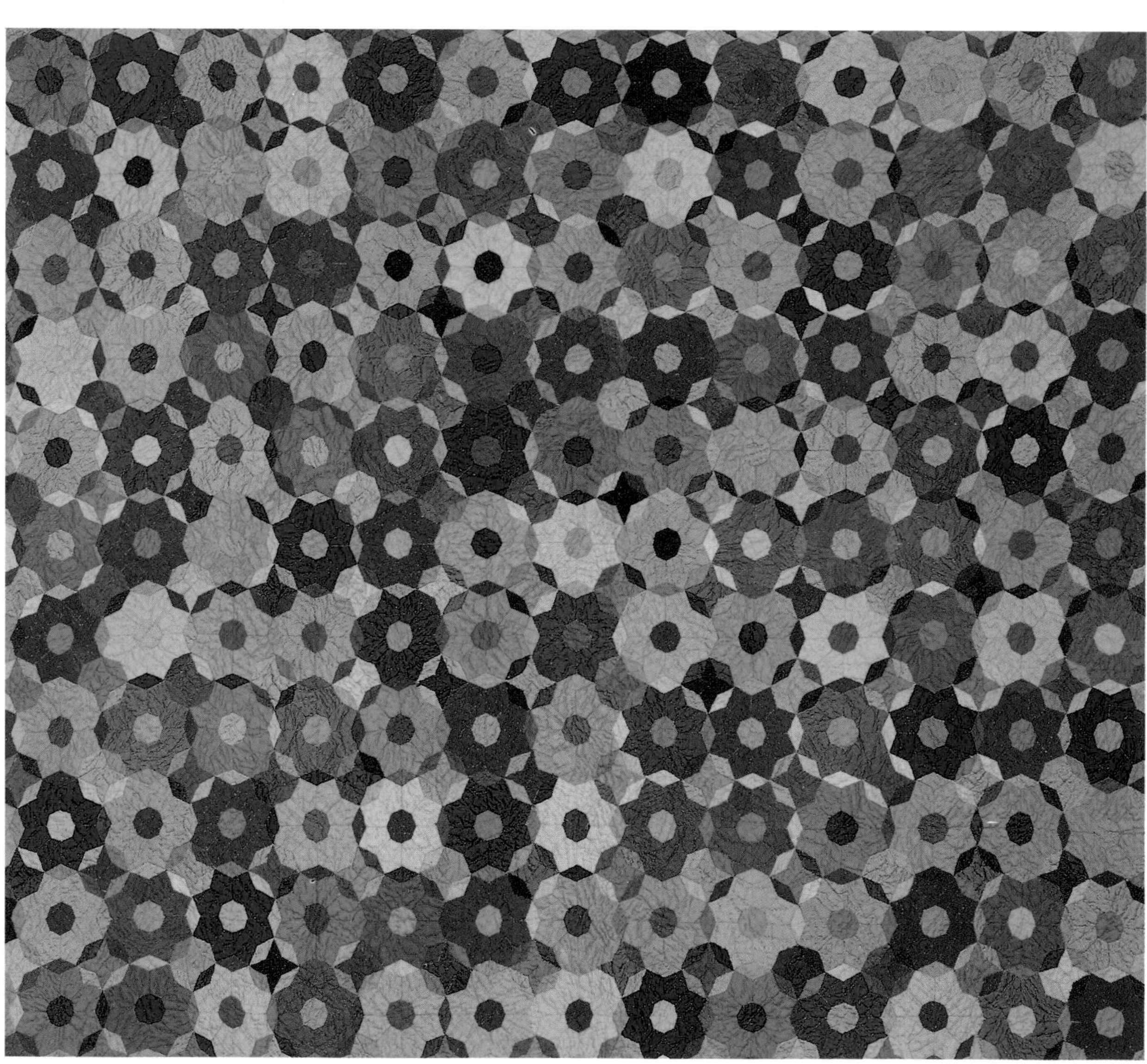

The red dye used on this quilt, dating from the turn of the century, was known as Turkey Red and was one of the most popular colors for this kind of simple appliqué.

APPLIQUÉ

Appliqué has been around for many centuries; the first person to sew a patch on worn clothing was using appliqué. Traditional appliqué in quilts involved arranging fabric shapes – often natural forms such as petals, leaves, berries, animals, or feathers – in a pleasing design on a background. The fabric shapes were then sewn into place with tiny invisible stitches; raw edges were turned under so they didn't fray or were held in place with a decorative stitch.

Early appliqué quilts often used a simple color scheme, perhaps one or two strong colors on a plain white background. Some of these quilts were called turkey quilts because a certain shade of red known as turkey red was a popular choice. Another form of applied stitching was crazy quilting – random shapes of patchwork, often made from velvets and other fancy fabrics, were embellished with embroidery, beadwork, and patriotic slogans. Broderie perse was also popular; this method involved cutting motifs from several printed fabrics, arranging and stitching them onto a background fabric, and embellishing the new design, if desired.

A spectacular example of a Baltimore album quilt, featuring many complex and beautifully executed appliqué designs, including many typical garlands and vases of flowers, and several versions of the American eagle.

ALBUM QUILTS

Album, or friendship, quilts are a specialized type of quilt originating in America. The original album quilts were usually done as gifts, perhaps for a wedding or if a friend was moving. These quilts are generally stitched in blocks, but in true album quilts, each block is a different design and often was stitched by a different person. Christmas Cactus and Basket blocks were favorite designs, and occasionally three-dimensional flower motifs were appliquéd; the designs are sometimes breathtakingly detailed. The colors and patterns were usually carefully chosen so that the whole quilt harmonized when assembled; red and green on a white background was a favorite color scheme. On some examples the names of the

quilters were embroidered on the blocks.

The most spectacular examples of album quilts were done in the Baltimore area, so album quilts are often known as Baltimore quilts. Genuine Baltimore quilts are highly sought after and prized by collectors. Album quilts are still made today; they are popular as community and school projects.

SEMINOLE PATCHWORK

The Seminole Indians of Florida developed distinctive patchwork designs in strip-pieced patterned bands. The technique seems to have developed in the late 1800s when the sewing machine became available to them.

The technique involves strip piecing two or more long pieces of fabric and then cutting the new fabric into secondary strips. The secondary strips are then laid out and joined in a new relationship to each other, forming patterned bands which can be quite complex. The Seminoles generally use the bands on garments, but they can be used to create large decorative pieces as well.

Many different geometric patterns can be seen in this striking example of Seminole patchwork, worked in a limited color scheme of bright solid fabrics set off by the black border.

The spiky plant design worked in a solid-colored appliqué on a white background, is typical of Hawaiian Kapa Lau work.

HAWAIIAN APPLIQUÉ

Hawaii has developed its own form of appliqué called Kapa Lau. It is made by stitching one large, carefully shaped piece of fabric onto a plain background. American missionaries showed the islanders how to fold paper and cut it into shapes like simple plants or snowflakes; the unfolded paper was then used as a pattern for cutting the appliqué fabric. Hawaiians soon developed their own designs, and the original small patterns became larger and larger, many of them based on the luxuriant foliage of the island such as pineapples, breadfruit trees, ferns, palms, and paw-paws.

Once the design has been cut out, it is basted to a background fabric and the edges are carefully turned under and stitched down. This is a very time-consuming process, for some of the designs are extremely complicated. Once the appliqué is complete, the area beyond the appliqué is usually quilted with echo quilting – lines of stitching that echo the outline of the appliqué shape.

TRAPUNTO QUILTING

Trapunto, or stuffed, quilting is a specialized technique that involves stitching two layers of fabric together in shaped pockets which can then be stuffed. Stuffing is inserted through the backing fabric (if it is loosely woven) or through a slit which is later sewn closed. Raised appliqué work of this kind is common in ecclesiastical embroidery.

In 18th and 19th century trapunto quilts, most of the quilt would be quilted in the ordinary way, then a central motif or medallion was given an extra layer of stuffing to raise it. It is an effective way to draw attention to a particular part of a design.

This quilt shows an attractive combination of appliqué and quilting in a subtle color scheme; the border of grapes and the delicate outer border provide an attractive frame for the geometric central design.

ITALIAN QUILTING

Italian, or corded, quilting involves threading cords through channels stitched in a double layer of fabric; the corded design stands out in relief from its background. Despite its name, it did not develop solely in Italy; corded quilting is found in artefacts from many Asian and Middle Eastern countries as well as European ones. Wonderful examples have survived from the 18th and 19th centuries in England of whole bedcovers decorated with tiny, elaborate, intricate corded quilting designs.

Linear designs lend themselves well to Italian quilting, but the design can be as fine or as bold as you wish. Modern quilters have experimented using everything from thin yarn to rope for the cording and leather to net for the fabric.

This corded and quilted hat dates from the early 20th century; it was made in Northern India.

2

Quilting basics

Making a traditional quilt is not an activity that can be rushed; that is part of its charm. There are several different stages, from choosing the fabric and working out the design, through cutting, piecing, backing and quilting, to the final finishing by binding the raw edges. The main stages of quilt making have a logical order, and in the pages that follow we take you through them one by one. Occasionally, a stage

QUILTING BASICS

Elements of a quilt

may not be necessary; for instance, you will not need to draw a design and make templates if you are using commercial templates, but generally each step will be covered in some way.

But first you'll need to understand the terms that quilters use; like every other art and craft, quilting has its own special vocabulary. Words and phrases like basting, batting, piecing, sashing, setting blocks, and quilt top can all seem strange and bewildering if you're a beginner, but you'll quickly become used to them, and like the stages in quilt making, they are all perfectly logical. On these pages, we introduce you to the common terms for the different parts of a quilt and the various processes involved. The same terms will be used throughout the book.

Binding *is the edging of the quilt, and covers all the raw edges neatly. It also contributes to the overall effect of the design. There are several ways of binding quilt edges (see page 98).*

A block *is a section of patchwork stitched in a regular shape, usually a square. Traditional quilts are often built up from several individual blocks; the blocks may be identical or may vary in design. In our sampler quilt, we use nine different square block designs.*

Piecing *or* **patchwork** *refers to pieces of fabric cut in specific shapes and then stitched together in a decorative design.*

Basting *is used to hold the three layers of the quilt together; the lines of basting threads, worked in a grid across the quilt (see page 52), hold the layers in place while they are being quilted.*

Backing fabric *provides a neat finish for the back of the quilt; the batting is concealed between it and the quilt top.*

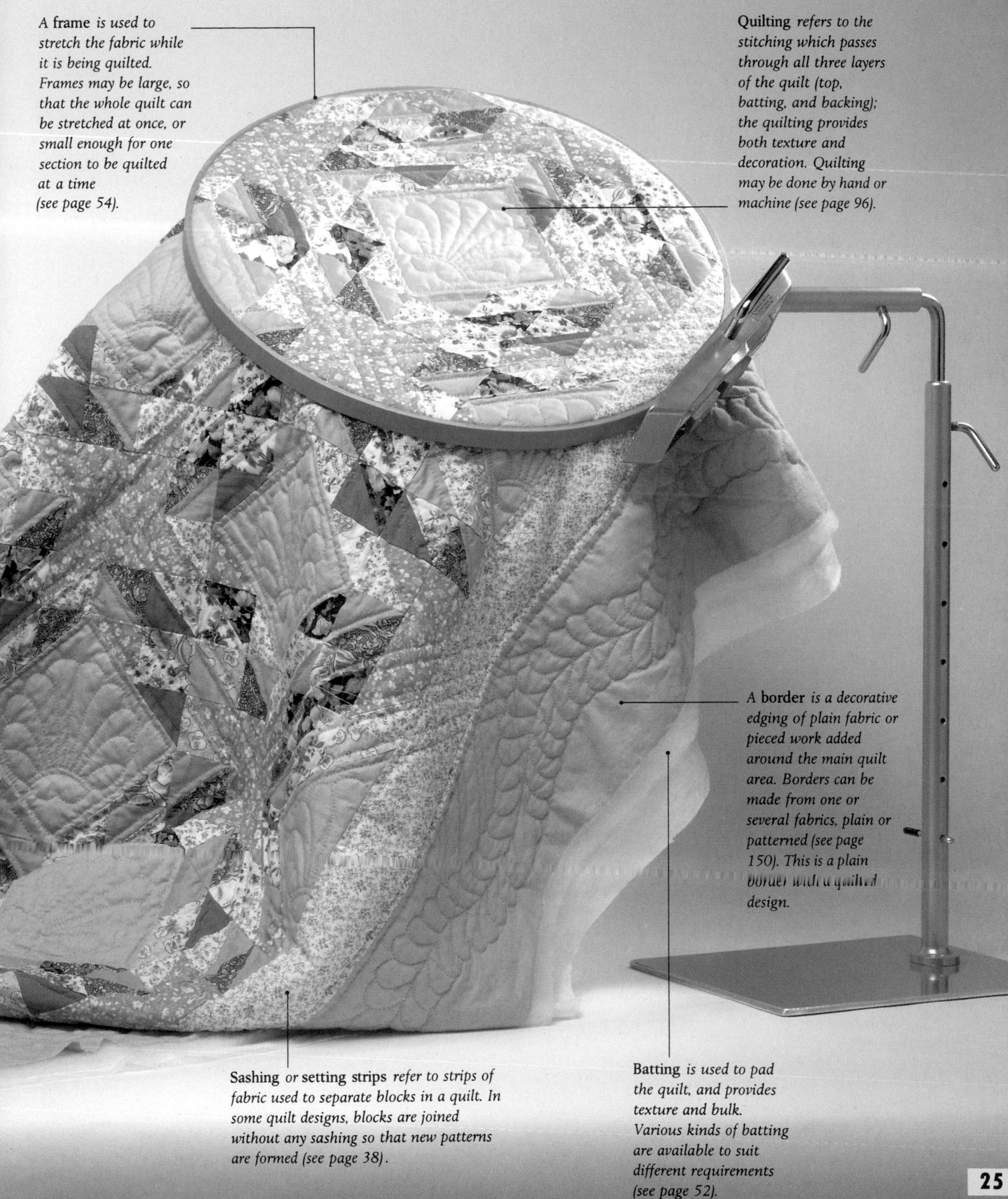
A frame *is used to stretch the fabric while it is being quilted. Frames may be large, so that the whole quilt can be stretched at once, or small enough for one section to be quilted at a time (see page 54).*
Quilting *refers to the stitching which passes through all three layers of the quilt (top, batting, and backing); the quilting provides both texture and decoration. Quilting may be done by hand or machine (see page 96).*
A border *is a decorative edging of plain fabric or pieced work added around the main quilt area. Borders can be made from one or several fabrics, plain or patterned (see page 150). This is a plain border with a quilted design.*
Sashing *or* **setting strips** *refer to strips of fabric used to separate blocks in a quilt. In some quilt designs, blocks are joined without any sashing so that new patterns are formed (see page 38).*
Batting *is used to pad the quilt, and provides texture and bulk. Various kinds of batting are available to suit different requirements (see page 52).*

Equipment

While there is plenty of specialized equipment available to help the quilter, not very much of it is essential; most of the tasks of making templates, cutting and piecing fabric, and marking and stitching quilting patterns can be done with general drawing and sewing equipment that you will probably already have in your house. If you are just beginning quilting, start off with the essentials, marked with a bullet (•) below; they will provide all that you need to make the projects in this book. As you want to extend your quilting skills, acquire the more specialist items listed: they will save you time as you cut and stitch.

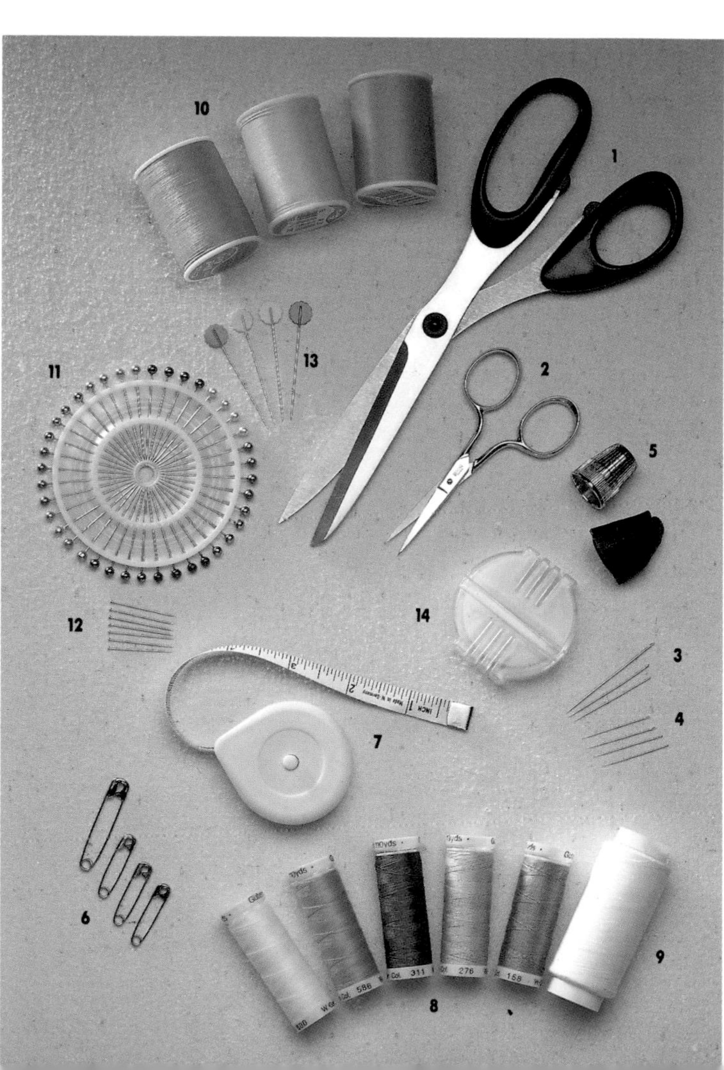

► General sewing equipment

- **1** *Large scissors for cutting fabric*
- **2** *Small, sharp-pointed embroidery scissors*
- **3** *Selection of sewing needles*
- **4** *Quilting needles*
- **5** *Thimbles*
- **6** *Safety pins*
- **7** *Tape measure*
- **8** *Cotton or polyester sewing thread*
- **9** *Basting thread*
- **10** *Quilting thread*
- **11** *Pins, preferably glass-headed (they are easily visible and can't accidentally be ironed over)*
- **12** *Extra-fine pins for silks and satins*
- **13** *Flat-headed pins (useful when machine-stitching as they don't catch in the foot)*
- **14** *Beeswax and beeswax holder*

Even-feed foot for sewing machine
Sewing machine
Thumble (used on the thumb of your quilting hand)

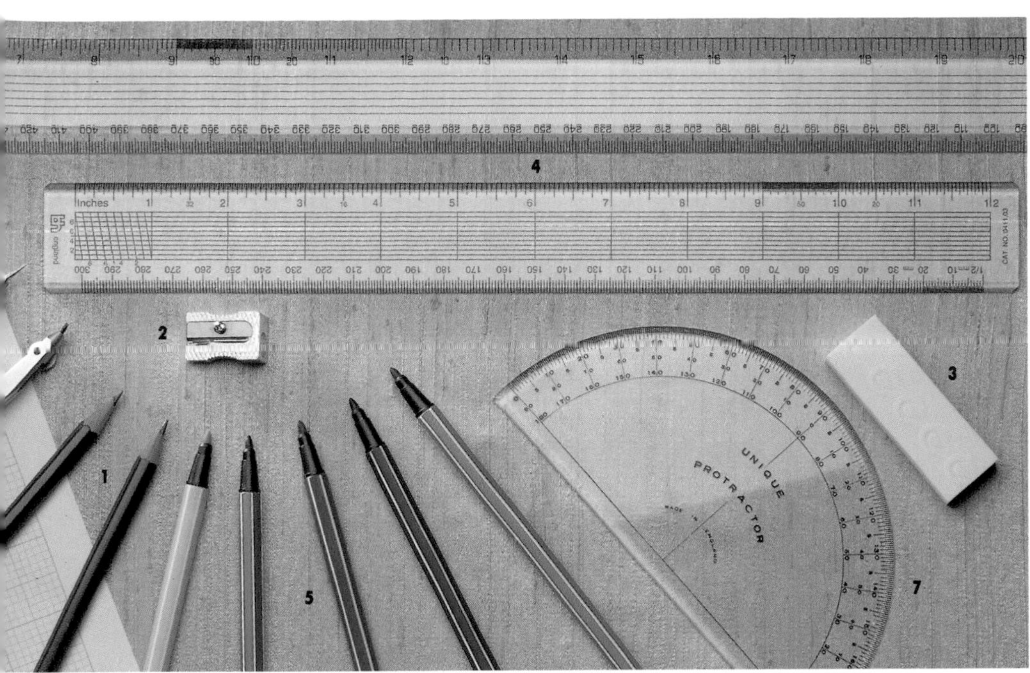

◄ **General drawing equipment**

- **1** *Pencils – both medium-hard and soft, HB and 2B*
- **2** *Pencil sharpener*
- **3** *Eraser*
- **4** *Short and long rulers (12 in. and 24 in.)*
- **5** *Crayons or felt-tip pens*

6 *Set square*
7 *Protractor*
8 *Graph paper*
9 *Compass*

▼► **Frames**

- *Quilting frames (you will only need one type: circular, rectangular, oval, rolling, slate, floor-standing, full-size)*

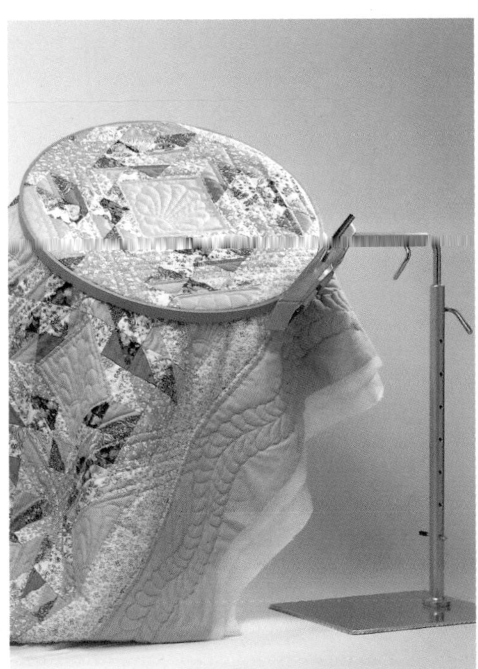

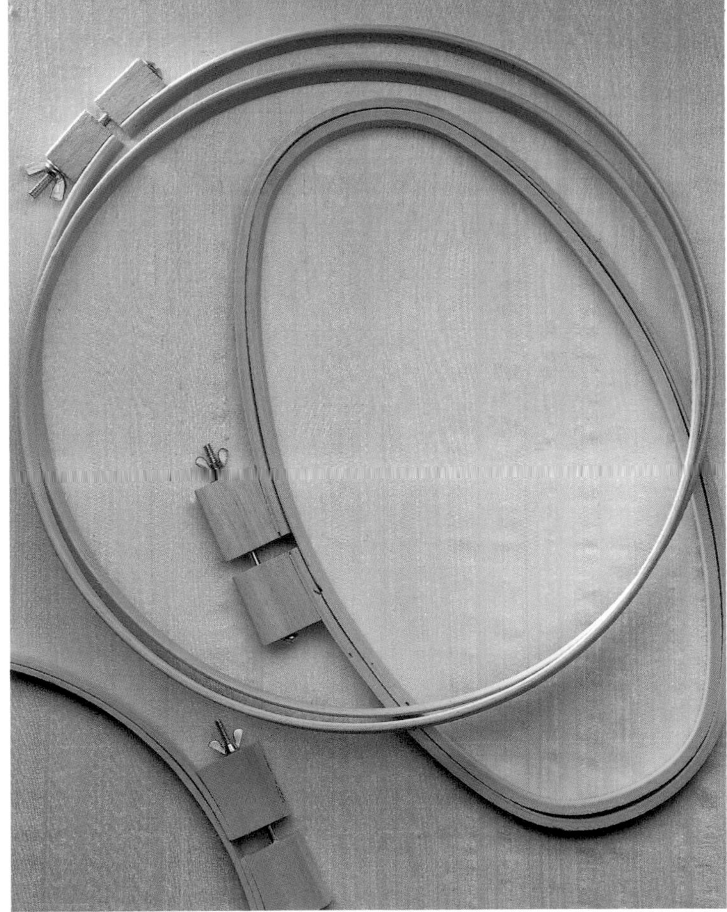

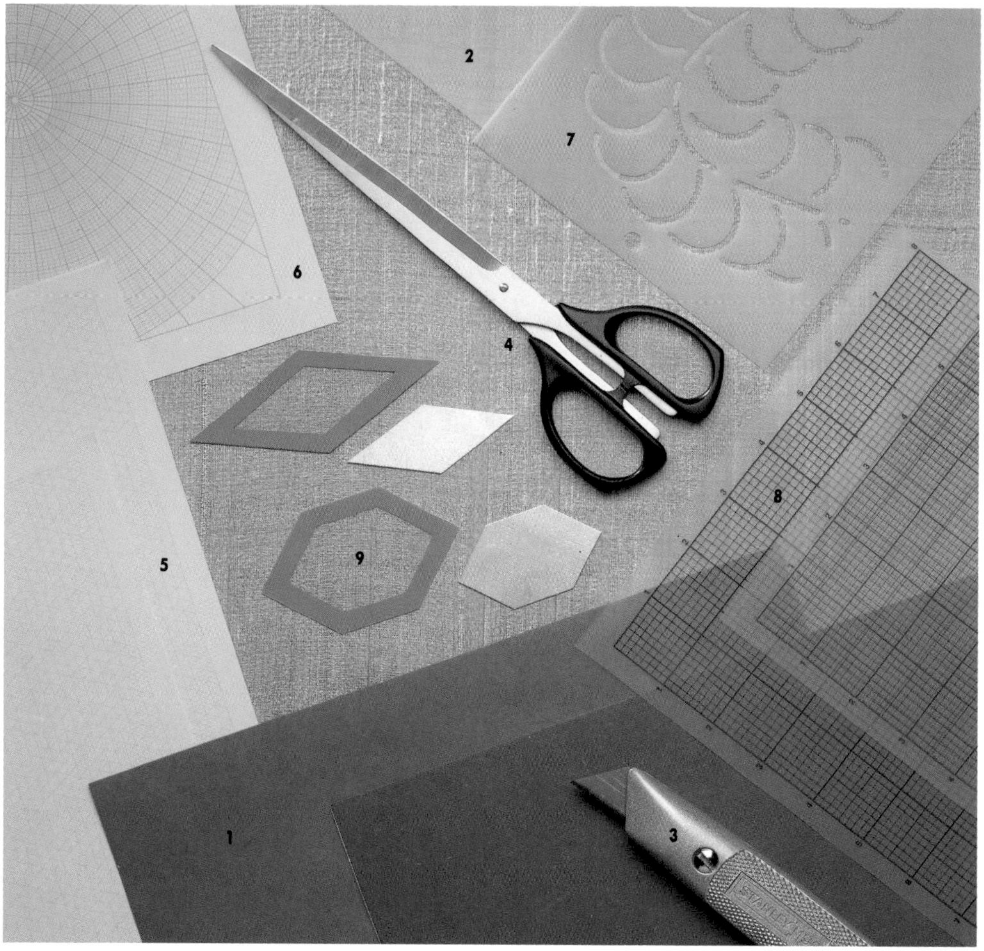

◀ **Templates and template materials**

- **1** *Cardboard*
- **2** *Plain template plastic*
- **3** *Craft knife*
- **4** *Paper scissors*

5 *Isometric graph paper*

6 *Polar coordinate graph paper*

7 *Quilting templates in different designs*

8 *Sheets of template plastic marked with guide rules*

9 *Window template (for positioning a printed motif accurately within the template shape)*

Patchwork templates in different designs

▶ **Equipment for cutting accurate fabric patches**

- **1** *Rotary cutter*
- **2** *"Self-healing" specialized cutting mat with cutting guides for templates*

3 *Sandpaper grips (used on the corners of rulers and templates to stop fabric from slipping while you cut)*

4 *45° Kaleidoscope wedge ruler*

5 *Omnigrid (a useful guide for cutting many different templates)*

6 *Multi Miter (a guide for miters of different angles)*

7 *Scrapsaver ruler*

8 *BiRangle for cutting half rectangles*

9 *Magic Star for cutting 8-pointed stars*

10 *Quilter's Rule*

11 *9 inch Circle Wedge*

Quilt and Sew ruler
Easy Angle (for cutting accurate triangles)
Lip edge ruler
Pineapple ruler (measures accurate 45° sections)
Salem ruler (a guide marked with 60° and 45° angles)
Super Seamer ruler (for adding seam allowances to templates and fabric pieces)

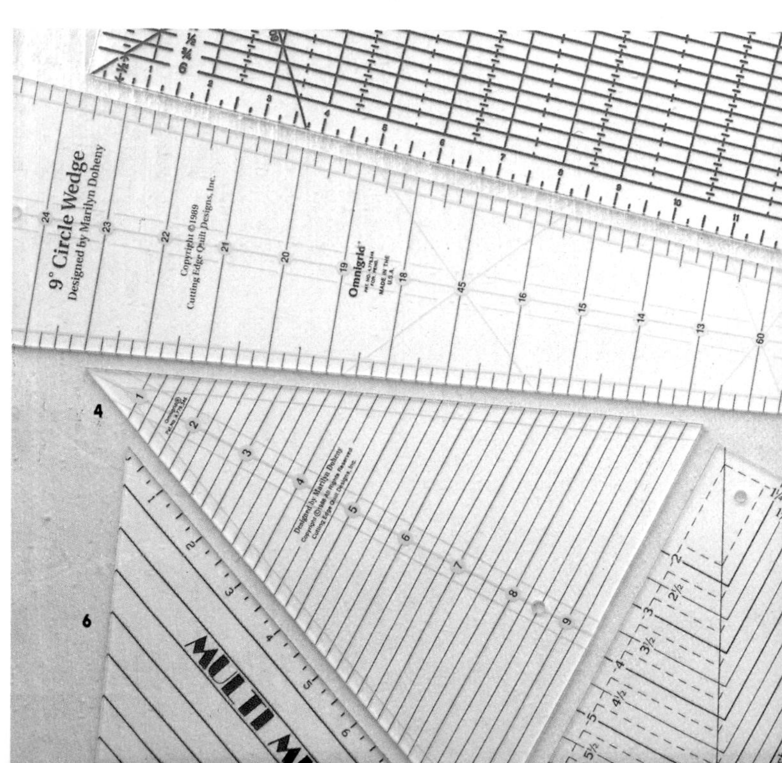

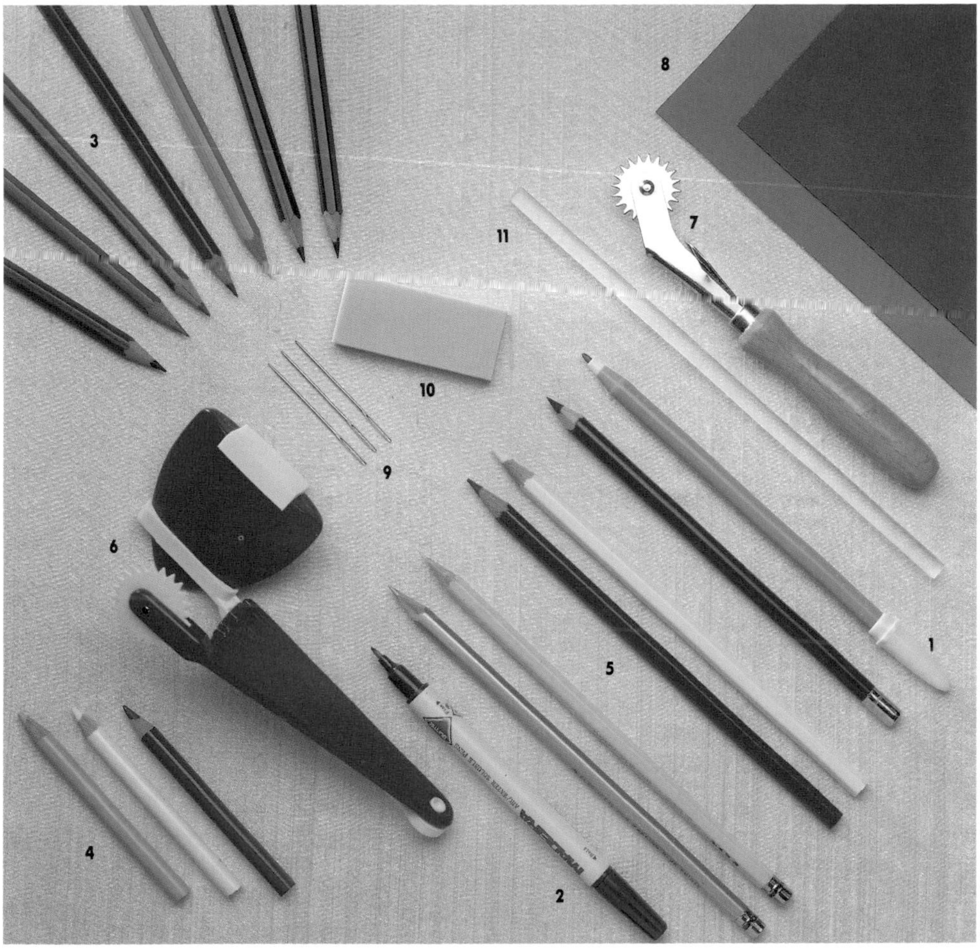

◄ **Equipment for marking fabrics**

- **1** *Soluble-ink pens (marks can be removed with cold water)*
  2 *Fading-ink pen (marks fade gradually when exposed to air)*
  3 *Colored pencils*
  4 *Cloth markers*
  5 *Colored marking pencils*
  6 *Tracing wheel with chalk holder*
  7 *Prick and pounce wheel*
  8 *Dressmaker's carbon paper (available in several colors)*
  9 *Blunt tapestry needles*
  10 *Fabric eraser (for removing ordinary pencil marks from fabric)*
  11 *Quilter's quarter (adds 1/4 in. to straight edges)*

Bodkin
Silverpoint (pencil-shaped metal implement used for marking fabrics)
Transfer pens (for drawing on transfers)

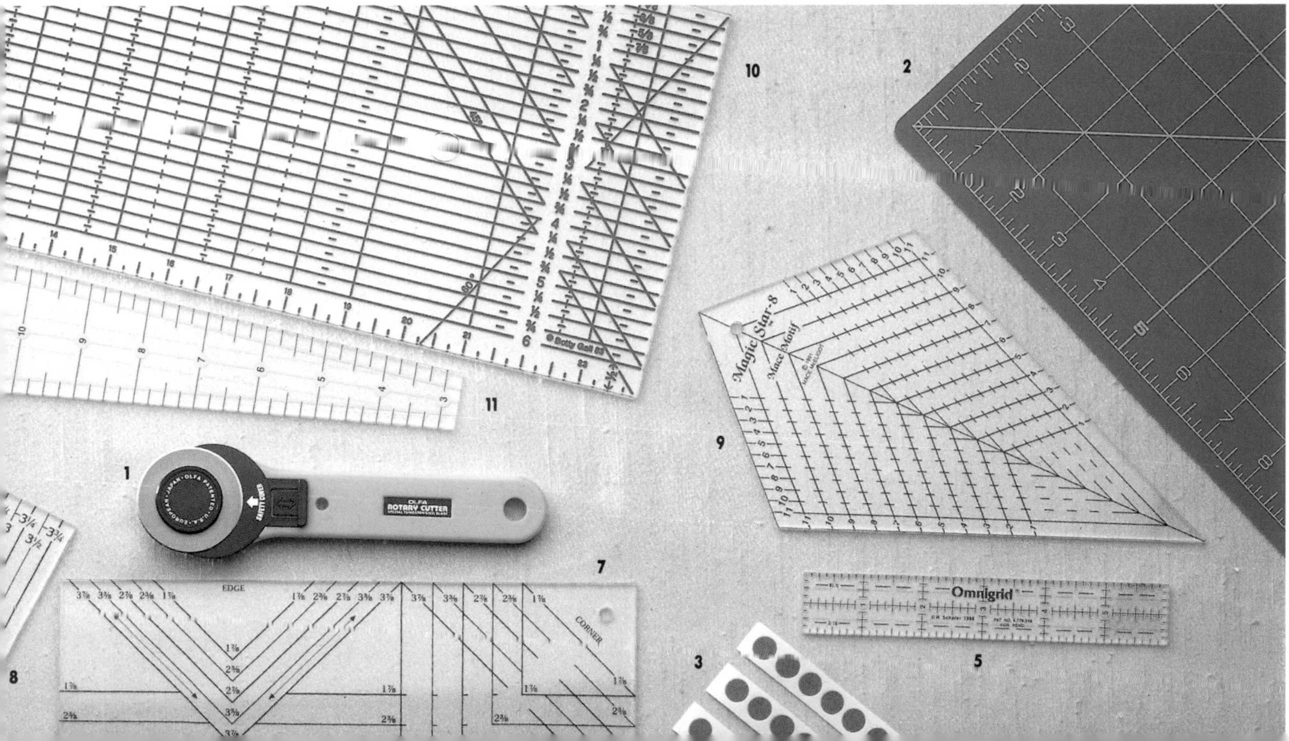

Choosing fabrics

In the early days of patchwork, people would simply use what was available, usually the best parts left in worn-out clothing or bedding. In fact, that was how the whole craft of patchwork began; it was born from necessity, when fabric was expensive and thrift was the order of the day. Nowadays, most of us buy patchwork fabrics new for each project, and there is an endless variety to select from: wool, cotton, synthetics, and novelty fabrics such as lamé, fur, plastic, and leather. In addition, many of these fabrics are available in a multitude of solid colors, prints, and textures, which can make your choice bewildering. How do you decide whether to use solid or printed fabrics? Large or small prints? Should you mix different types of fabric?

Although it seems a very mundane consideration, the first thing to decide is whether the finished article will need to be washed. Obviously, if you are making a quilt for your bed, a pillow cover, or a garment, at some stage the item will need washing, so you will have to use a fully washable fabric. The most suitable is lightweight 100% cotton, which holds its shape well, is washable, and is easy to stitch through several layers if you are quilting. Cotton/polyester blends are available in many pretty solids and prints, but generally they aren't so satisfactory for quilting; they slip around more while you are working on them, can be rather translucent, and are often more difficult to quilt through several layers.

All the fabrics you plan to use in a washable item must be soaked in warm water to pre-shrink them and to test them for color fastness. Light- to medium-colored ones can be washed by machine on a warm cycle, but dark colors are more likely to run and should be washed separately. Rinse the fabric until the water runs clear; if color is still bleeding from it after about six rinses, discard it – it could ruin

◄ **Cotton**
All of these fabrics are 100% cotton in different thicknesses. Cottons come in myriad prints and solid colors, and are the ideal quilting fabrics. Polished cotton and chintz have a shiny finish which looks very pretty in plain quilted areas; the glaze is diminished, though, by hot washing, and it makes it more difficult to work the quilting.

◄ **Cotton/polyester blends**
These fabrics are attractive, but don't have the density or firmness of cotton.

◄ **Polyester fabric**
Many polyester fabrics are unsuitable for quilting because they are slippery and loosely woven, but others, such as the firm polyester silks shown here, can be used to great effect in patchwork and quilting.

◄ **Satin**
Satin has a wonderful sheen and can be very dramatic used in stained glass patchwork (see page 108).

many hours of work if it runs when your finished patchwork item is washed. Once the fabric is dry, check whether the grain is straight; the visible horizontal and vertical threads (warp and weft) should be at right angles. If they aren't, gently pull the fabric diagonally to straighten the grain. Then press the fabric to remove the creases caused by washing. If you wash and press your fabrics as soon as you buy them, when inspiration strikes, you're all ready to cut and sew!

Some types of silks and satins can be washed; others have to be dry-cleaned; check with the supplier when you buy them, and don't mix the two types. Generally it's better to use the same kind of fabrics in a patchwork item – for instance, all cottons or all silks – unless you are mixing them for a particular effect. If you want the look of silk without the expense and the washing difficulties, polyester silks are available.

Finally, if you're making something which won't be washed, you can use any fabric. Thick fabrics such as linen, sailcloth and twill are usually too thick to be pieced or quilted successfully, while wool fabrics such as chambray are often too thin and too loosely woven. However, there are plenty of other fabrics to experiment with. Lamé patches here and there on a jacket or wallhanging give a wonderful sparkle; nets and voiles can be layered over other fabrics to create new tones and depths of color; fur fabric and leather could make realistic animals on a child's wall quilt. Exotic silks, satins, and velvets make a rich setting for the embroidery on a crazy quilt.

◀ **Silk**
Silk is available in many different weights, weaves, colors, and textures. The firmer weaves are very satisfactory for patchwork; the finer ones can be very slippery. Some silks are woven to produce novel effects, such as heavy slubs; "shot" silk has different colors for the warp and weft threads and shimmers between the two shades.

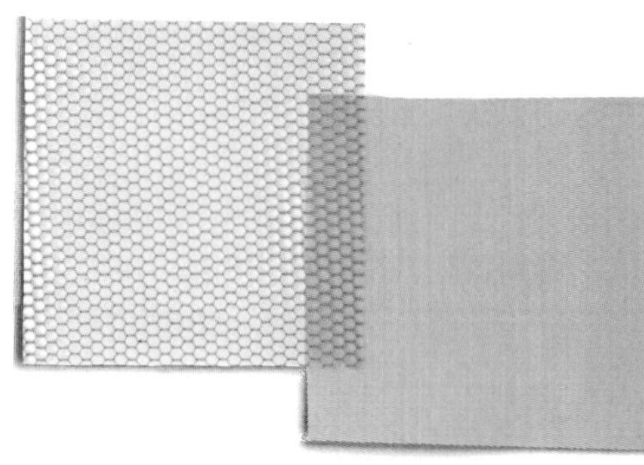

◀ **Net and voile**
These fabrics aren't firm enough to use for patchwork on their own, but they produce interesting special effects in experimental work.

◀ **Metallic fabric**
Metallic fabrics are generally wholly or partly synthetic, and come in a dazzling variety of finishes. They can be used with conventional patchwork patterns to make exotic items such as evening jackets and glittery bags, but have the drawbacks of other synthetic fabrics. Also, they have a very strong visual impact, so don't overdo them.

Good fabric should have the long grain running parallel to the selvage (the finished edge). Check this before buying, because if the grain is not true your pieces may become distorted. Templates should always be placed straight along the grain. In a woven fabric such as cotton, the long grain is sometimes known as the warp, while the yarn woven across this at a 90° angle is the weft.

Choosing colors

Once you've decided on a patchwork pattern, the next important decision is color. You may want to match or contrast with something in your decor or an outfit, and this may determine the dominant color for your patchwork. Or, you may want the patchwork to have a certain "feel", for instance, a vibrant look, or a soft, gentle effect. Patchwork patterns themselves often suggest to the quilter the kind of color schemes that would suit them. However, it is possible that you don't have any ideas about color and are starting from scratch; in this case, you can have great fun working out your color scheme.

Certain colors go together naturally, especially when they have a similar underlying color. For instance, blues that tend toward green rather than purple move toward yellow in the color wheel; green-blues tend to look harmonious with yellows and creams. In the same way, purple-blues go well with pinks because they both move toward red in the color wheel. Other colors create a vibrant reaction and set each other off in different ways; this is especially true of the complementary colors,

◄ **Shades of one color**
Although we divide the color wheel into six basic colors – red, orange, yellow, green, blue, and purple – each individual color can have an almost infinite number of shades or variations in hue. The fabrics here are all green, but you can see the enormous variety of shades, from acid lime-green to a dark olive green.

◄ **Light and dark**
All colors range from dark – very dark in some cases – to pale. The lightness or darkness of a color is known as its "value." Aim to have fabrics of several different values in your block; otherwise it may look bland and lacking in contrast.

COLOR WHEEL

Even a simple color wheel like this can help you to understand how colors relate to one another. Colors close together, such as the blues and purples, harmonize because they are the same family. The colors shown far right are the complementaries, which are opposite one another on the color wheel. These set up strong contrasts, so use them sparingly unless you want a particularly vibrant, dramatic effect.

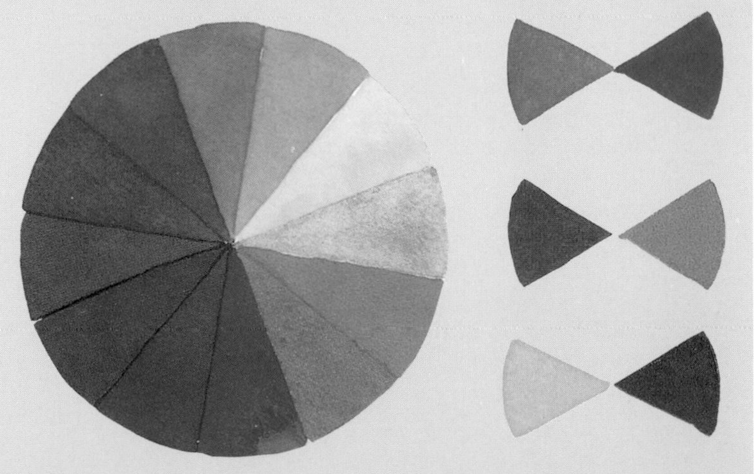

which are directly opposite each other on the color wheel – green and red, purple and yellow, orange and blue. Colors which are quite close to each other in the color wheel can create dramatic clashes – for example, red and puce, purple and turquoise, blue and lime-green.

If you're starting your color scheme from scratch, visit a fabric store or department which has a wide choice of cotton fabrics and pick two or three which please your eye when they are put together. Stand back to check the overall effect. If one is "killed" by the others, discard it and choose another. Continue until you are completely satisfied with your selection. In the end, it's your decision: if you like it, use it.

◀ **Vibrant colors**
Red and green, the strongest pair of complementary colors, create strong contrasts which can be effective on a small scale. You can play down the contrast by varying the proportions of the colors or by introducing some neutrals.

◀ **Clashing colors**
Some colors set up a discordant effect which can be dramatic. The lime green and dark turquoise are not natural partners, but such colors can be used successfully if separated by another color such as peachy-orange.

◀ **Harmonious colors**
Here, pink and mauve-pink is combined with a gentle slate gray. The effect is harmonious, with all the fabrics blending well with each other. Colors like these would give a gentle "country" feel to a bed quilt.

◀ **Adding neutrals**
Neutral colors are those which don't appear as pure color mixes in the color wheel: black, white, cream, brown, beige, dark gray, muddy green etc. All neutral colors can be used to great effect in patchwork, especially in backgrounds and to set off other colors.

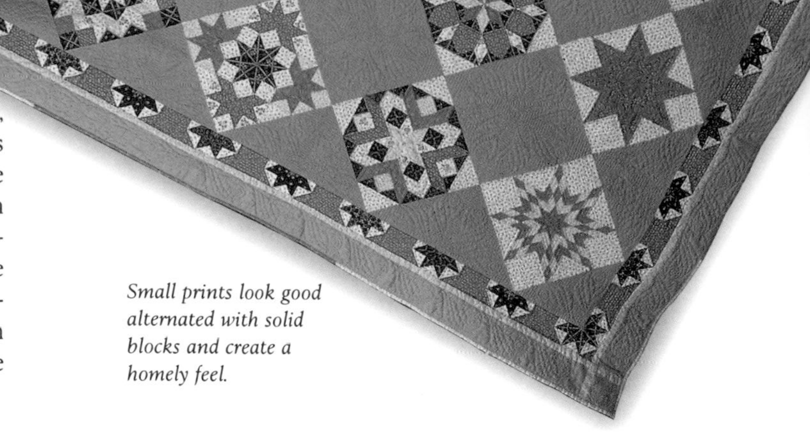

Small prints look good alternated with solid blocks and create a homely feel.

Some fabrics, such as gingham and damask, have patterns woven into them, but this process tends to alter the characteristics of the fabric, especially the texture. Generally, when you want to use a mixture of solid and patterned fabrics in patchwork, fabrics which have patterns printed on them are best. The patterns may be small or large, seemingly random or printed in a very regular design; some

Prints and solids

patterned fabrics have individual motifs which can be picked out and placed in specific arrangements in your work.

Patchwork patterns can look very bold worked entirely in solid fabrics, but adding a print or two will often give an extra lift to the design and keep it from looking stark. It is possible to use more than one print in your patchwork; in fact, you can piece it entirely from print fabrics if you choose them carefully. The main rule of thumb is not to choose strong patterns that fight visually with each other, or which obliterate the lines of the piecing itself.

Striped fabrics can be very striking and lend themselves to special effects, but avoid striped designs which are not printed along the straight grain of the fabric – they can deceive the eye into believing that the patches are cut crookedly. If the pattern isn't straight, cut with it rather than with the fabric grain.

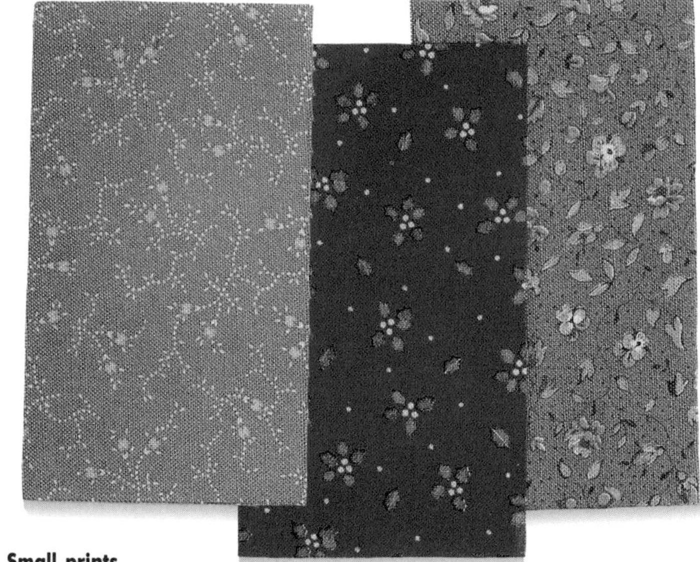

▲ Small prints
Small all-over prints are particularly suitable for patchwork; they provide texture without distracting the eye.

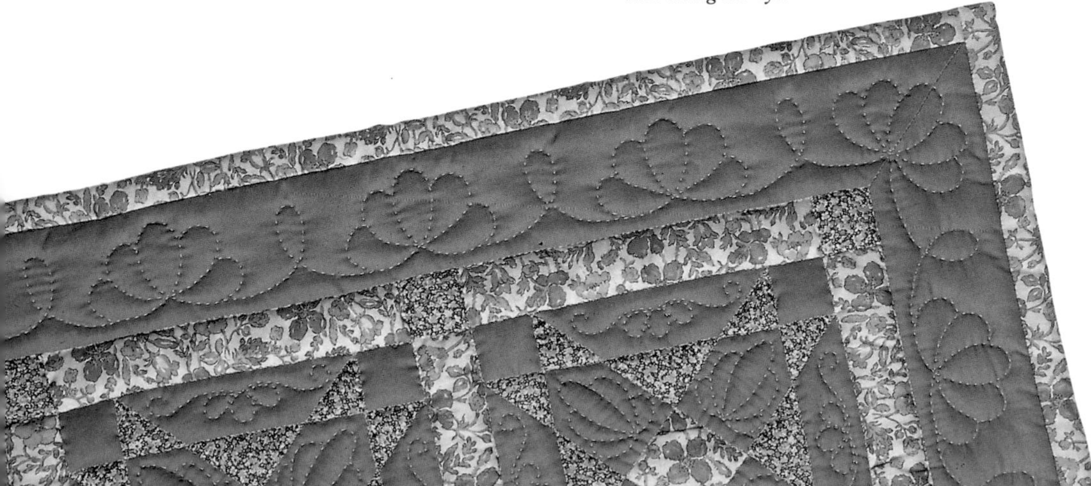

Large blocks of solid color create impact and have an immediate effect.

◀Large prints
Large all-over prints can be very effective if used carefully, but if you use several large patterns together, you may lose the lines of the patchwork shapes themselves.

◀Striped fabrics
Striped fabrics can have simple or complex patterns, ranging from a straightforward two-color stripe to a multicolored design in a random color sequence.

USING INDIVIDUAL MOTIFS OR AREAS

You may want to use just one part of a printed fabric – perhaps a particular motif or section of a design. In this case, you will need a transparent template, so that you can be sure that you have positioned it exactly where you want it on the fabric. This technique is rather wasteful of fabric, but it does allow you to produce some very dramatic effects.

QUILTING BASICS

Working it out

Buying fabrics for a quilt can be a costly business, so you want to be sure that you've chosen fabrics that will work well together before you invest in large amounts of them. Coloring in a sample block will give you a good idea whether your chosen color scheme works well, but once you have a basic idea in mind, you need to start working with real fabrics. One of the best ways is to lay out a sample block using scraps of fabric cut to shape. If you have a good collection of fabrics, you may have enough to try this out without buying anything; if not, most stores will sell short lengths or small patches of fabric. Move the shapes around until you have a good balance of color and intensity. If one fabric doesn't seem right, replace it with another one until you are satisfied with the result.

You may need to buy one fabric to blend in with several others you already have; if so, making a color fan may be useful. Glue long thin strips of your existing fabrics on thin cardboard, making sure that you don't leave a border of cardboard around the fabric – this way, you can lay your fabric right up against fabrics on the bolt and see how they look side by side. Secure all the strips together in one corner with a safety pin, or punch holes and put a ring through them; then you will be able to fan them out as necessary so you can see different combinations of fabric together.

Here you can see how some of the ideas in this section work in practice. All of the nine-patch blocks shown here have been made in the same design – the Churn Dash – and the same size. You can see, though, that each block looks different from the others, because of the fabrics that we have chosen and the ways that the fabrics have been arranged.

Making a shape come forward
When you want to emphasize a particular motif or part of a design, work the motif in the lighter fabric and set it on a dark background.

Individual motifs
This floral print has been carefully cut so that a flower appears in the center of each triangle, and in the center of the middle patch. Use a clear template when you want to position individual motifs accurately in this way.

▼ *This color fan has been made with strips of fabric glued to cardboard; the strips have then been hooked together in one corner. The strips can be fanned out in different combinations so that they can be laid against new fabrics in the shop to assess their effect together.*

Making a shape recede
A dark shape placed on a light background seems to move away from you. Use this effect to reduce the emphasis of a very dramatic fabric.

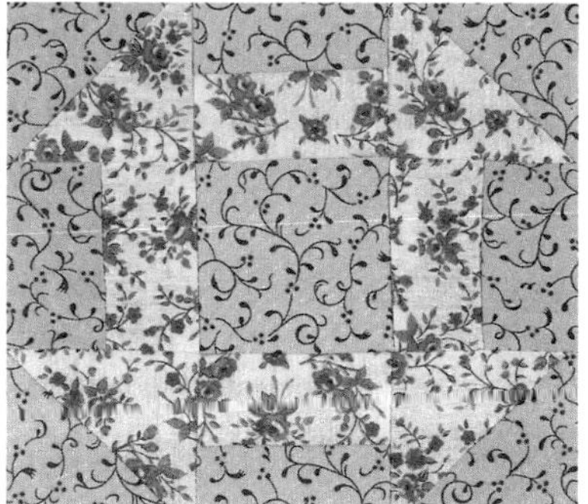

Fabrics too close in shade
Although the patterns on these two print fabrics are quite different when you look carefully, they are so close in shade that they merge together, losing the lines of the block design.

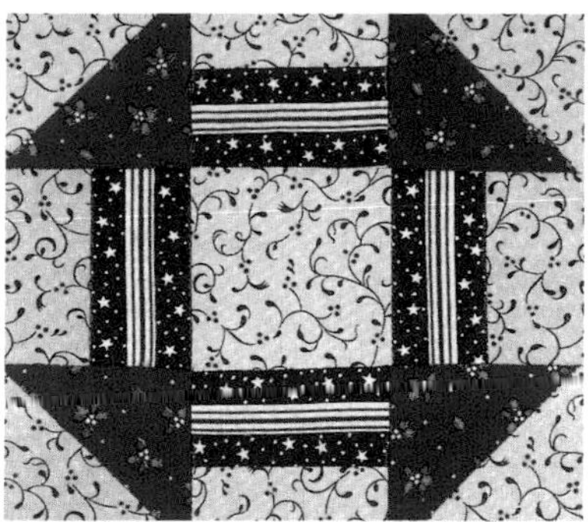

Well-balanced shades
This block has a background fabric similar to the previous one, but stronger fabrics have been chosen for the other patches, so that the lines of the block design can be seen clearly.

Asymmetric arrangements
In this block, the shades fade from light to dark diagonally. This can look very dramatic if you join several blocks made in the same way, so that the shading alters in a regular pattern.

Bright and bold fabrics
This block uses bright, acid solids and bold, brightly colored prints, giving a very modern look to the block. The asymmetrical arrangement of the fabrics add to the jazzy effect.

Exotic fabrics
Although cotton is the traditional choice for patchwork, you can use many other fabrics. This block has been made in subtle shades of silk, hand-dyed to give a soft and delicate appearance.

MAKING TRIAL GRIDS

If you draw your patchwork pattern (see page 40, Drawing designs) and photocopy it several times, you can use these grids to try out different color schemes and arrangements. Use colored pencils or felt-tip pens, depending on the intensity of color that you want in your finished patchwork.

QUILTING BASICS

Putting it together

When you are planning your quilt, you need to decide how the different elements will go together. If you are using several blocks, will they look best joined directly to one another, or separated? For the edges of the quilt, do you want a decorative border, or will you simply bind the edges?

When blocks are joined side by side, they can produce intriguing secondary designs (see opposite and page 146). You may decide, though, that you want each block to be seen on its own, and the best way of doing this is by adding sashing, or setting strips. Sashing is particularly important if you have made blocks in several different designs or techniques, such as for our sampler quilt; blocks in very different patterns rarely look good joined directly without sashing. Sashing should be made from a fabric that will show off the more decorative blocks to their best advantage; you might want to choose a neutral color, or one of the solid fabrics from your patchwork. Sashing can be in a patterned fabric, but since it is intended as a frame for the stronger patterns, it is best to use a small all-over print that doesn't distract the eye too much from the blocks.

Borders go around the whole quilt top and add extra visual interest; they are also a good way of increasing the size, for instance, if you want to extend a double-bed size to fit a king-size bed. A pieced quilt really calls for a pieced border, which will look most effective if it uses elements from the quilt itself – stars or diamonds for star quilts, borders with curved elements for Drunkard's Patch or Grandmother's Fan designs, squares and triangles for quilt designs made up from these basic shapes. Use the same fabrics as you used for piecing the blocks; plan the design on graph paper, and work the corners out carefully so that they carry the design around well.

Sashing can be used in many ways to create different visual effects. The quilt above uses sashing at angles with a half-fan motif to give a feel and look of shells or scales. The quilt right uses sashing across the block motifs to create "quarter" blocks which are then echoed in the border.

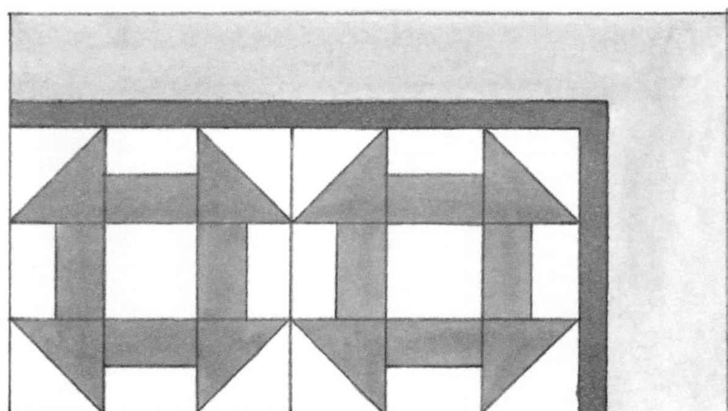

Here, a Churn Dash quilt has been designed with the blocks joining directly and edged with a narrow plain border.

This border for a quilt made from Card Trick blocks uses smaller versions of the shapes in the blocks.

This pieced border for the same Churn Dash design uses one third of the basic block in reversed colors, with a corner made from a square divided into two triangles. The whole quilt top is then edged with a narrow border.

In this variation, sashing one third of the width of the block has been added between the blocks and around the edges. Because of the extra width produced by the sashing, a new element has been added to the patchwork border, repeating the rectangular shapes.

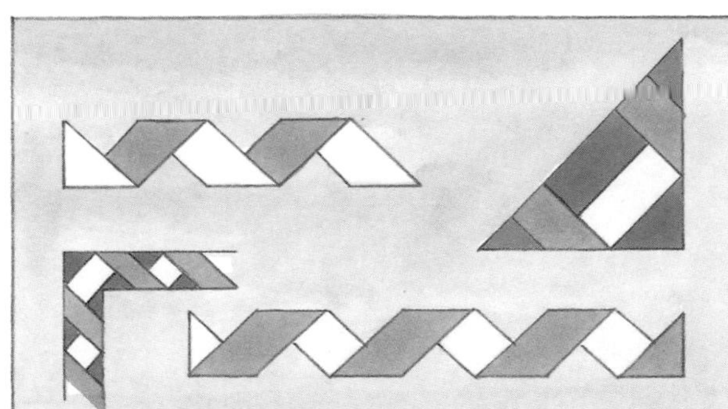

These examples show two variations of a pieced border known as Twisted Ribbon.

These pieced borders look very attractive around simple pieced quilts. Here they border Shoo Fly and Jack-in-the-Box blocks.

Drawing designs

Many patchwork quilts are constructed from square blocks which are then joined, with or without separating strips of fabric (sashing, or setting strips - see page 38), to make the quilt top. Other designs are based on equilateral triangles, or circles divided into different segments, or other arrangements of shapes. Whatever basic design you choose, it is important to know how to draw accurate patterns at the right size so that you can calculate how much fabric you need and make perfect templates from your drawings. Once you have learned the basic principles, it is then very easy to change the size of a pattern or to change the design by altering a line or two.

Good-quality graph paper is essential for drafting patterns. It is available from stationery shops and art suppliers, and from quilting supply outlets, in both standard and metric measurements. A transparent plastic ruler is a great help, along with soft-to-medium pencils, a good pencil sharpener, and an eraser.

Graph paper makes it unnecessary to measure many of the angles, such as the angles of the triangles in a nine-patch design, but you will find polar coordinate graph paper or a compass and protractor (see page 27) useful for patterns such as Dresden Plate, which are formed from segments of a circle. Isometric graph paper (see page 26) is divided into equilateral triangles and is useful for patterns based on 60° angles and their multiples.

Once you have a full-size pattern, use it to cut pattern pieces for templates, or photocopy it and color in different versions to try out different color schemes and examine the effect of several blocks joined side by side.

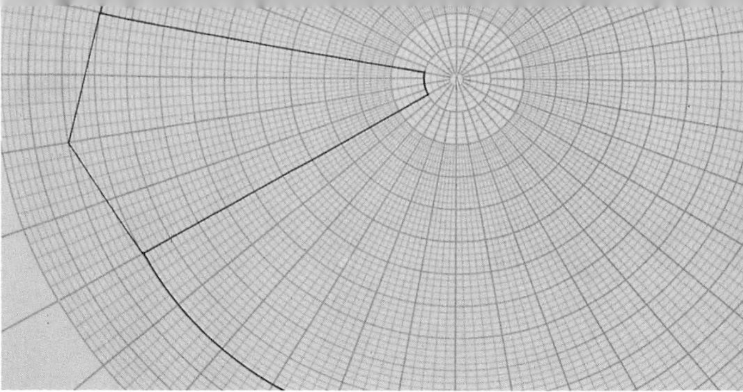

▲ *For patterns using segments of a circle, draw your design onto polar coordinate graph paper at the correct size, dividing the circle into the number of segments that you need. Mark the pieces you need for templates in the same way. If the graph paper is too small for a full pattern, use it to draw the correct angles in the center of the circle and simply extend the petal shapes out as far as needed.*

ENLARGING AND REDUCING

When you are working with irregular patterns such as appliqué shapes you may want to enlarge or reduce them. To do this draw a grid of squares across the original pattern. Draw another grid containing the same number of squares, but making them larger or smaller depending on whether you want to enlarge or reduce. Now copy the main lines of the shape onto your grid; the squares will help you to see where the lines go.

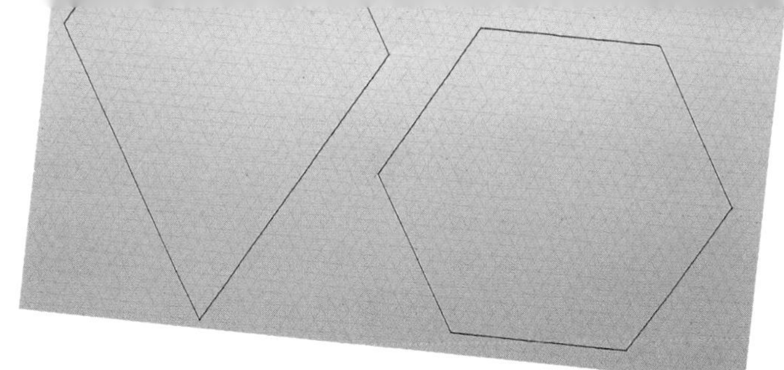

▲ *For patterns using 60° angles and their multiples, draw your design on isometric graph paper at the correct size and mark the pieces you need for templates in the same way.*

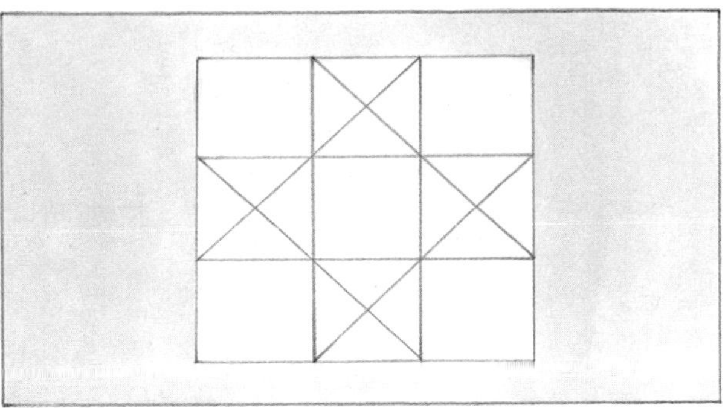

1 *Choose your pattern, and decide on the size of the block that you need. Your chosen size will depend on the kind of block you have chosen (see above), the number of blocks you need in your project, and the size of your finished project. For this example, we will use a 12 in. block and draw the Ohio Star design.*

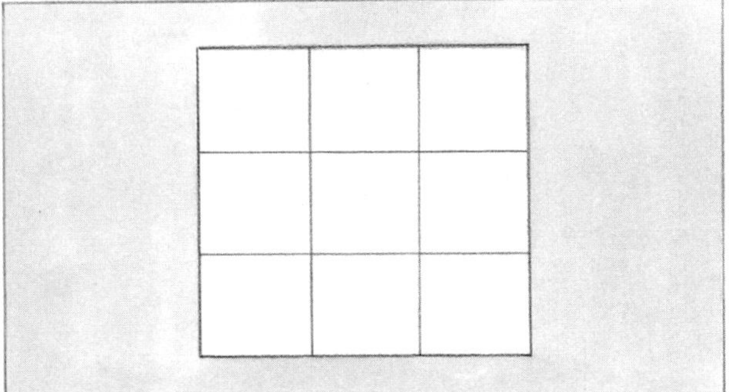

2 *Draw a 12 in. square on graph paper, and divide it into 9 equal squares, each measuring 4×4 in.*

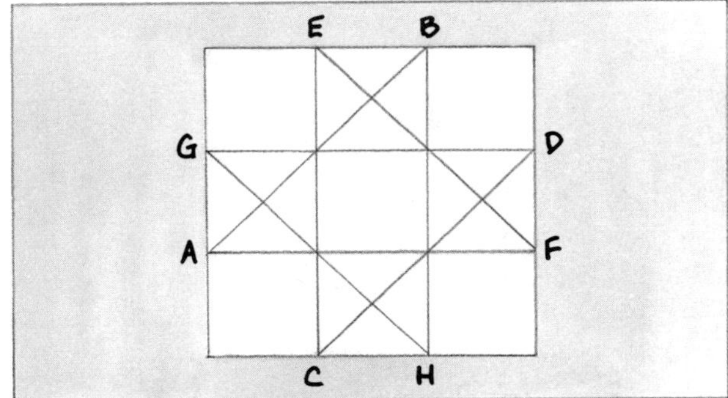

3 *Draw in the diagonals. In this example, they run from A-B, C-D, E-F and G-H. Draw each of the diagonals in one line for accuracy, even when they go across several squares.*

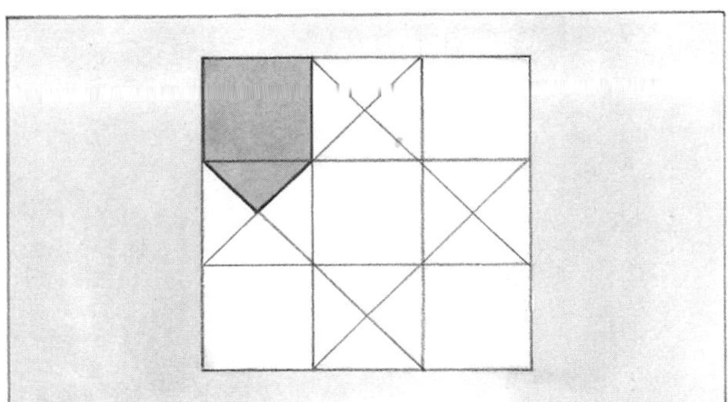

4 *Now work out how many individual template pieces you will need. If you look carefully at this block, you will see that although it is pieced from 21 different pieces of fabric, only two shapes are used – the 3 in. square, and the right-angled triangle which makes up a quarter of it.*

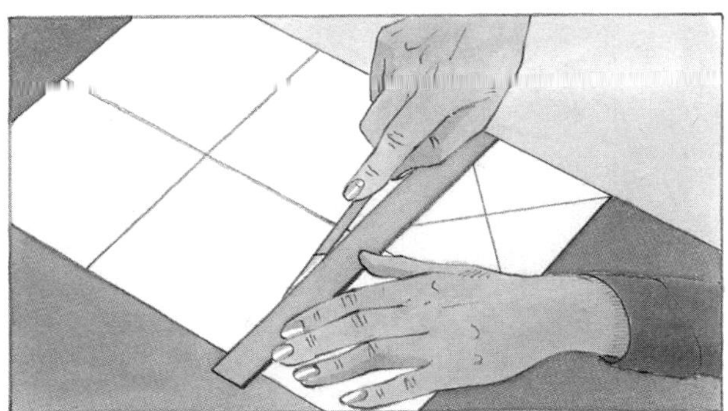

5 *Use a craft knife to cut out one example of each piece needed. If you don't want to spoil your full-size drawing make careful copies of the pieces needed on a separate piece of graph paper and cut them out. You now have accurate guides which you can use for making templates.*

Making templates

Commercial templates are available for most patchwork designs, but it's far more satisfying and of course cheaper to make your own. Also, if you know the principles of making templates, you will be able to copy designs that you see, such as those in antique quilts.

If you only intend to use a particular template a few times, thin cardboard is adequate. After about 20 tracings cardboard templates start to become worn and are therefore inaccurate. The most durable materials are metal and plastic; for home use, plastic is better as it can be cut much more easily. Special template plastic, which is transparent and easy to cut and mark, is readily available from art, craft, and quilting suppliers.

If you are making templates for hand-pieced work (see page 46, Piecing), you should make them the exact size of the finished piece – i.e., without seam allowances. However, if you are making templates for machine piecing, you should include the seam allowances on your final template.

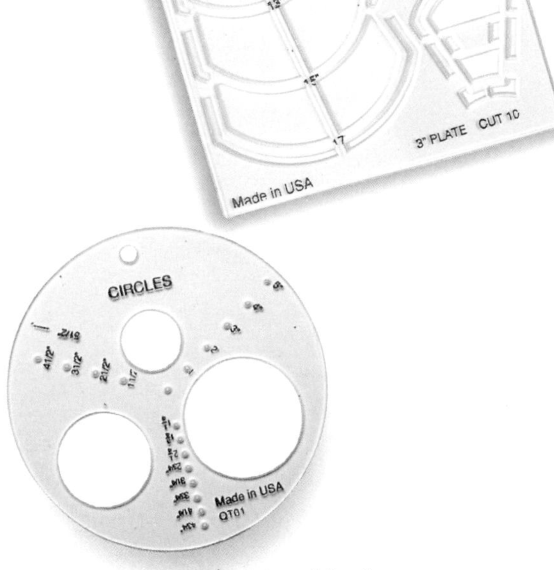

▲ *It is useful to know how to make your own templates, and some quilters enjoy the challenge. Nowadays, however, ready made templates are available in a wide range of shapes and sizes.*

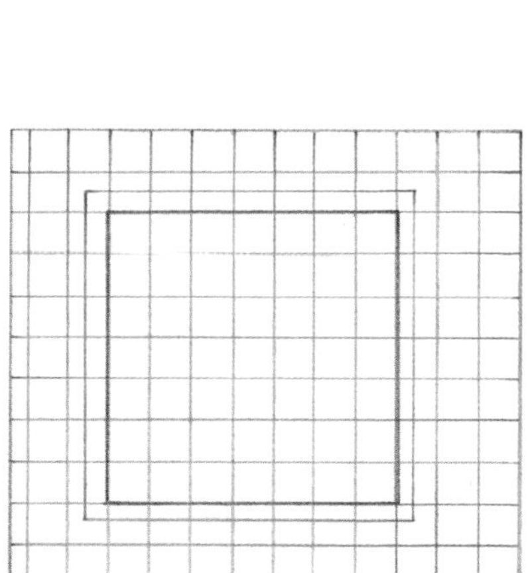

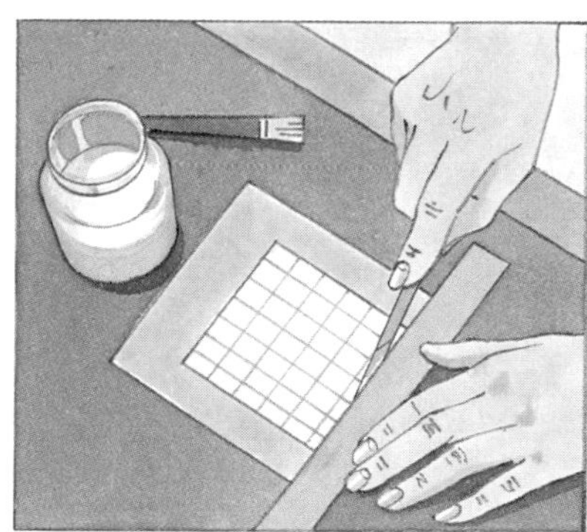

Making a square template from cardboard

1 *Draw a square of the required size on graph paper. Use a very sharp pencil so that the shape isn't distorted.*

2 *If you are sewing by hand, cut along the marked lines. If you are sewing by machine, add ¼ in. all around and cut along the outer line.*

3 *Glue the paper square face up on a piece of cardboard, then cut the card around the edges of the paper, using a steel ruler and craft knife for accuracy.*

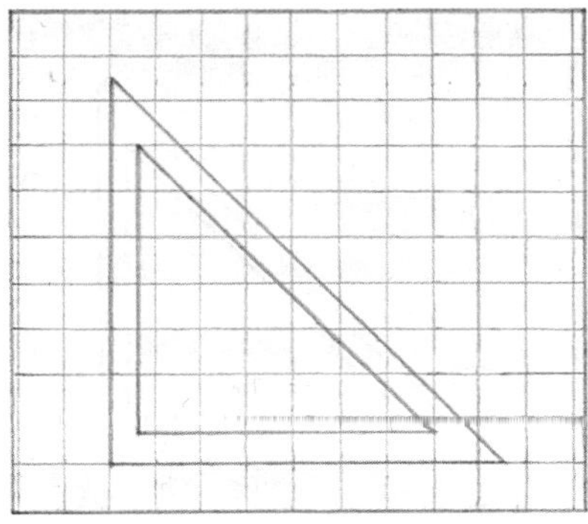

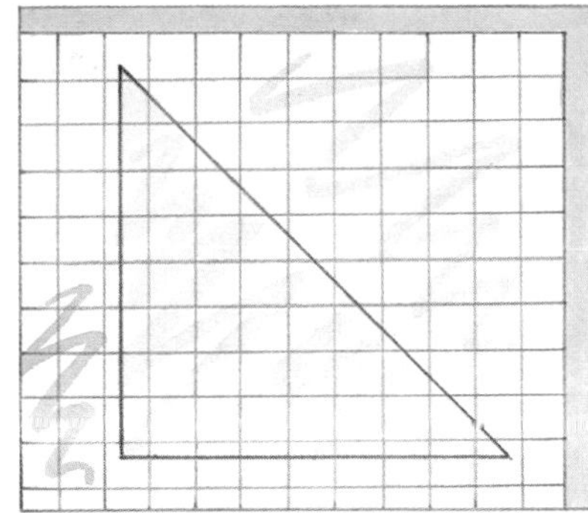

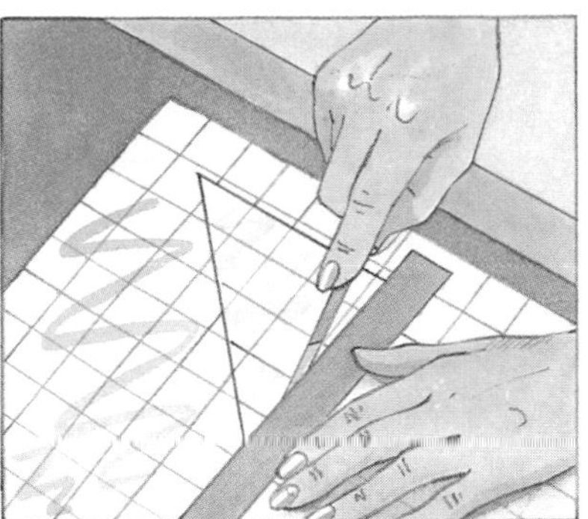

Making a triangular template using template plastic

1 *Draw a triangle of the required size on graph paper. Add seam allowances if necessary.*

2 *Place the plastic over the graph paper and trace the shape. If you have a specialized ruler for cutting triangles (see page 26, Equipment), you can draw onto the plastic.*

3 *Using a craft knife and a steel ruler, cut out the template. Keep your fingers away from the cutting edge.*

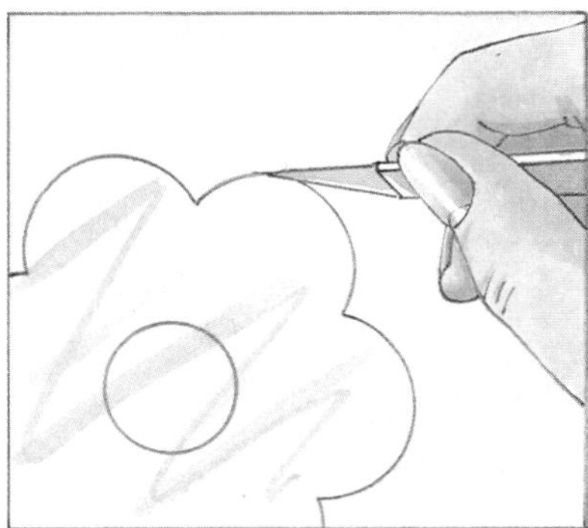

Making appliqué templates

1 *Draw or trace the shape onto paper, cardboard, or template plastic. If you are using a shape that isn't the right size, follow the instructions on page 40 for enlarging or reducing.*

2 *Add ¼ in. seam allowance around all the edges of the shape.*

3 *If you are using paper, glue it on cardboard, then cut around the outside line; if you are using template plastic, simply cut around the outside line.*

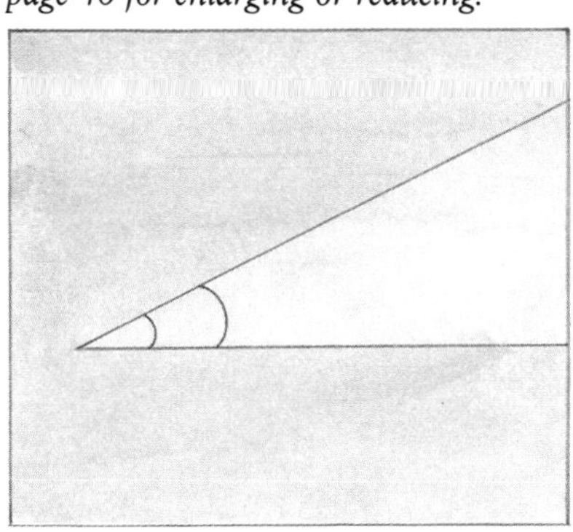

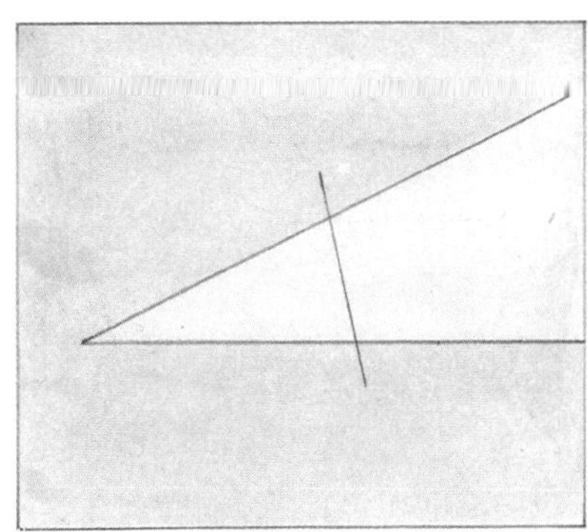

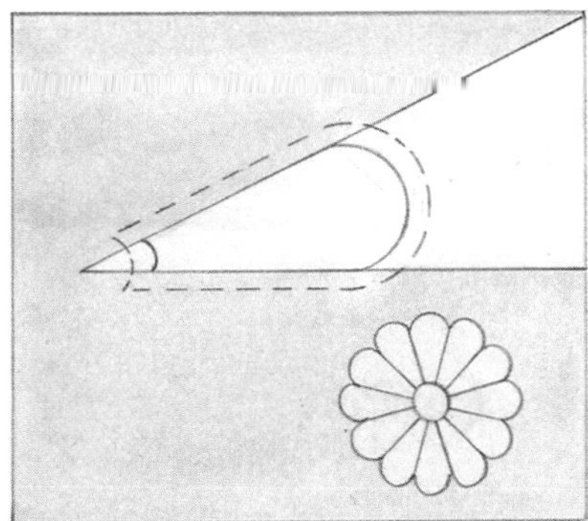

Making a Dresden Plate template

1 *Draw two straight lines at an angle to each other. The angle will be 360° divided by the number of petals that you want; a 12-petal design needs an angle of 30° (360÷12).*

2 *From the point, measure out the same distance along both lines. The distance will be half the diameter of the design, so for an 8 in. plate, measure 4 in. from the corner.*

3 *Join the two marks with a faint line, then draw in a point or a curve depending on the shape you want. Draw an inner curve a short way in from the angle. Add ¼ in. seam allowance, and cut the shape out.*

Cutting fabrics

The most important thing to remember when you are cutting your fabric into pieces for patchwork is *accuracy*. If your patches aren't cut accurately, they won't fit together properly. The finished piecing may be too large or too small if you have cut the pieces with too much or too little seam allowance.

Make sure that your templates are very precise, checking them against your full-size pattern. Always use a very sharp pencil for marking your fabric, pressing it tightly against the template so that your line is accurate. A small piece of sandpaper glued to the back of your template will stop it from moving out of position while you are marking – this is also a useful trick if you are using a rotary cutter. Cut exactly on the line you have drawn, not either outside it or inside it.

Before you do any cutting, make sure that you have prepared your fabric by washing, pressing, and straightening any raw edges, and cutting off the selvages (this is because the selvage is more tightly woven than other areas and therefore pulls the fabric slightly). If you are a beginner, you may prefer to mark and cut one piece of fabric at a time, but experienced quilters cut several layers at once if they are using scissors, and up to eight thicknesses of fabric using a rotary cutter.

If you prefer to use scissors, choose a very sharp pair of dressmaking scissors and keep them only for cutting fabric. Never cut paper or cardboard with them; the fibers lie in numerous different directions and blunt the blades very quickly. If you are using a rotary cutter, you will also need a cutting mat and a quilter's transparent ruler (see page 26). Always sheath the blade of a rotary cutter after use; the blade is very sharp.

ESTIMATING YARDAGES

For an accurate estimate, make a chart with a column for each of your chosen fabrics as the example shown here. Down the left-hand side, list each piece needed for the patchwork, sashing, borders, and backing. Now draw each of these requirements on graph paper (you don't need to draw all 96, of course; just draw two or four and then multiply). Add up all your requirements for each fabric, and you will have exact yardage requirements. It is, however, worth adding a little extra as a safety margin in case you cut some pieces wrong.

Pieces Required	Fabric 1	Fabric 2	Fabric 3	Fabric 4	Fabric 5	Fabric 6
Border 82" x 4" 180 x 10cm		2				
Border 62" x 4" 150 x 10cm		2				
Sashing 82" x 2" 180 x 5cm			3			
Sashing 2" x 12" 5 x 30cm			20			
Squares 4" 10cm	24					
Rectangles 2" x 4" 5 x 10cm	96			96		
Triangles 4" 10cm	96				96	
Backing 62" x 90" 150 x 228cm						1

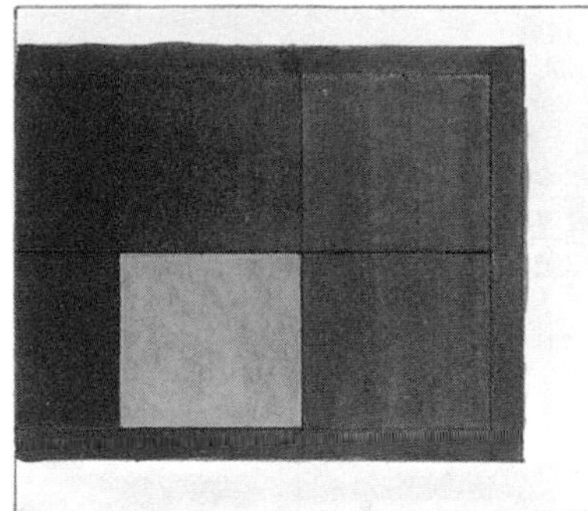

Cutting with scissors

1 *For hand piecing, position your template on the fabric and draw around it. Mark a $^{1}/_{4}$ in. seam allowance for each piece and reposition the template.*

2 *For machine piecing, butt the edges of the templates right up to each other and cut along the solid lines, as the seam allowances are included in the templates.*

3 *If you want to cut more than one layer at a time, mark one layer and stack it on top of two or three other pieces. Pin, then cut through all the layers together.*

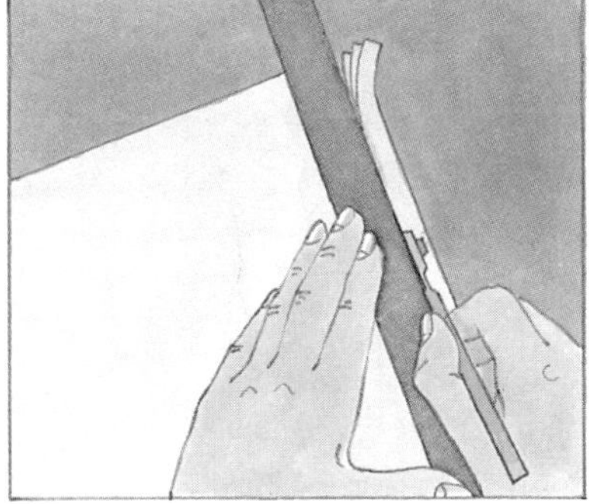

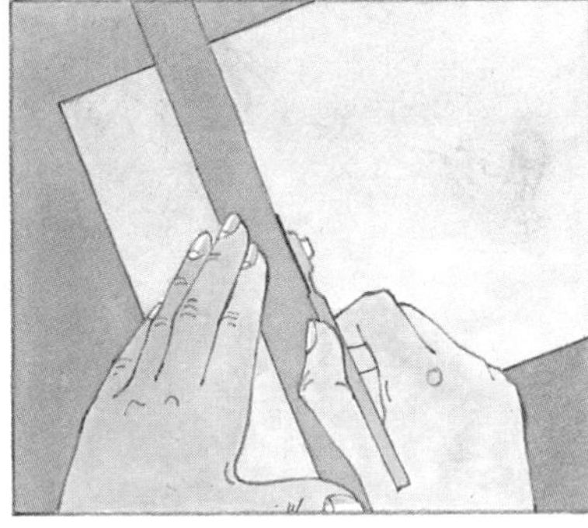

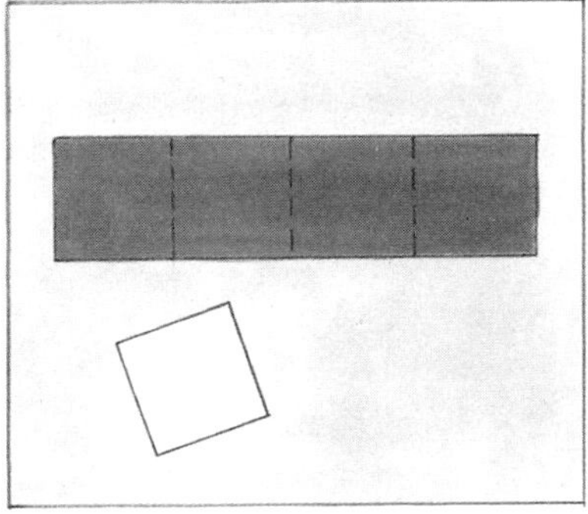

Cutting with a rotary cutter

1 *To minimize the number of cuts needed, the fabric is first cut into strips. Fold in half lengthwise twice. With a transparent ruler held at right angles to the fold, trim the raw edges.*

2 *Turn the fabric around so that the layers are to the right of the ruler (reverse if you are left-handed). Line up the ruler along the width needed for your strips and cut along the edge.*

3 *Now use your templates or special cutting rulers to cut the strips into squares, rectangles, triangles, or parallelograms, as needed.*

GENERAL CUTTING PRINCIPLES

Always mark, or allow for, the largest pieces on your fabric first. So, for instance, mark borders, sashing, and large pattern pieces on your fabric before cutting lots of small elements – otherwise, you may find that the areas you have left are not the right shape for your larger pieces. Make sure that the grain lines of your fabric are square, and position your templates so that the grain line arrow is straight along the grain. Always mark on the back of your fabrics.

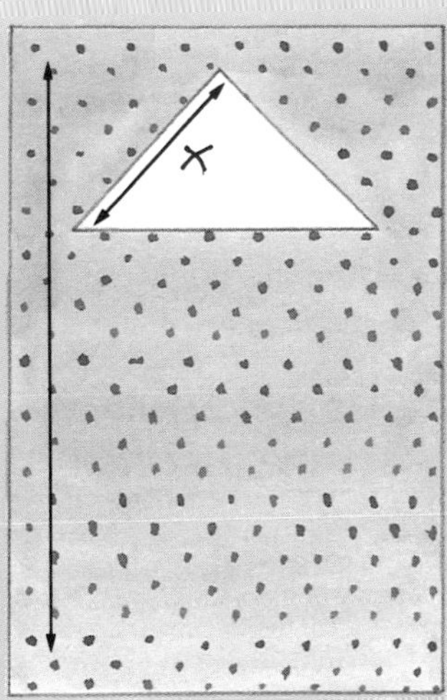

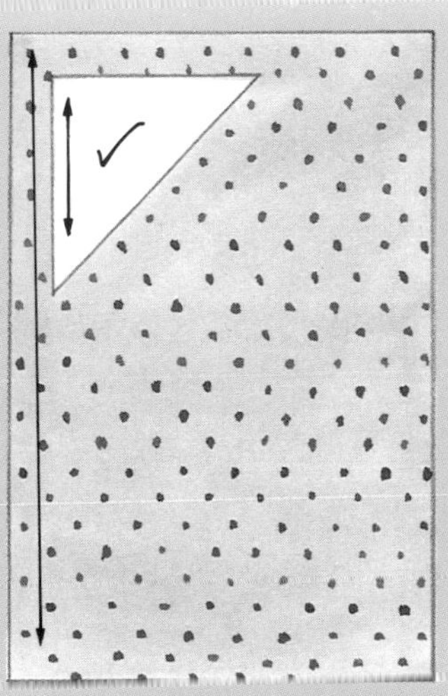

Pieced quilt with Flying Geese borders

QUILTING BASICS

Piecing

Once you have chosen the fabrics for each part of your patchwork, you need to decide how you are going to join the patches. Piecing may be done by hand or machine, and there are advantages to both methods.

If you decide to stitch by hand, you will be able to carry your work with you wherever you go. It will be slower, but you will often find a few moments when you can sew a few patches together. It is also easier to "fudge" a slightly inaccurate seam by hand and make seams meet where they should.

Much more accuracy is needed when you are stitching by machine, but of course it is much faster. More and more quilters are using their machines for piecing – not to mention quilting (see page 56) and embroidery embellishment. In fact, machine piecing has been used for quilts for about 100 years. A design with lots of small pieces is sometimes easier to piece by hand, but the choice is yours entirely.

Before using your machine for piecing, it is a good idea to use a spare piece of fabric to practice stitching an accurate $^{1}/_{4}$ in. seam. Make several parallel rows, using the pressure foot as a guide for spacing them. Or, place a length of masking tape on the throat plate of your machine exactly $^{1}/_{4}$ in. from the needle and use this as your guide.

Each seam should be pressed after it is stitched. The general rule is to press the seam allowance toward the darker fabric; this will stop the extra fabric from showing through lighter patches. With complex patterns where several seams join in one place, you may end up with the bulk of several seam allowances all pressed toward the same piece of fabric; if this happens, you can trim away some of the fabric, or press one seam in a different direction.

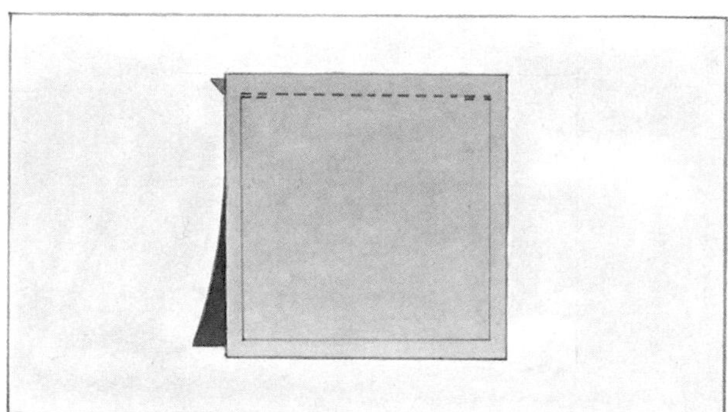

Piecing by hand
Your pieces will have been cut with the stitching lines marked (see page 42). Pin the two pieces right sides together and sew with small running stitches along the stitching lines, beginning and ending with a few backstitches for extra strength.

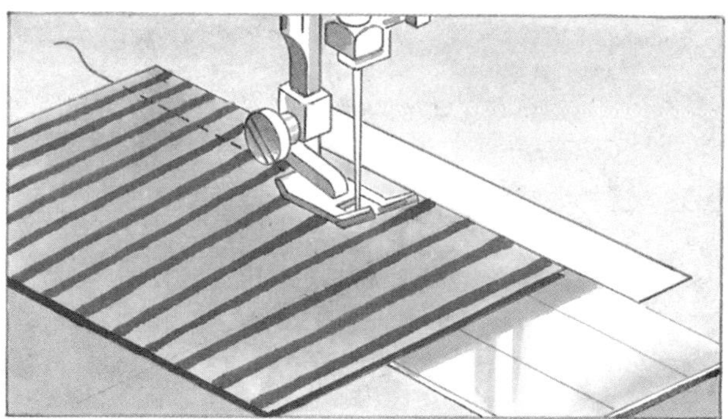

Piecing by machine
Your patches will have been cut with the seam allowance added and with no stitching lines marked. Pin the two pieces right sides together and sew $^{1}/_{4}$ in. away from the edge.

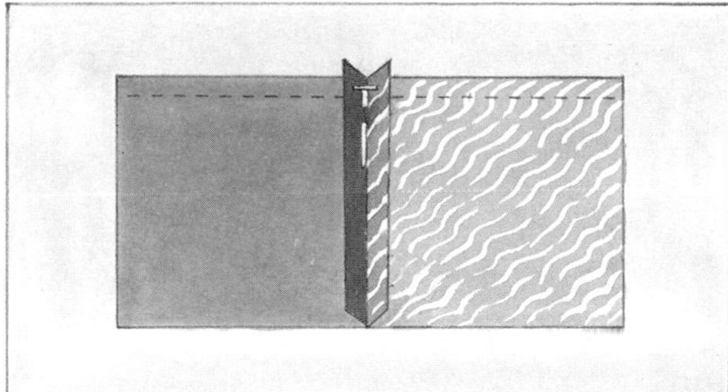

Matching seams

When you need to match the seams of two composite patches, put the fabrics together and then pin across the seam allowances. If you're careful, you should be able to sew across the pin while it is still in place.

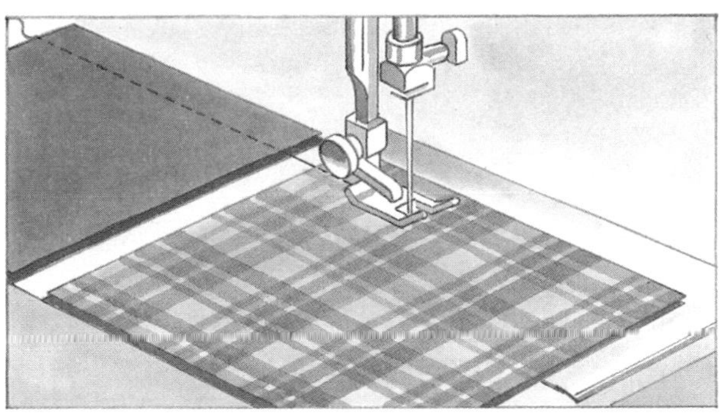

Assembly-line method

To save time when you are sewing several sets of patches, put them together in pairs, then stitch them on the machine one after another, without breaking the thread between each pair. When all the seams have been stitched, cut between the pairs.

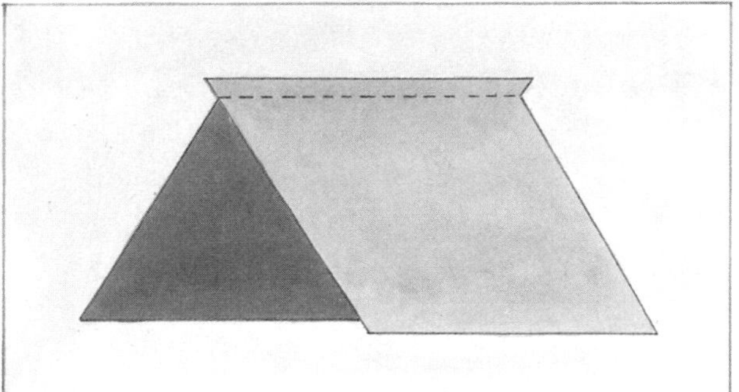

Offset seams

If a seam is between two angled pieces, position them right sides together so that the ends of the seam allowances, rather than the ends of the patches themselves, are aligned.

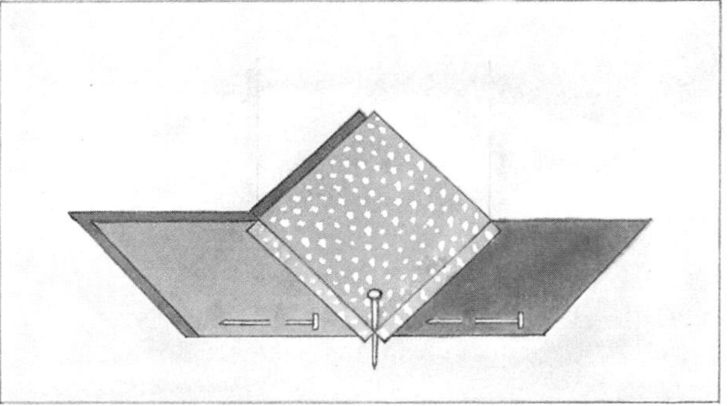

Joining multiple seams

To get an exact alignment, put a pin through one patch where the seams join, then push it through the seam in the other patch, right sides together. Pin the two patches across the seam allowances, then remove the first pin.

Mark the center of each seam with a pin or a notch. Match the pins or the notches at the center, right sides together, and pin in position, then pin the ends of the seams. Ease the seam allowances together evenly, pinning at right angles as you go.

Stitch along the seam line by hand or machine, then remove the pins and press the seam allowance toward the darker side. If the seam allowance doesn't lie flat, clip it slightly so that it can be pressed into position.

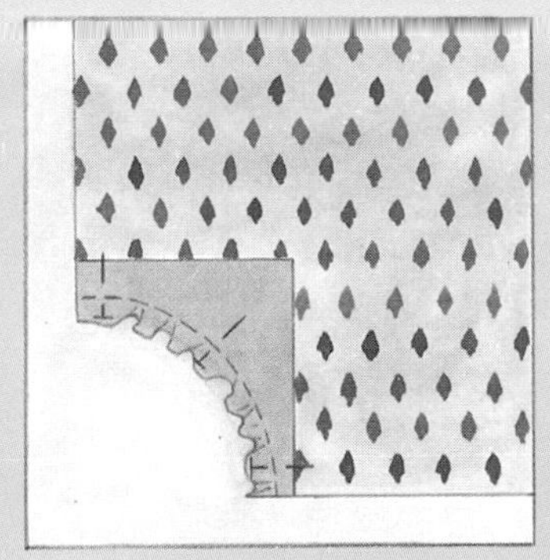

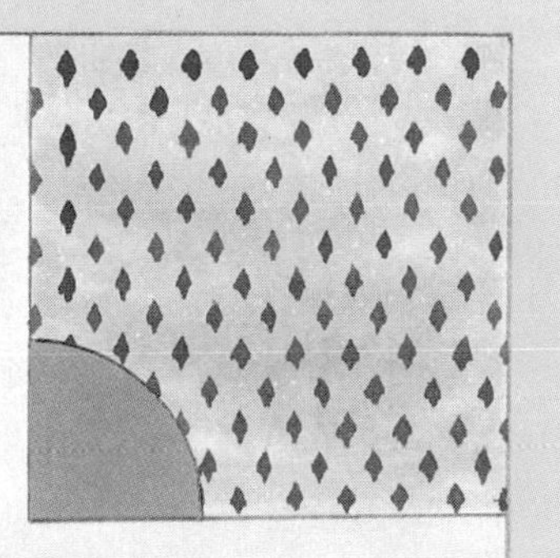

There are several basic ways of marking quilting patterns. Each method has its pros and cons, and some are more suitable for certain fabrics or for certain tasks than others; experiment with the methods shown here and see which ones you find most comfortable.

For making the actual marks on your fabric you can use several different tools. An ordinary medium-hard pencil, sharpened to a good point, will make clear marks, but won't necessarily wash out, so only use this method if you are confident that your stitching will cover all of the pencil marks – for instance, if you are quilting a particular area with chain stitch. Pens with water-soluble ink, which produce strong marks that disappear when wetted, can be extremely useful. Pens with fading ink also produce strong marks which fade sometimes within a few hours, so don't mark a large area at one time! Fading-ink pens are useful if you don't want to have to wet the finished item. Colored pencils are often ideal for marking solid fabrics; choose a shade just slightly darker than your fabric and sharpen it to a good point. You will find that the marks are unnoticeable when the quilting is complete. Iron-on transfers and transfer pencils make a strong mark that doesn't usually wash out, so again make sure that your stitching will cover the line – some quilting patterns use a silver-gray transfer line, which is less noticeable. For marking patterns on stretched plain quilt tops, some people like to use a blunt needle or a silverpoint pencil; these make fine indented lines which, again, are unnoticeable when the quilting is complete.

Marking quilting patterns

▼A marked quilt pattern

This is a pattern for a wholecloth pillow cover, marked on the fabric with water-soluble ink to produce a strong line.

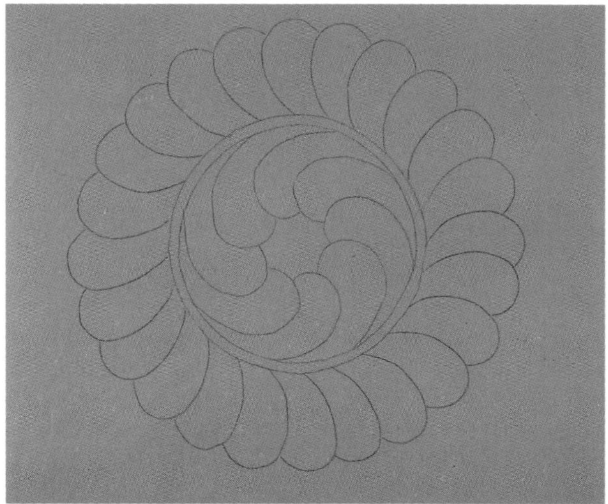

Tracing around templates

If you are quilting a pattern without any internal lines, or if you have a template with the internal lines cut out, you can simply trace around the shape using pencil or colored pencil, soluble or fading ink, or a blunt needle or silverpoint pencil.

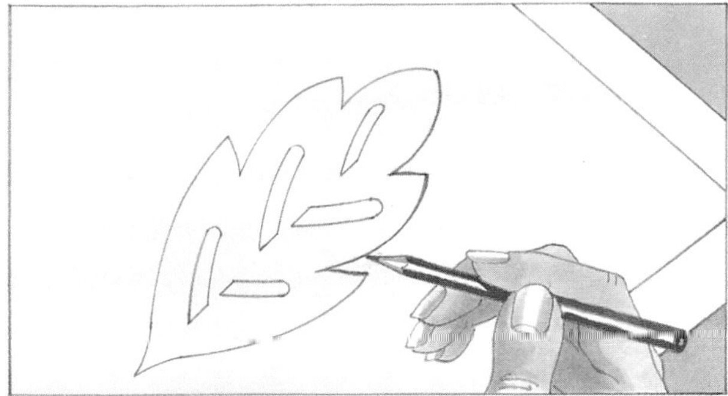

Tracing through fabric

When your fabric is very pale or very fine, you may be able to trace through it. Lay your pattern face-up on a flat surface, place your fabric, right side up, on top, and trace the pattern using pencil or colored pencil, or soluble or fading ink (see page 29).

Lightbox

If you have access to a designer's lightbox, it can be used to make a medium-shade fabric more transparent so that you can trace through it. Lay the pattern on the lightbox with the fabric right side up on top, and trace the pattern.

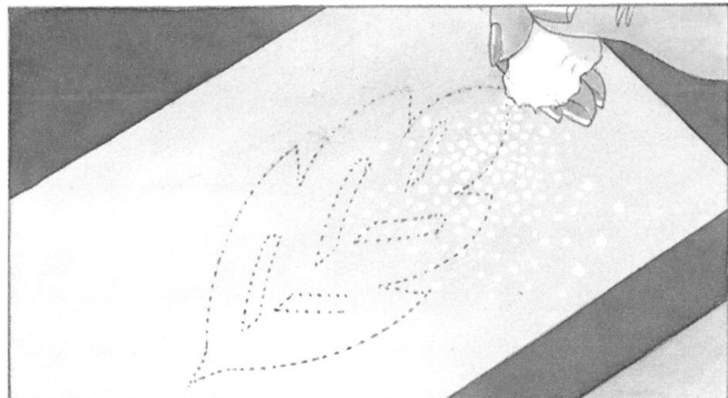

Prick and pounce

This method is useful for dark fabrics. Perforate your pattern along all the lines with a pin or machine stitching, lay it on top of your fabric and dust chalk, or talcum powder through the holes with a cotton ball.

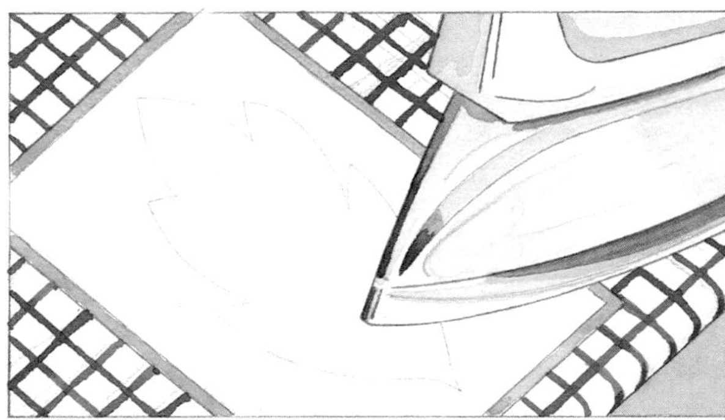

Iron-on transfers

Iron-on transfers are available for some patterns, and you can also buy transfer pencils for drawing your own design on paper. Lay the transfer face down on the right side of the fabric, then press with a warm iron. Remember that the design will be reversed.

Dressmaker's carbon paper

This is available in several different colors, so you can choose a color that will work well with your fabric. Lay the carbon paper face down on the right side of your fabric and place your pattern on top; run a dressmaker's tracing wheel over all the lines of the pattern.

Blunt needle or silverpoint

This method works best on solid-colored fabrics that have already been stretched taut on a frame. Lay your template down on the right side of your fabric and trace around all the lines with the blunt needle or silverpoint, which will make an indented line on the fabric.

Quilted border designs add interest to a quilt top. They can be added to plain sashings and fabric borders (see page 152), or stitched around the edges of wholecloth projects (see page 100) to provide visual contrast and interest. In many ways working a border design is similar to working with other quilted designs such as individual medallions or background textures; they are marked onto the fabric using

Adding quilted borders

A simple but effective example of a quilted border

the same methods (see page 48), and stitched in the same way by hand or machine (see page 56). However, quilted border designs present some extra challenges to the quilter, and you need to plan your border pattern carefully, watching out for some of the common pitfalls.

The first task is to choose your border pattern; you may decide to pick out some elements from your pieced or quilted center design, such as flower shapes or diamonds, and make a border using those, or you may choose a pattern that contrasts. Most border patterns are made of repeating shapes, and you need to choose a pattern that will fill your border area with whole repeats. If the measurement doesn't quite work out, you may find that you can adjust it by enlarging or reducing the border pattern slightly.

Continuing the border pattern around the corners of the quilt can be a little tricky. Some commercial quilting patterns for borders also include extra templates for corners. If you are making up your own border, you may need to make some sketches first to experiment with different ways of carrying the pattern around the corner. If it proves too difficult, you can finish the edges of the border neatly on each side of the corner and fill the corner itself with a complementary motif or medallion.

The notch method

1 *This method will help you to mark even borders for twisted designs such as cables, using just one small template. Draw your chosen pattern full-size very accurately onto paper; draw several repeats of the basic shape so that you can see exactly where each repeat begins and ends.*

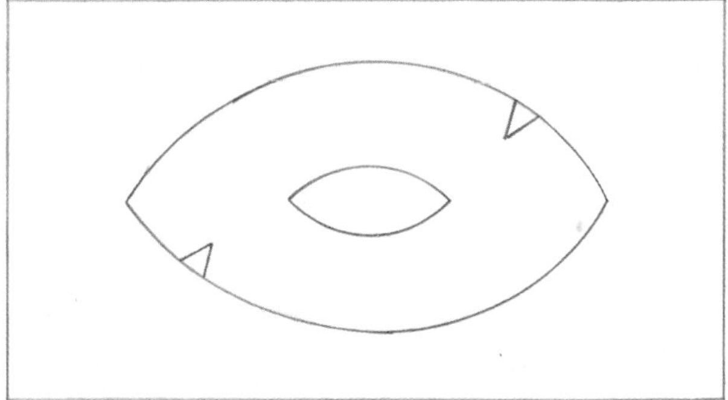

2 *Using either template plastic or sturdy cardboard (see page 42) so that you have a durable surface for marking against, cut the basic template for one repeat of your chosen pattern. Cut or mark a notch on each side of the shape where the next repeat begins.*

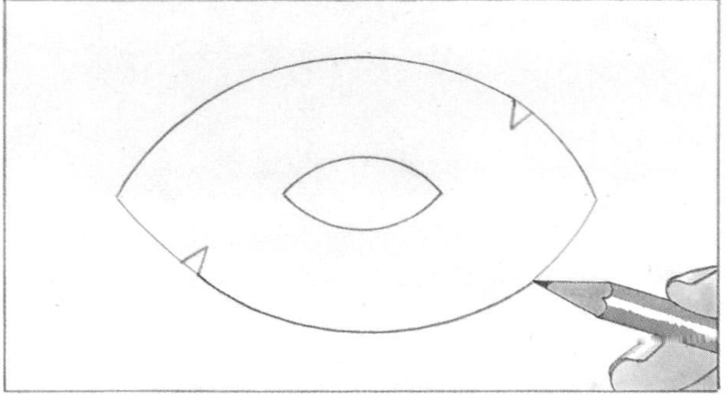

3 *Use this template as a guide for marking your fabric. Mark around the long outside edges between the tips of the template and the notches. Mark the inside edge all around.*

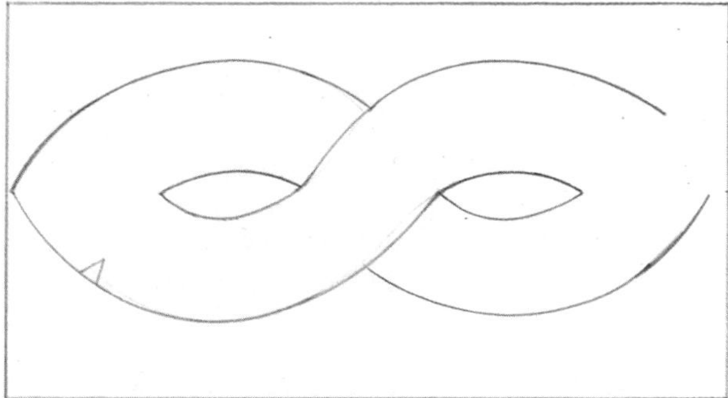

4 *Move the template along so that the tips and notches align with the previous marks, and mark the next pattern repeat in the same way. Continue this process until the border is as long as you need it.*

Working with corners

1 *If you have a matching corner template, mark it first in one corner and then work outward along each side to the other three corners.*

2 *If you don't want to take the border around the corner, finish off the border pattern neatly on each side of the corner and fill the space with a complementary motif.*

Working with one-way patterns

1 *If you are working with a pattern which moves in one direction, for instance a feathered design or a twisted cable, you may want the pattern going in the same direction all the way around the quilt border.*

2 *If you prefer the quilt design to be symmetrical, work a motif or medallion in the center of the side of the quilt and mark the border design outward from this, reversing the template so that each section goes in a different direction. Do the same on the other sides of the quilt.*

Before a block, or a whole quilt top, is quilted, a "sandwich" is made of the top fabric, a padded filling known as batting, and a backing fabric. Batting comes in several thicknesses and is made from several different fibers. Polyester is the most popular. It is light, easy to stitch, and has the great advantage of being washable. It comes in several different thicknesses, which are usually described by weight. The most common weights are 2 oz. (thin), 4 oz. (medium), 6 oz. (thick) and 8 oz. (extra-thick). If you want something that doesn't quite fall into any of these categories it is possible to combine two weights, or to separate the layers of batting. Dark-colored polyester batting can be used behind dark fabrics.

Batting and backing

▲ *These examples show the effects of different weights of batting; the same design has been quilted on the same fabric using 2 oz., 4 oz. and 6 oz. batting.*

In the past, the type of batting used generally depended on what material was most readily available in that particular region; so, for example, North American quilters generally used cotton whereas British quilters tended to use wool. In both countries, silk batting was expensive, and kept for very special items. These older types of batting are becoming popular again for specialized projects; some quilters choose cotton or wool batting when they want a more compact filling for a quilted item, or use a silk batting to line a silk garment. When you are making a quilted garment, you don't want a lot of bulk, so flatter batting such as flannelette can be useful. Check the washing instructions on the batting before you use it, as many silk, cotton and wool battings can't be machine-washed.

If you don't want your quilting stitches to show on the back of the quilt, use a piece of cheesecloth or a similar fabric as an inner backing while you are quilting, and then attach the final backing fabric.

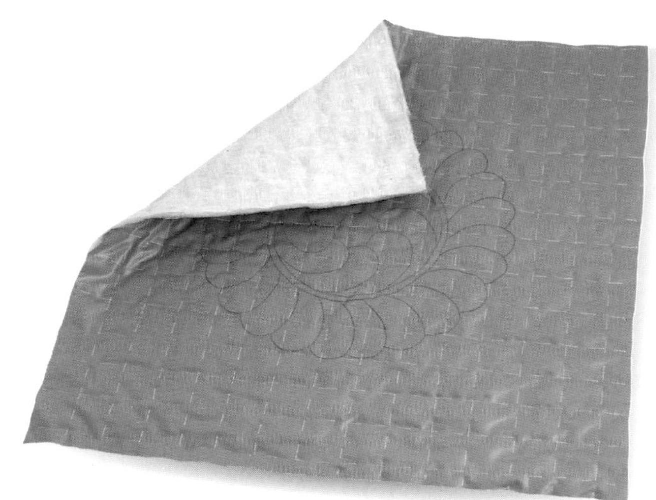

▲ *This is a wholecloth pillow ready for quilting; the fabric has been marked with the quilting pattern and then sandwiched together with batting and cheesecloth.*

The quilts below show how different backing fabrics work. The one on the left clearly shows the outlines of the quilting patterns, while the backing fabric on the right almost camouflages the stitching.

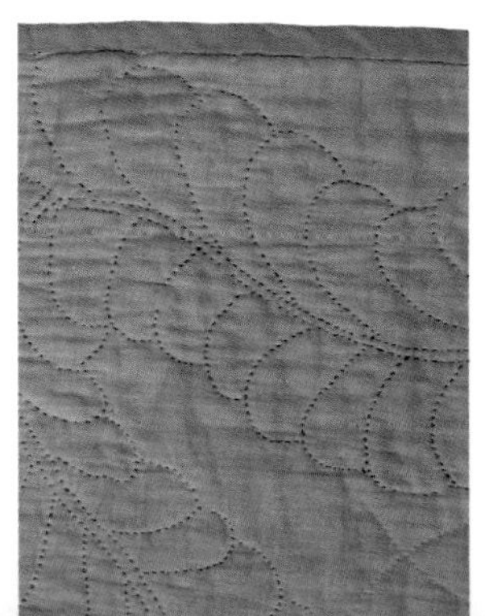

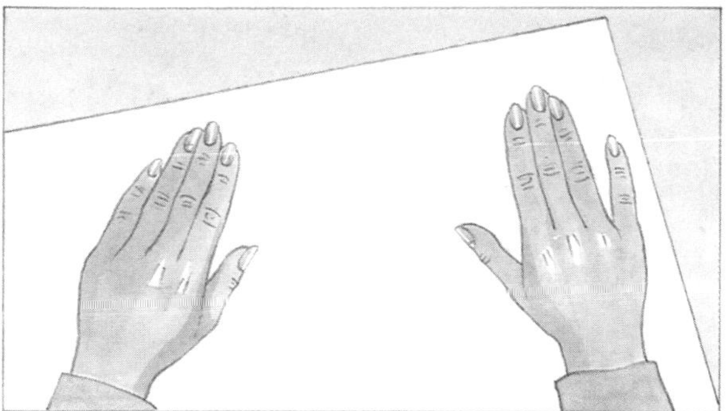

1 *To prepare a piece of fabric for quilting, place the ironed backing fabric right side down on a flat surface and smooth it out. If you are quilting a particularly large item, you may need to work on the floor.*

2 *Place the batting on top of the backing fabric and smooth out any creases. Place the fabric to be quilted right side up on top of the batting.*

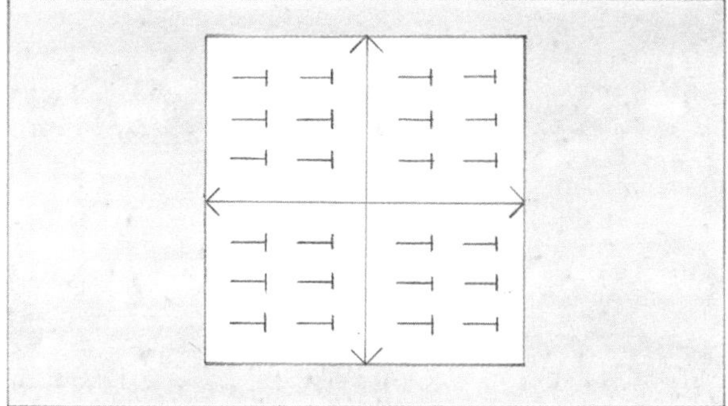

3 *Beginning in the center of the quilt and working out to the edges, pin through all three layers in rows spaced approximately 3 in. apart.*

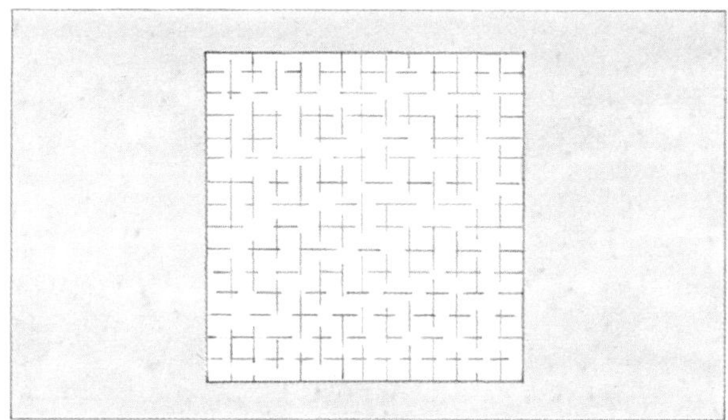

4 *Baste through all three layers in parallel horizontal rows, about 2 in. apart. Then baste even rows of stitches vertically, forming a regular grid of basting across the sandwich of fabrics. This will keep the layers from moving around while you are quilting. Remove the pins.*

SAFETY-PIN METHOD

Stitching an even grid of basting can be time-consuming, and some quilters prefer quicker ways of securing their work. If you are in a hurry, try this method: make the sandwich of backing, batting, and top fabric as above, then secure the three layers together with large safety pins at regular intervals.

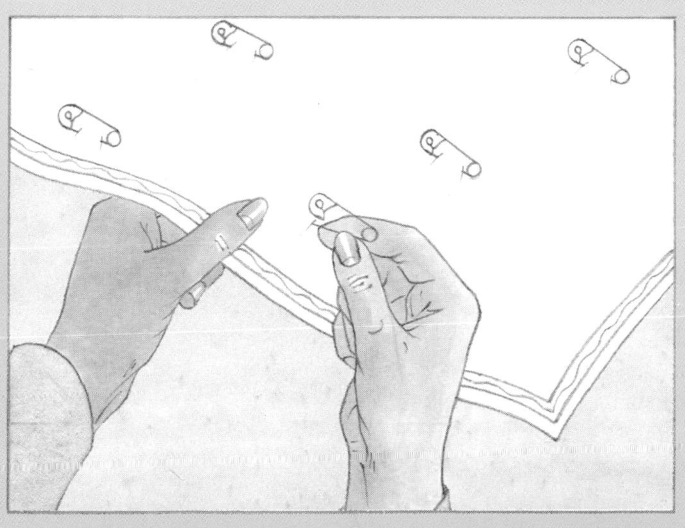

When you are quilting by hand or machine, each quilting stitch introduces tension into the work because you are pulling three layers together – the quilt top, the batting, and the backing. This process produces the slightly gathered effect which gives quilting its attractive texture, but the tension can cause the quilt top to become distorted. To prevent this problem from occurring, handwork is stretched

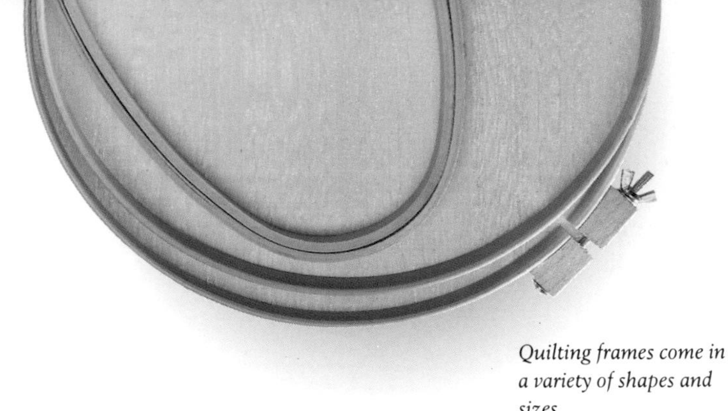

Quilting frames come in a variety of shapes and sizes

Using a quilting frame

fairly taut while it is being quilted; if your project is small, you may not need to stretch it, but if it is medium-sized or large, you will need some kind of frame.

Hand-held frames don't have any extra means of support and are used for stretching small areas of a quilt at a time. Hand-held frames can be circular or oval; they look like large embroidery frames and are used in the same way, catching the fabric sandwich between an inner and an outer ring.

Floor-standing frames are similar to hand-held frames, but you don't need to support them in your lap or on the edge of a table; they come with their own stands.

Full-size frames are large, free-standing frames which are used for stretching the entire quilt at once. Many quilting groups in the past used flat frames, which made the whole quilt top accessible so that it could be worked on by many quilters simultaneously. These days, few people have sufficient space, so they use a rolling frame, an adaptation of the same principle. The quilt top is attached to two rollers, and the bulk of the quilt is rolled up onto them, leaving an area exposed for quilting.

When you are quilting by machine, it is difficult to stretch your quilt top in the same way, since few frames will fit under the arm of the machine. If you have an oval frame, it may be useful for stretching machine quilting; if not, use your hands to spread the fabric evenly.

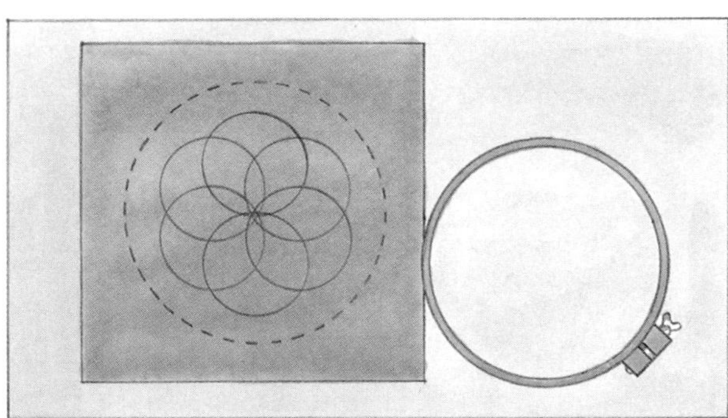

How to use a quilting hoop

1 *Separate the inner and outer hoops of a hand-held or floor-standing frame, and lay your basted quilt top smoothly across the top of the inner hoop.*

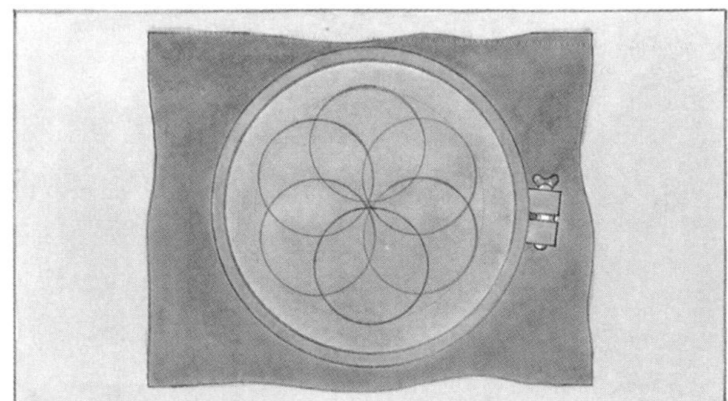

2 *Lay the outer hoop over the top layer of fabric so that it catches the quilt top between the two hoops; tighten the tension screw at the side so that the fabric is held firmly between the two rings.*

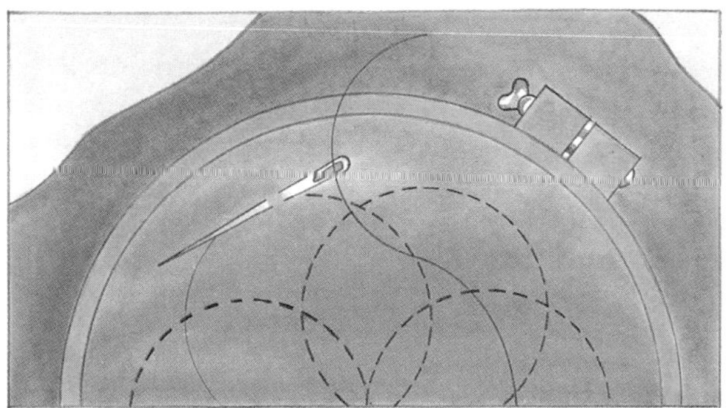

3 *Quilt the area within the hoop, then move the hoop to the adjoining part of the quilt; continue in this way until you have completed the quilting.*

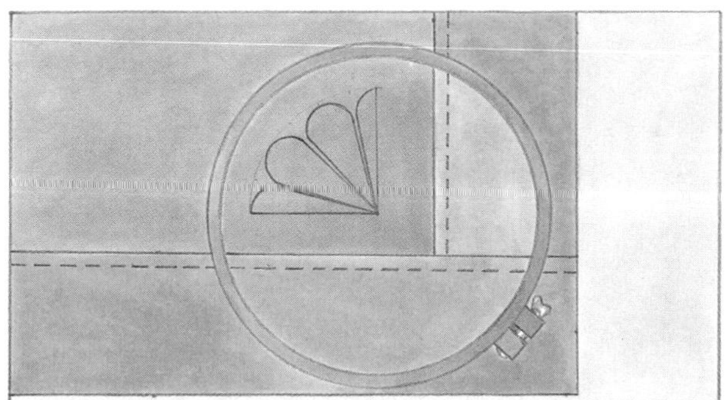

4 *If you find it difficult to quilt the corner, baste some extra fabric to the edges so that you can stretch it in the frame. When the quilting is complete, remove the extra fabric.*

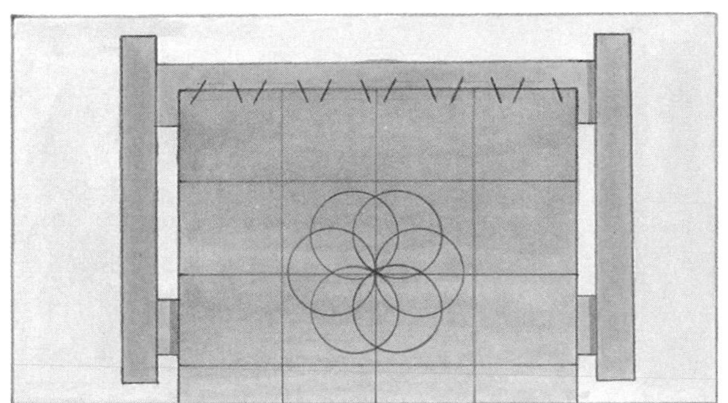

Using a roller frame

1 *Lay your quilt top right side up over the frame so that the longer sides are parallel with the flat stretchers at the sides of the frame. Baste the shorter sides of the quilt to the tapes on the rollers.*

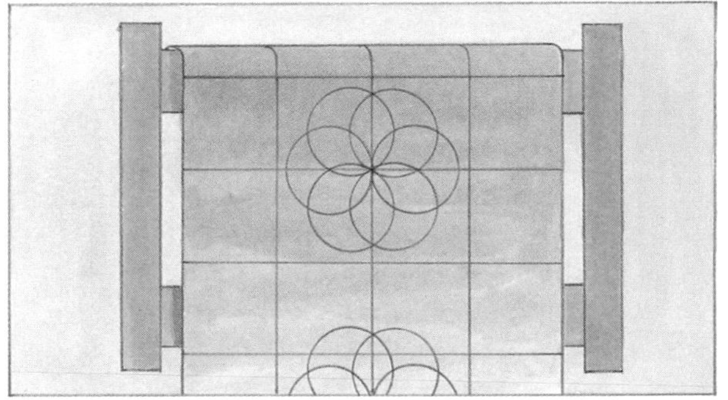

2 *Turn the roller at one end so that it takes up the bulk of the quilt, leaving one end of the quilt top stretched across the frame. Secure the rollers to maintain an even tension.*

3 *Stretch the sides of the quilt top by winding tape around the stretchers and pinning it in place on the quilt top with large safety pins.*

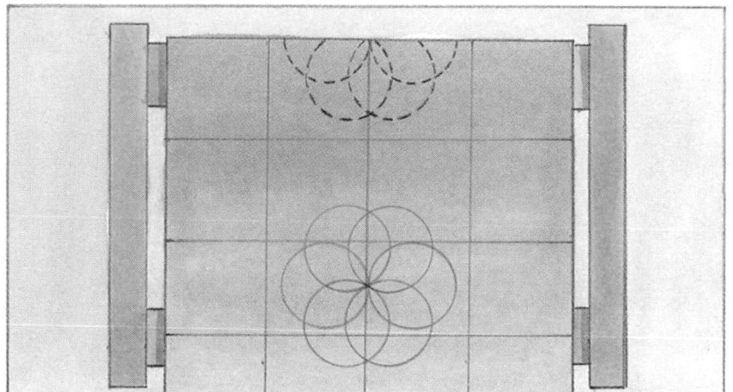

4 *Quilt the exposed area of quilt top, then unpin the tape and loosen the rollers. Rewind the rollers until a fresh piece of quilt top appears for stitching, then secure and quilt it in the same way.*

QUILTING BASICS

Quilting

Quilting is the stitching you work through the layers of quilt top, batting, and backing fabric. The quilting is functional in that it holds the three layers together, but it is also decorative; as you stitch, you form a textured pattern on the quilt top which enhances your design.

It is possible to work quilting by hand or by machine. Many traditionalists always quilt their quilt tops by hand even if they have pieced them by machine, but there is no reason at all why you shouldn't quilt by machine if you want to. Your stitching will show more, but that isn't necessarily a disadvantage; also, quilting by machine is quicker. Don't worry about how many stitches there are to an inch, but practice working stitches of uniform size and tension and you will produce good results. If you are working a long chain or cable design by hand, you may find it useful to work your way along each portion of the pattern using a separate needle and thread for each line, rather than stitching one whole line first and then coming back to do the next one; this helps to keep the tension even.

TIP

MACHINE QUILTING

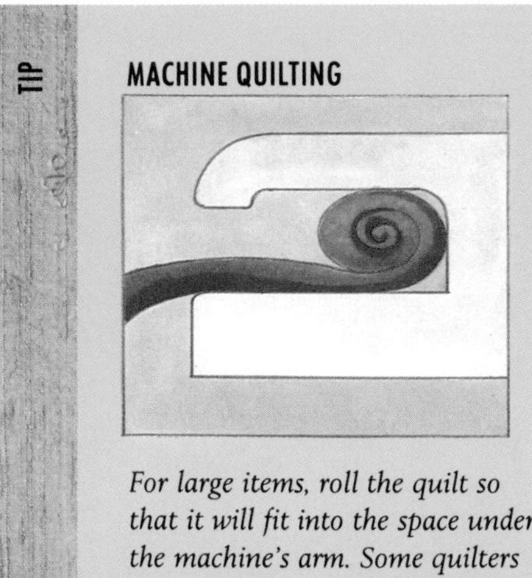

For large items, roll the quilt so that it will fit into the space under the machine's arm. Some quilters use bicycle clips to hold the roll.

HAND QUILTING

Use a thimble or thumble (see *page 26)* *on your stitching hand, and wind a piece of masking tape around whichever finger you use under the quilt; this will help you to guide the needle tip back up without pricking your finger.*

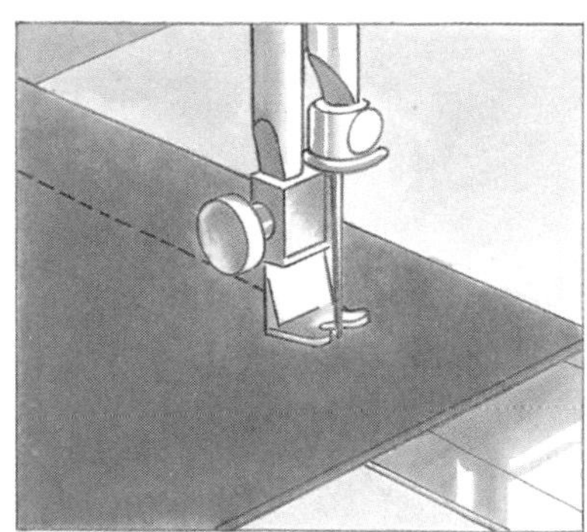

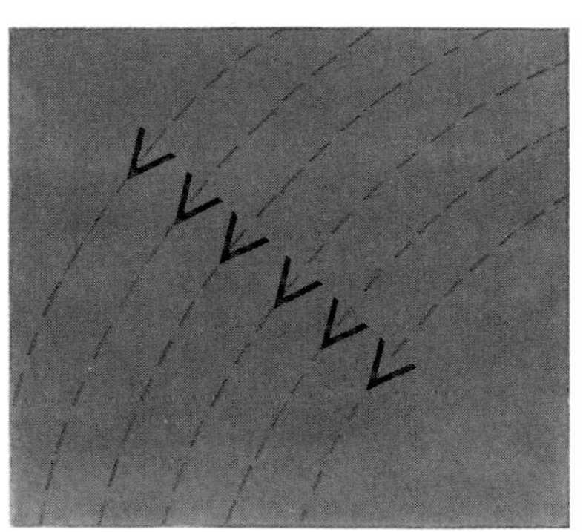

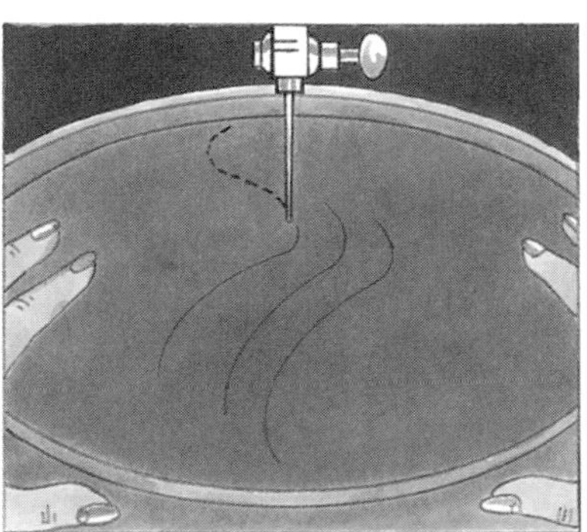

Quilting by machine

1 *Set your machine for a fairly long straight stitch, and stitch along the stitching line. To change direction, stop with the needle down, then lift the foot and pivot the fabric.*

2 *If you are quilting long parallel lines, stitch each row in the same direction; otherwise, the fabric may show slight puckering marks.*

3 *For quilting intricate designs, attach a darning or embroidery foot and lower the feed dog. Use either an embroidery frame or your hands to keep the fabric stretched, and move it freely around.*

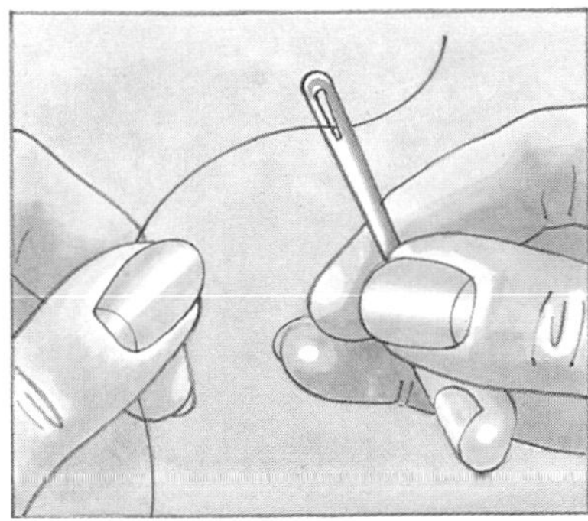

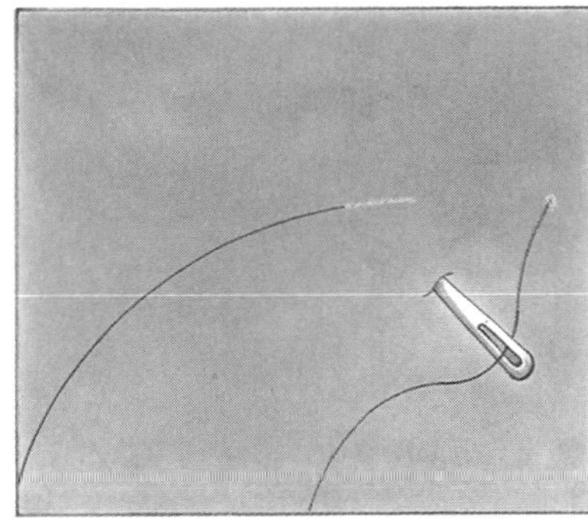

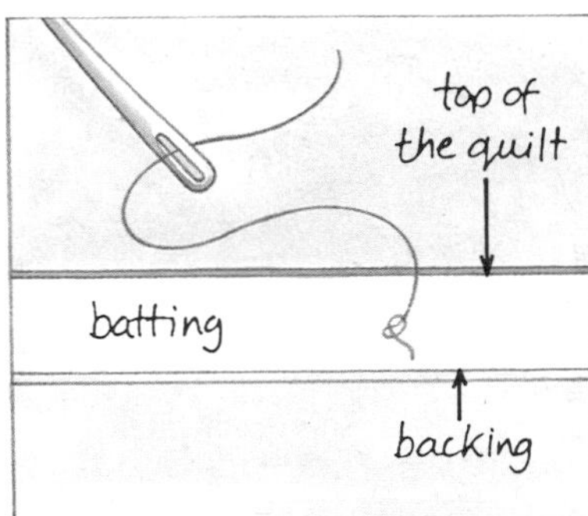

Quilting by hand

1 *Cut a length of thread about 18 in. long, and thread one end through the eye of your quilting needle. Tie a small knot at the longer end of your thread.*

2 *Put the needle into the fabric, on the right side, about 1 in. away from the beginning of your quilting line.*

3 *Bring your needle up at the beginning of the stitching line and pull gently. The knot at the end of the thread will pop down under the surface fabric and remain hidden from view.*

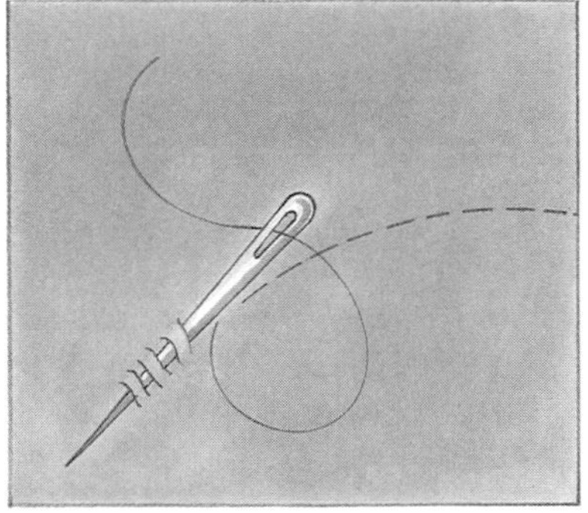

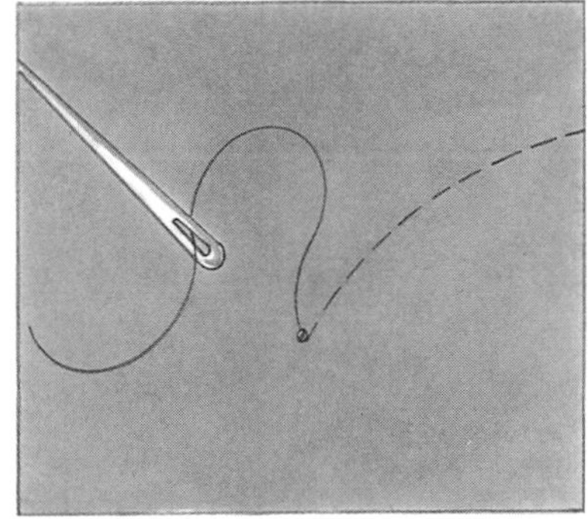

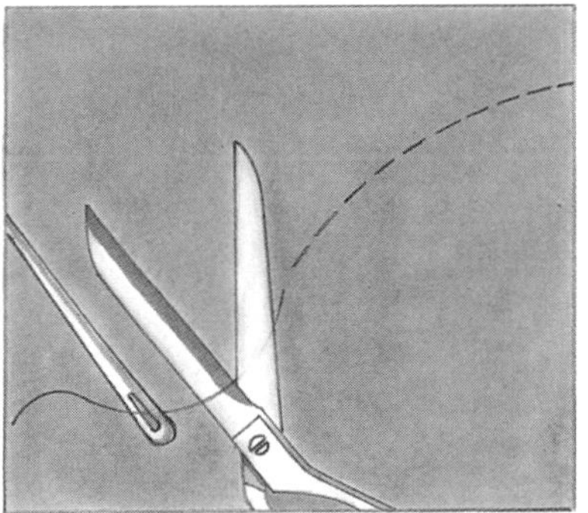

4 *Sew with small, even running stitches, making sure that you go through all the layers of the quilt. Take several stitches at a time on your needle before you pull it through.*

5 *When you are near the end of your thread, wind it around the needle twice and draw the knot close to the fabric.*

6 *Insert the needle into the stitching line, making sure that you draw the knot down into the batting. Then pull the needle back through the fabric about 1 in. from the end of the stitching and cut the thread.*

PROS AND CONS

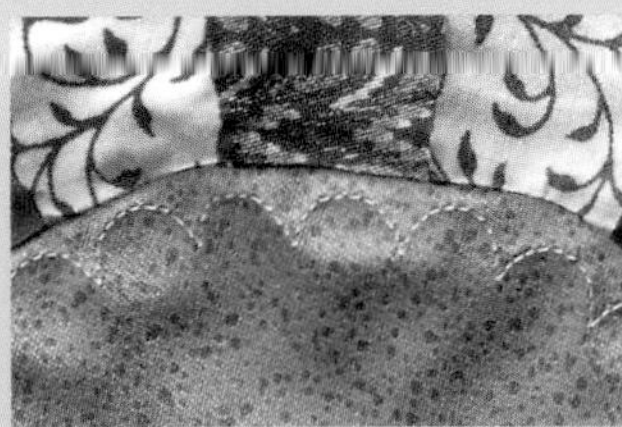

Machine quilting

Hand quilting

Machine quilting: pros

It is very quick, so your project takes shape rapidly. It is useful for large, regular patterns. Specialized accessories such as quilting guides make the stitching very accurate. The stitching is always even.

Machine quilting: cons

You can't carry your work with you. It is harder to keep layers wrinkle-free. The stitching shows more on the right side. Large quilts are difficult to manipulate under the arm of the machine.

Hand quilting: pros

It is attractive because the stitching shows less. It is easier to "fudge" difficult areas of a design. It creates a soothing rhythm. You can carry small pieces with you to stitch.

Hand quilting: cons

It is very time-consuming. It requires short lengths (18 inches) of thread, so you are constantly rethreading needles. Long sessions lead to sore hands, pricked fingers, and tired eyes.

If you are quilting patchwork or appliqué designs, you can often use the patchwork or appliqué patterns themselves as starting points for your quilting design. The seam lines on pieced work, and the edges of appliqué pieces, can be followed or echoed by your lines of stitching. Or, if you prefer, you can quilt a traditional or modern design over the top of the pieced work, ignoring the lines made by the

Different ways of quilting blocks

fabric patches, or combine the two techniques, perhaps by quilting small motifs inside some of the patches. Here you can see several ways of quilting the same pieced block, the Churn Dash; all of these methods can be done by hand or by machine.

On this quilt, the shapes of the fabric patches have been used to suggest shapes for quilted patterns and spirals. Along the border, triangles and points have been built up with rows of quilting stitches at different angles.

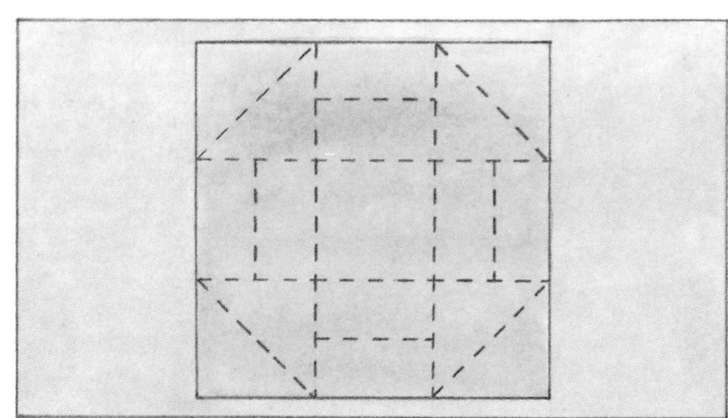

Quilting "in the ditch" is probably the fastest and the simplest method of quilting patchwork: stitch just next to the seam, on the side away from the seam allowance.

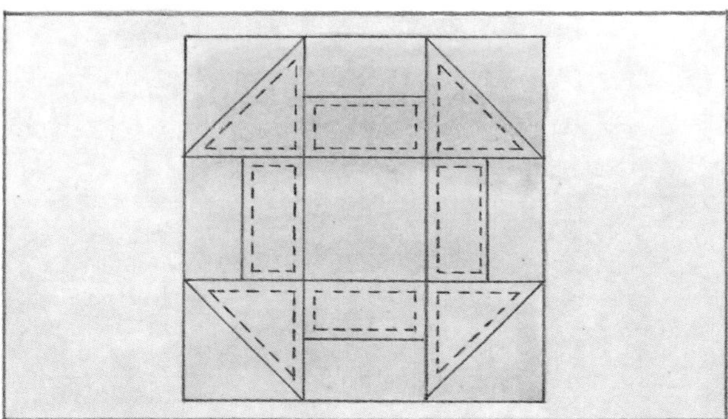

Outline quilting is done on each patch: stitch a row of quilting stitches 1/4 in. inside each patch, being careful to avoid the seam allowance.

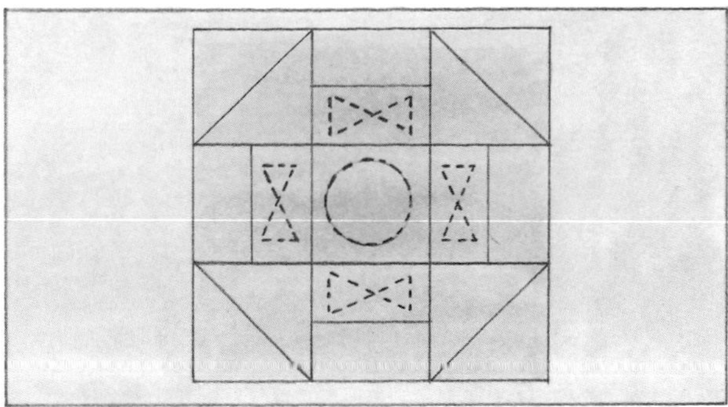

On this block, small individual motifs have been quilted inside some of the patches. This method can be combined very effectively with quilting in the ditch.

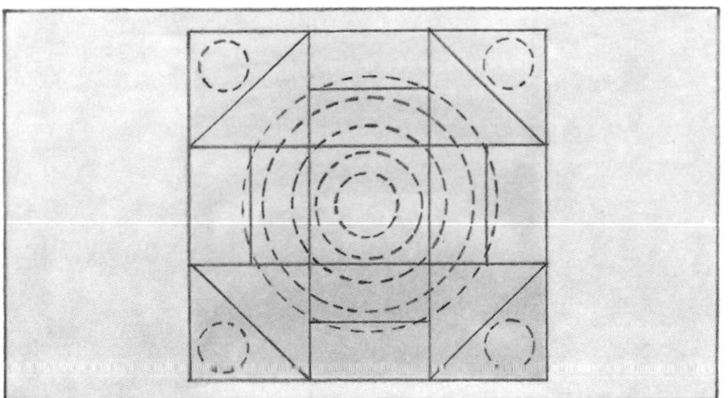

Here, the lines of the patchwork design have been ignored completely, and the whole block has been quilted over with concentric circles, adding tiny circles in the corners.

Here, the corners of the patchwork pieces have been used as guides for straight lines of quilting intersecting at the centers of the pieces.

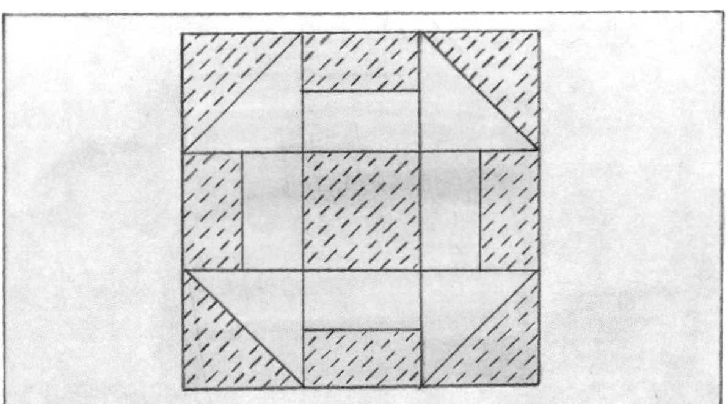

This design uses straight lines of quilting stitched diagonally across the outside and central fabric pieces and keeping the same direction each time.

QUILTING APPLIQUE BLOCKS

Hawaiian quilts often use a method known as echo quilting, where rows of quilting ¼ in. apart follow the outlines of the appliquéd design, filling in the spaces with flowing lines.

Background textures are popular for adding visual interest to appliqué blocks and quilt tops. The first line of quilting is worked close to the edge of the appliqué design or ¼ in. outside it; then the background fabric is quilted with a design to throw the appliqué into relief.

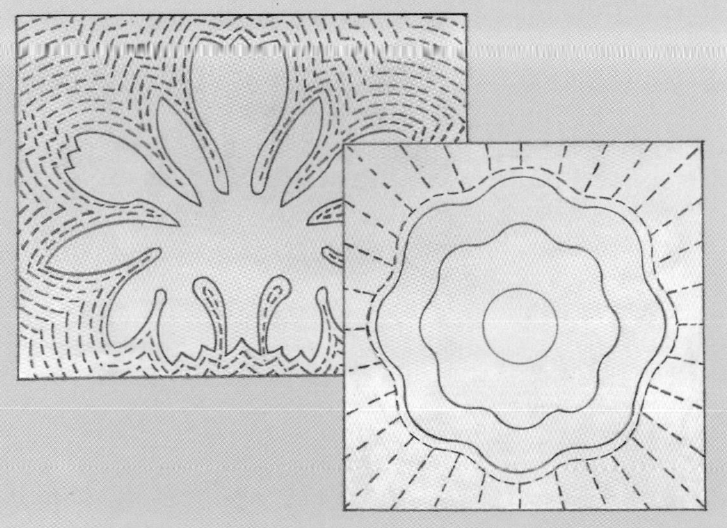

Finishing quilts

Once your quilt top has been quilted, the edges must be finished, and usually some kind of binding is used. For bed quilts, which will be subjected to quite a bit of wear, a good straight binding in a hard-wearing fabric is acceptable, but the ideal edging is bias binding – even better, a double thickness of bias binding. The first part of a quilt to show wear is usually the edge. If a straight binding is used, the single thread at the outside edge can disintegrate, making it necessary to replace the binding. Bias edges are composed of many threads criss-crossing around the whole perimeter of the quilt, so they are far less likely to wear out quickly. A bias binding is also quite elastic and can be coaxed along curves and around corners.

The fabric you choose for your binding should coordinate with the fabrics in the quilt, and although bias binding can be bought in several widths, it is usually better to make your own. Cutting bias strips takes a great deal of fabric, and you will need to allow for this when you are buying the fabrics for a quilt. If you are binding a large quilt, sheeting is strong and comes in very wide widths, so it is useful for straight and bias bindings. A pieced binding can be made using all the fabrics from the quilt; this is particularly effective if your quilt top has a wide plain border or sashing.

Many quilters bind their quilts by using either the backing or the quilt top to cover the raw edges. If you decide to do this, remember to make the backing or the quilt top about 1 in. wider all around than the finished size of the quilt. The edges of the quilt are then pressed under, turned to the front or back of the quilt as appropriate, and stitched down. An even simpler way of finishing a quilt top is to trim away about $\frac{1}{4}$ in. of the batting, turn in the edges of the quilt front and back, and stitch them together close to the edge.

A well-made quilt is a work of art to be proud of, so you might think about finishing it off with your name or initials, as artists do. Or, if it's intended as a gift, embroider the name of the recipient. This is a "friendship quilt," with the names commemorating two women's shared experiences.

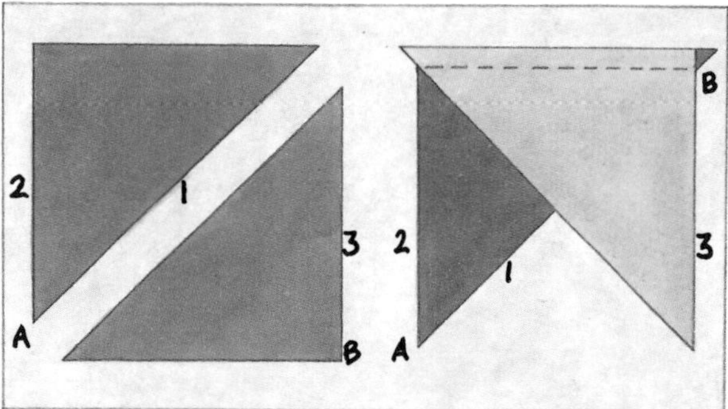

Making a continuous bias strip

1 *Take $1\frac{1}{4}$ yd. of 45 in. wide fabric. Remove the selvages and press the fabric. Fold the square across the diagonal and cut; you now have two large triangles. With the right sides together, place two of the short edges together as shown and stitch a $\frac{1}{4}$ in. seam by machine.*

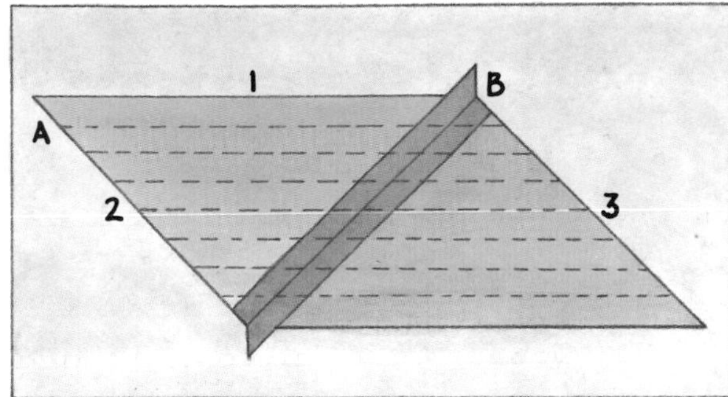

2 *Open out the piece and press the seam open; you now have a parallelogram. Mark the desired width of your strips, allowing for turning under the edges.*

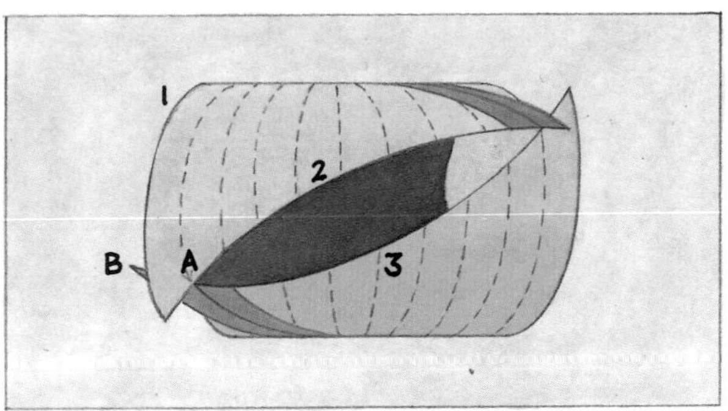

3 *With the right sides together, join side 2 to side 3, matching points A and B. Stitch a ¼ in. seam to form a tube; the end of side 3 will extend slightly at the end of the tube.*

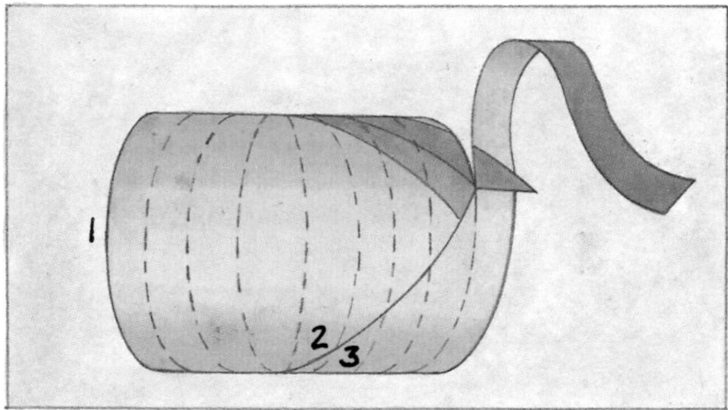

4 *Using the lines as a guide, cut around the tube until you reach the end. You will now have a long length of bias binding.*

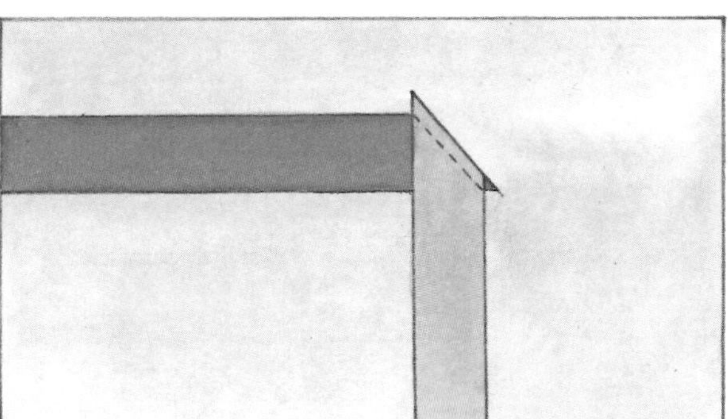

5 *If you have to join a bias strip, put the right sides together as shown and stitch a narrow seam either by hand or by machine.*

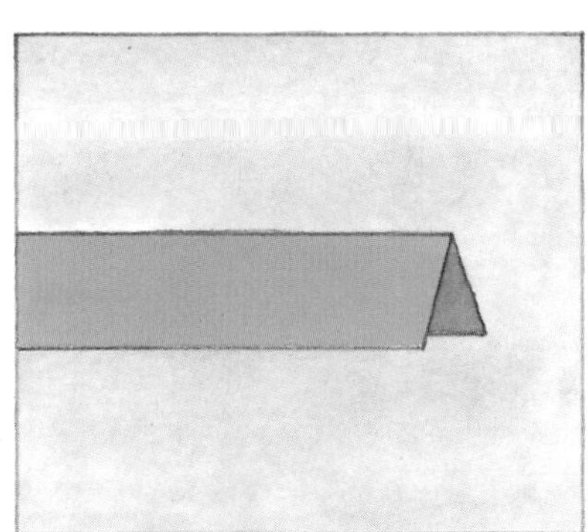

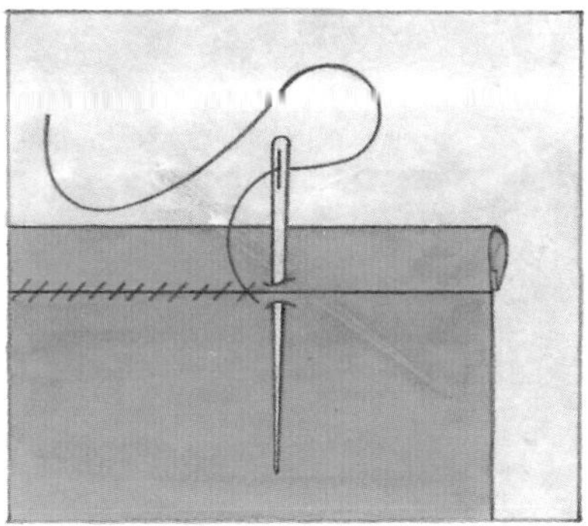

Making a straight binding

1 *Cut two strips 2½ in. wide by the length of the quilt, and two strips 2½ in. wide by the width of the quilt plus 1 in. Fold the strips in half lengthwise and press the fold.*

2 *Lay the longer strips face down along the longer edges of the quilt top; pin and sew them in position about ¼ in. from the edges.*

3 *Turn the strips over to the back of the quilt and turn under the raw edges; stitch into position by hand. Finish the other edges of the quilt the same way.*

3
The sampler quilt

Introduction to the sampler quilt

Now that you are familiar with the basic principles of making a quilt, it's time to put your knowledge into practice. This section will take you through all the steps necessary for making a sampler quilt, from cutting and piecing to binding the edges of your finished quilt. As you work your way through each lesson, you will be increasing your practical understanding of the piecing, quilting, and finishing techniques. We have chosen traditional blocks and quilting designs so that once you have finished the sampler quilt, you will have mastered most of the basic techniques needed for producing a wide variety of other traditional quilt designs.

In each lesson, you will find cross-references to the relevant pages in the Pattern Library in case you want to substitute one design for another. Remember that yardages of the different fabrics may need to be adjusted if you decide to alter the blocks or borders significantly.

All of the quilting on the sampler quilt can be done by hand or by machine, so you can choose the method which suits you best - or use a mixture of the two methods.

To complement the traditional design of the sampler quilt, we have chosen a traditional color scheme of pinky reds, gray greens, and creams. You may decide to choose a totally different color scheme. If so, choose fabrics that have similar values (see page 32) to the ones shown here (so, for instance, your new fabric A would be dark, while your new fabric B would be a lighter version of the same color). Simply substitute the appropriate fabric each time the relevant letter is mentioned.

Before you start the quilt, wash your fabrics (see page 30) to check that they are color-fast and to pre-shrink them. If necessary, pull the fabrics to straighten the grain; then press them so that they are ready to be cut.

▼ *These are swatches of the fabrics used in the sampler quilt. To make it easier to identify which fabric is being used in each part, every one has been given a letter. We have also given a brief description of the fabrics, all of which are medium-weight 100% cotton.*

Fabric A
Dark pink background with a small, light green flower-sprig pattern.

Fabric B
Light pink background with a small all-over pattern in white.

Fabric C
Solid dark green.

Fabric D
Light green background with small flower-sprig design in pink.

Fabric E
Solid medium green.

Fabric F
Solid light-to-medium pink.

Fabric G
Unbleached muslin.

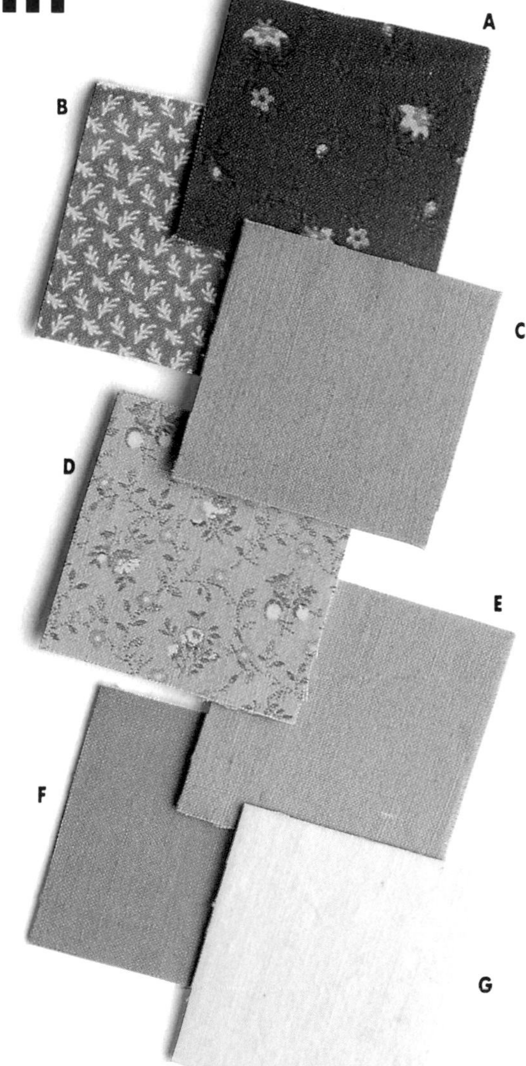

The nine blocks of the sampler quilt have been numbered for ease of reference and to correspond with the templates on pages 66-71.

1 *The Four-patch block (see page 72)*

9 *The Reverse Appliqué block (see page 88)*

3 *The Sugar Bowl block (see page 76)*

Sashing (see 10; page 90)

Pieced border (see 11; page 92)

Binding (see 14; page 98)

7 *The Star block (see page 84)*

8 *The Flying Geese block (see page 86)*

4 *The Appliqué block (see page 78)*

6 *The Strip-pieced block (see page 82)*

5 *The Log Cabin block (see page 80)*

Backing

Quilted repeat pattern

2 *The Nine-patch block (see page 74)*

Quilted corner motif

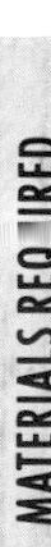

To make the sampler quilt, you will need the amounts given; all of the fabrics are 60 in. wide. The yardages given here should give you slightly more than you need, to allow for occasional accidents while marking or cutting; if you have large pieces left over, you could always make a pillow cover or two to go with the quilt.

Fabric A: $^3/_4$ yard
Fabric B: $^3/_4$ yard
Fabric C: $^3/_4$ yard
Fabric D: $^3/_4$ yard
Fabric E: $^3/_4$ yard
Fabric F: $^3/_4$ yard
Fabric G: 8 yards

You will also need:

2 spools of ordinary sewing thread in ecru
1 piece of medium-weight batting 78×78 in
Quilting thread in green, pink and ecru if you are quilting by hand, or sewing thread in your chosen colors if you are quilting by machine
1 water-soluble marking pen
Quilting needle if you are quilting by hand
A rotary cutter and cutting board
See pages 26-29 for general equipment for making templates, cutting, and sewing

SAMPLER QUILT

Sampler quilt templates

On these and the following pages you will find all the templates that you will need for the pieced blocks and the quilting patterns that make up the sampler quilt. All of the templates are full-size, so copy each of them carefully onto paper, cardboard, or template plastic (see page 42) and use them as cutting guides. All the seam allowances are included and are $^1/_4$ in. unless indicated otherwise. The arrows on some templates mark the straight grain of the fabric; the arrows should be lined up with either the warp or the weft threads on your fabrics. The blocks which don't require templates have full instructions in the appropriate lesson.

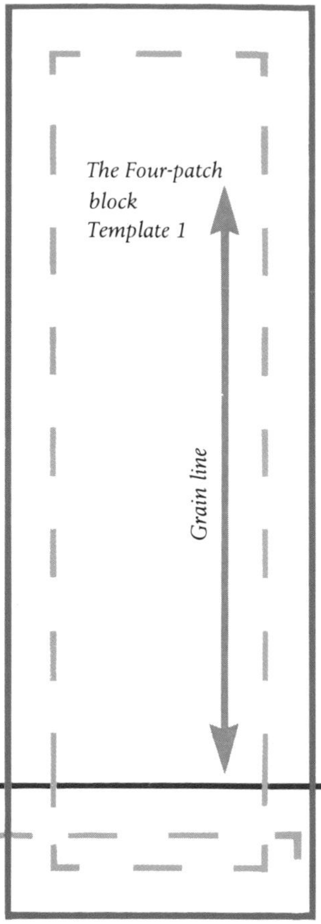

The Four-patch block
Template 1

Grain line

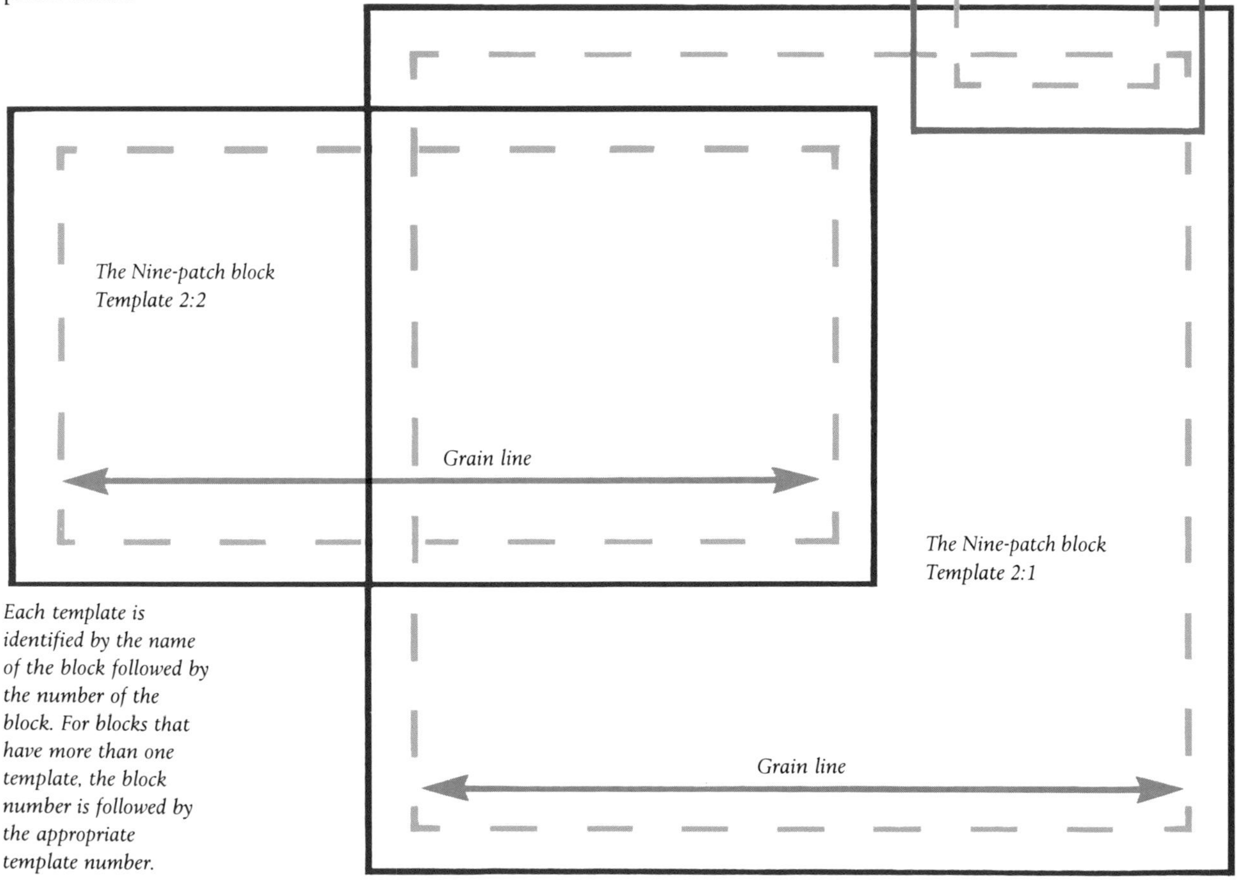

The Nine-patch block
Template 2:2

Grain line

The Nine-patch block
Template 2:1

Grain line

Each template is identified by the name of the block followed by the number of the block. For blocks that have more than one template, the block number is followed by the appropriate template number.

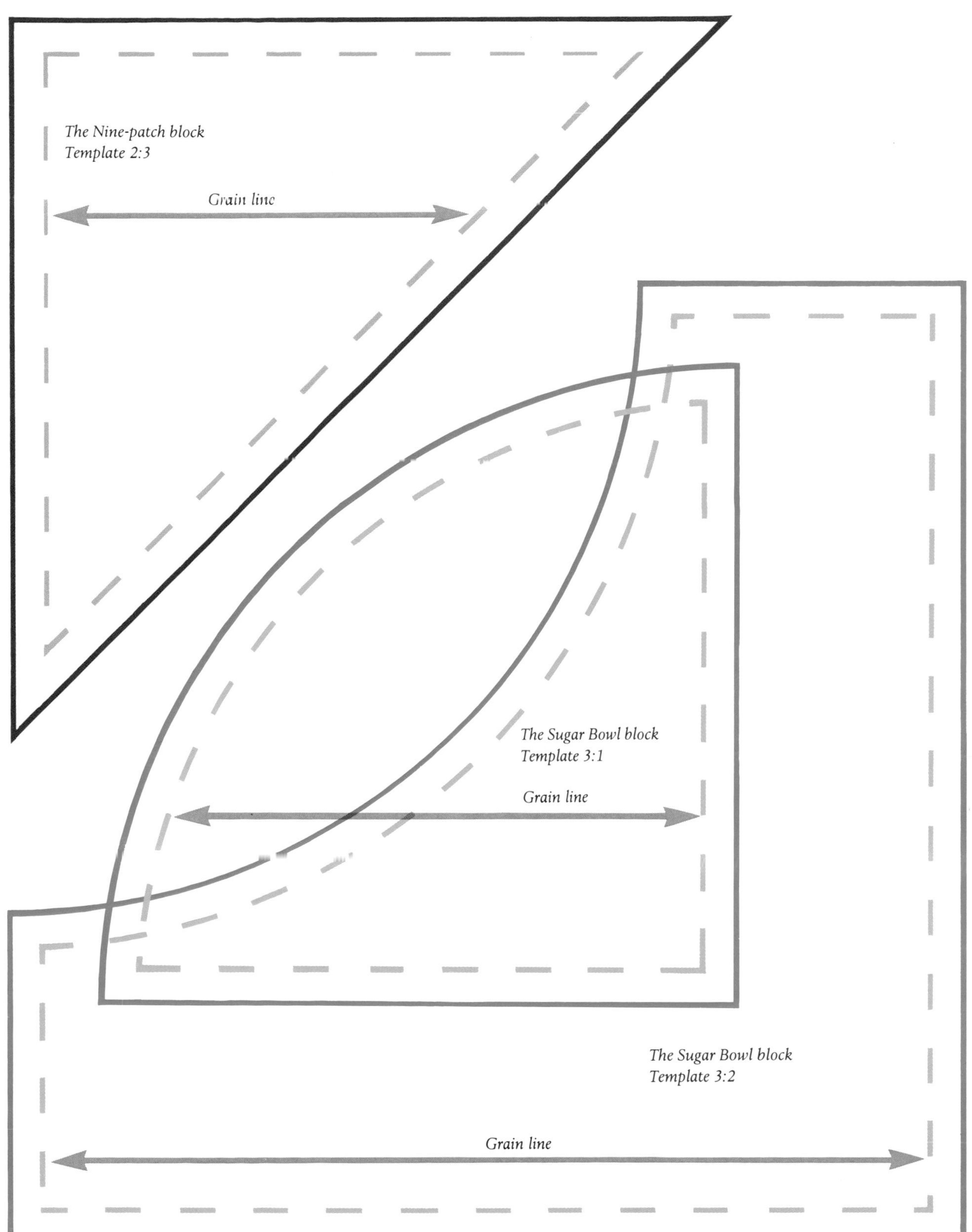
The Nine-patch block
Template 2:3
Grain line
The Sugar Bowl block
Template 3:1
Grain line
The Sugar Bowl block
Template 3:2
Grain line

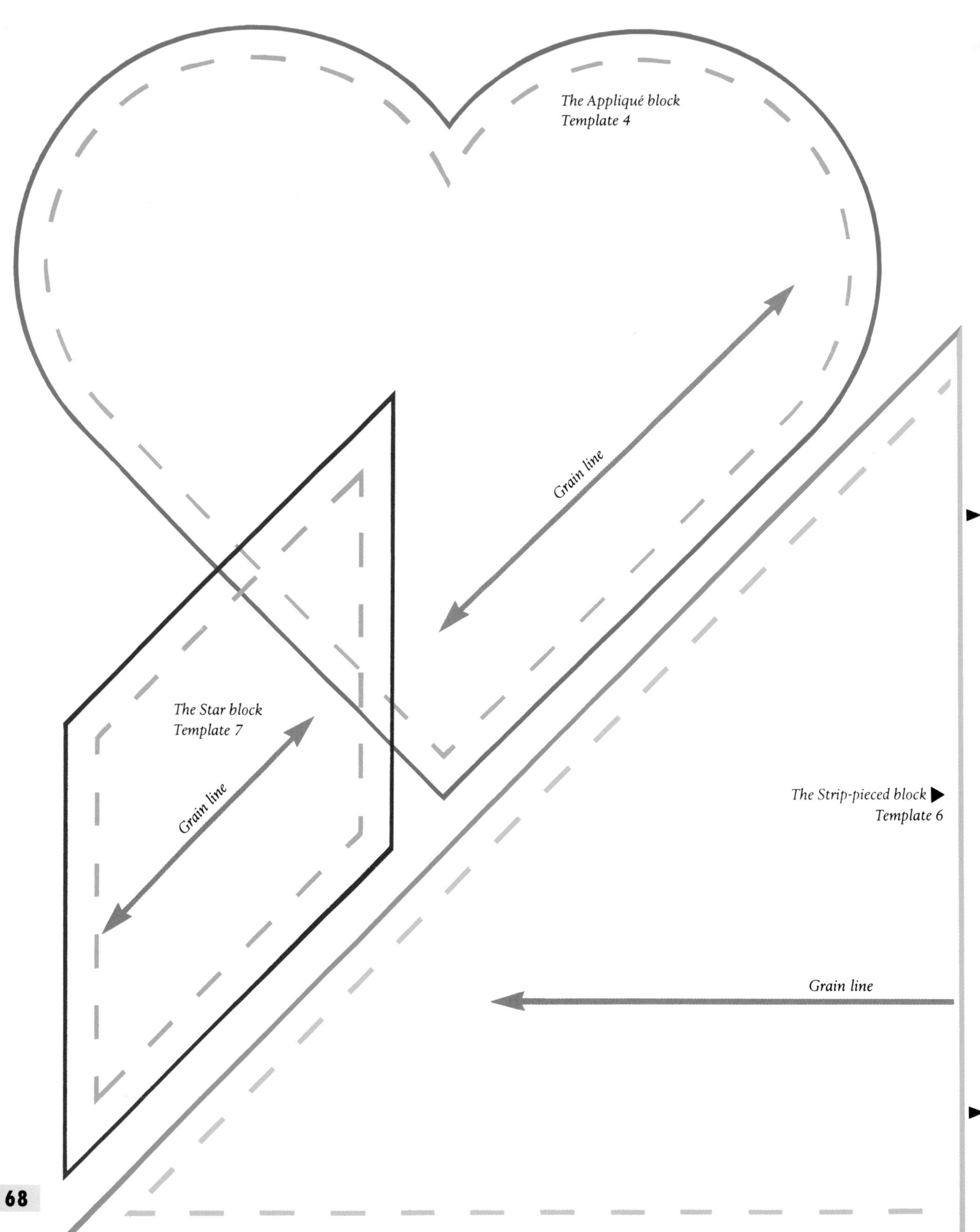
The Appliqué block
Template 4
Grain line
The Star block
Template 7
Grain line
The Strip-pieced block
Template 6
Grain line

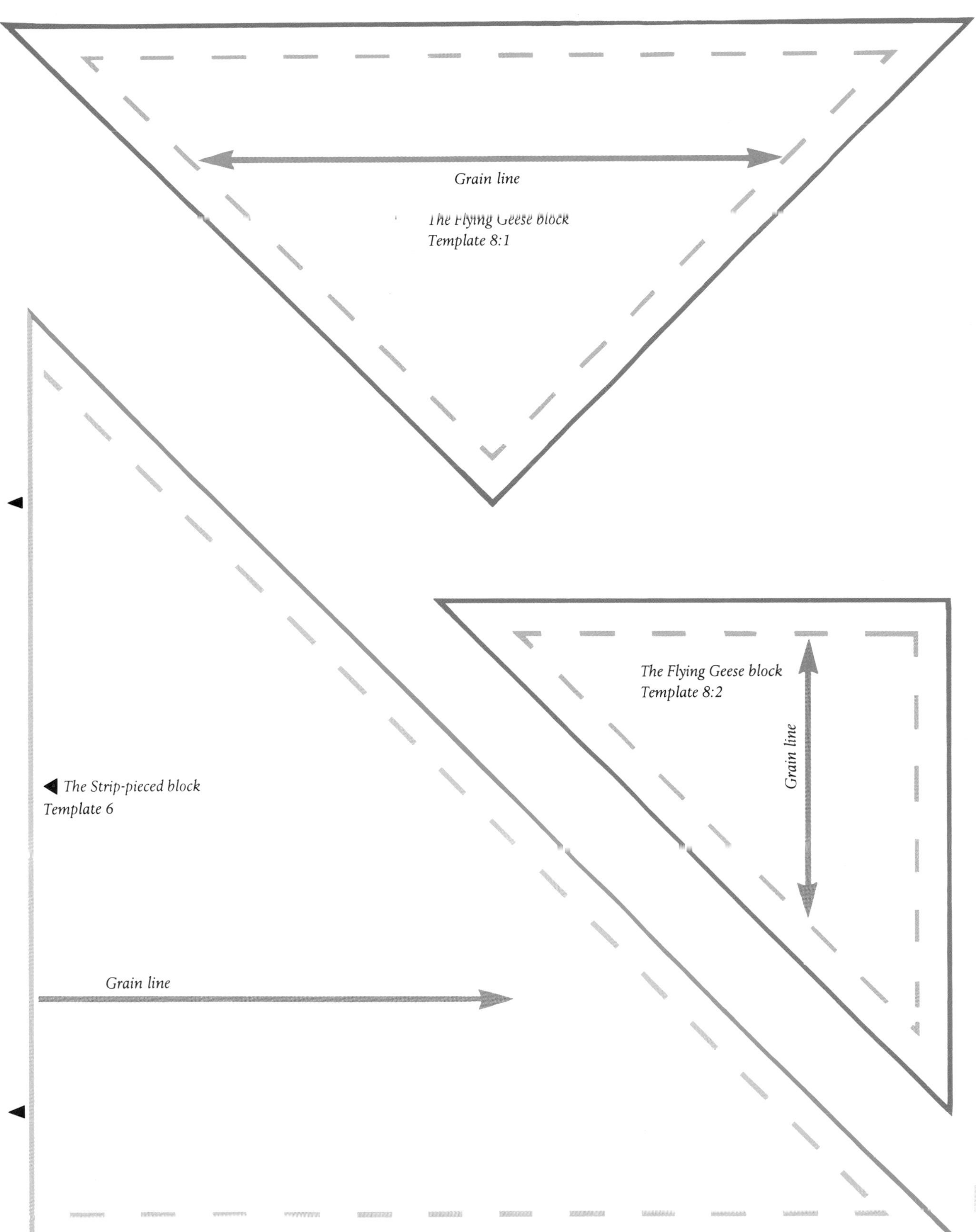
Grain line
The Flying Geese block
Template 8:1
The Flying Geese block
Template 8:2
Grain line
The Strip-pieced block
Template 6
Grain line

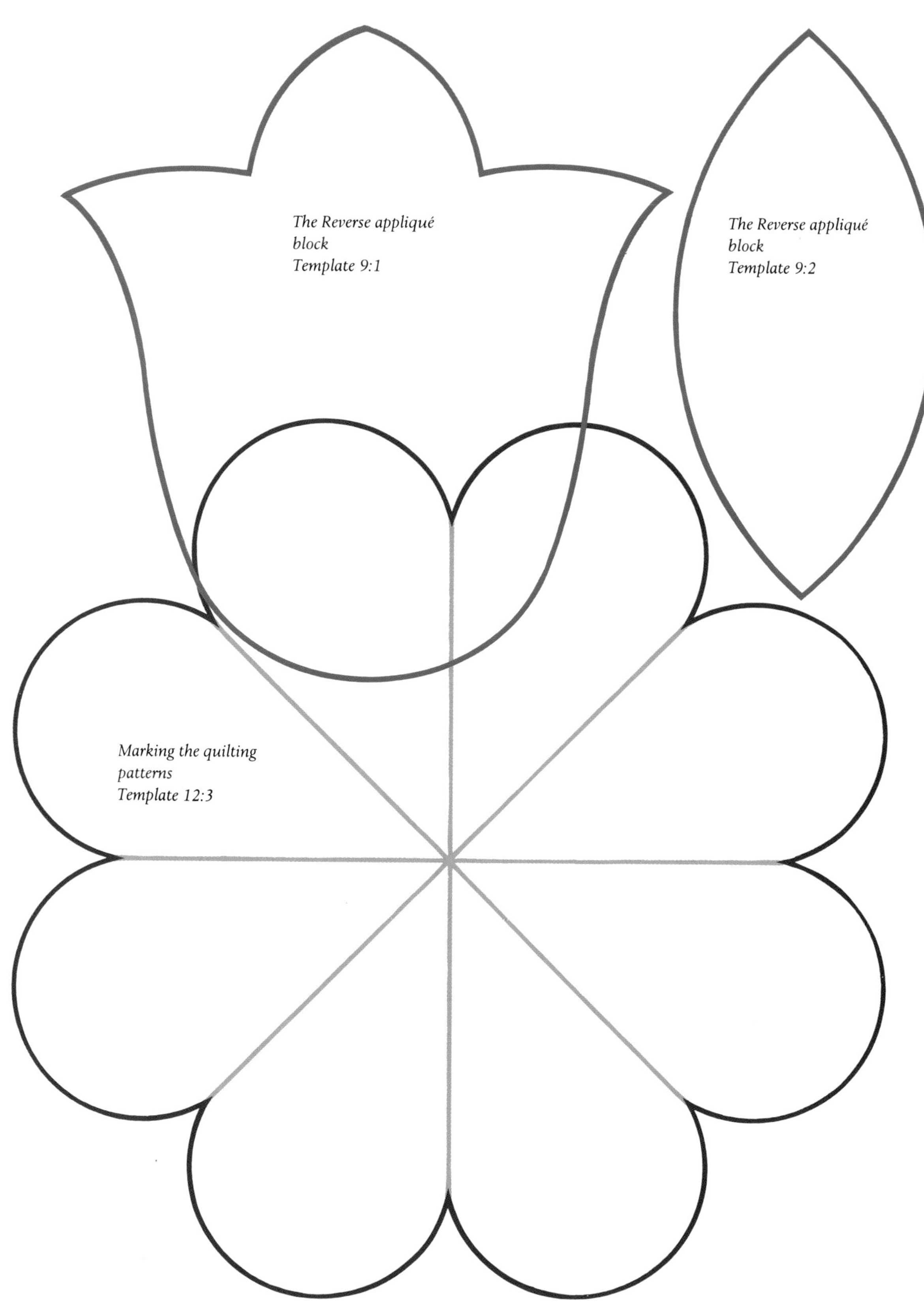
The Reverse appliqué block
Template 9:1
The Reverse appliqué block
Template 9:2
Marking the quilting patterns
Template 12:3

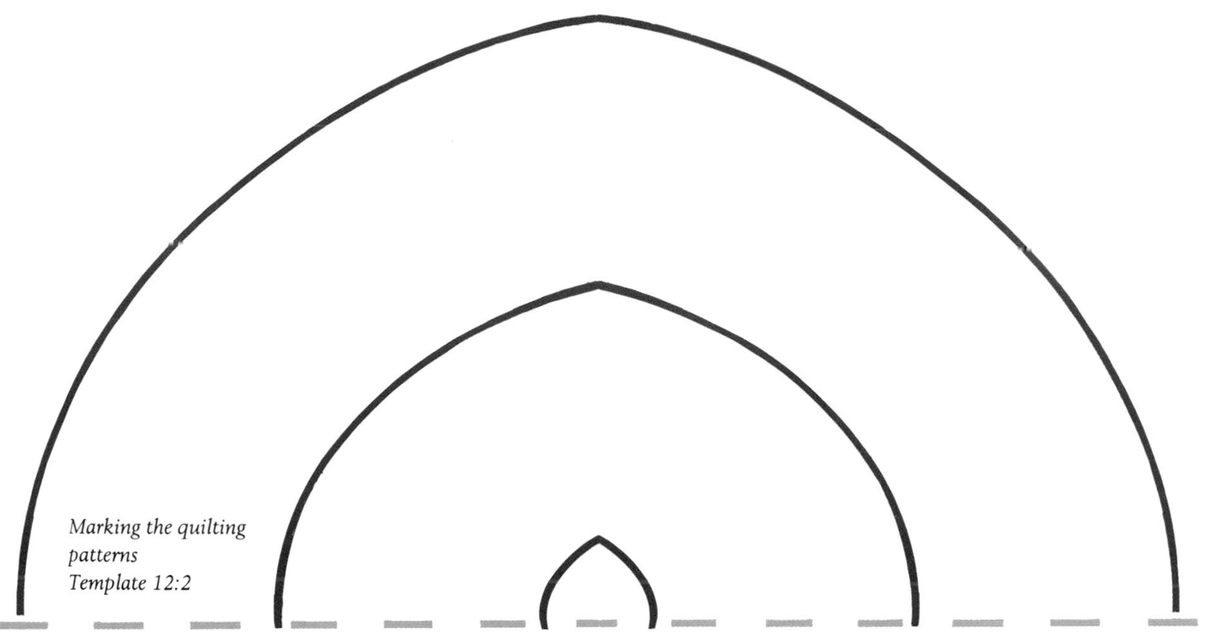

Marking the quilting patterns
Template 12:2

Marking the quilting patterns
Template 12:1

What exactly is a four-patch block? As its name suggests, it is a square design that is divisible into four separate basic patches, or units, which are constructed one at a time before being stitched together to form the complete block. There are many variations of four-patch blocks, and a selection is shown in the Pattern Library (page 122). In this lesson you'll learn how to construct the block called Rail

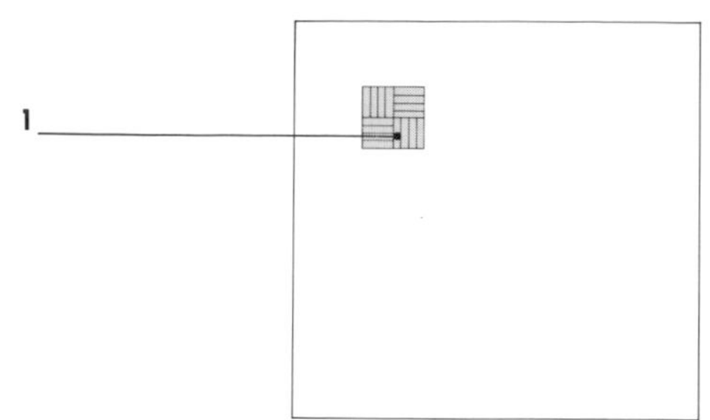

SAMPLER QUILT

1 The Four-patch block

Fence, which is a simple four-patch design. Only two fabrics are used in this, and only one template, but the way that the fabrics are alternated, with two of the patches turned on their sides, makes an attractive block design.

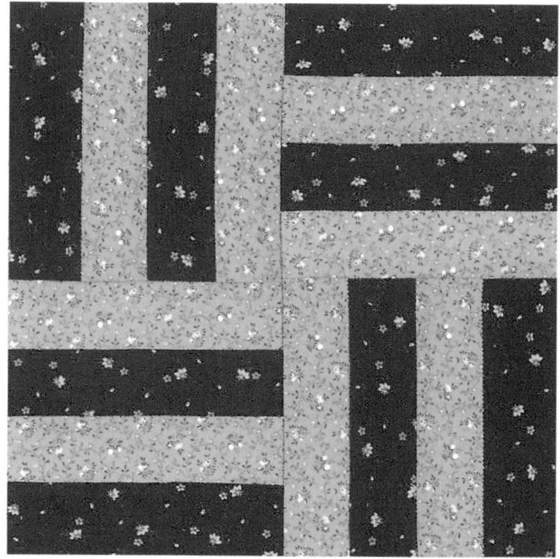

▲ *The alternating colors produce a dramatic effect from a very simple pattern.*

IDENTIFYING A FOUR-PATCH BLOCK

This might seem self-evident, but some designs which seem to divide neatly into quarters are actually more complex. A design is a standard four-patch block if you can divide it into four quarters without cutting into any of the shaped pieces.

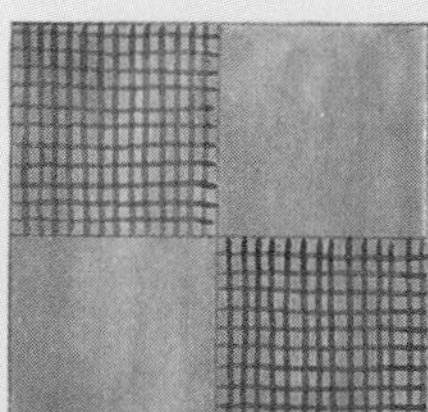

This is a four-patch design.

This is a four-patch design.

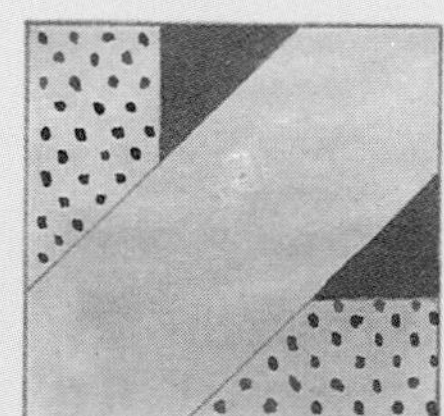

This is not a four-patch design.

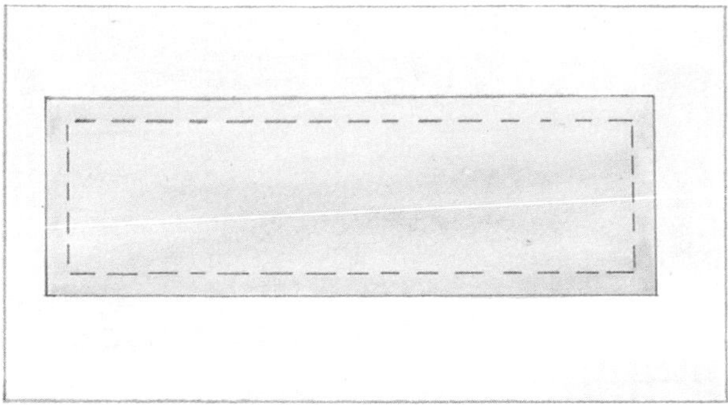

1 *Trace template 1 on page 66 full-size onto a piece of thin cardboard, and cut it out very accurately (see page 40, Making templates). Also mark the seam allowance lines and the grain line.*

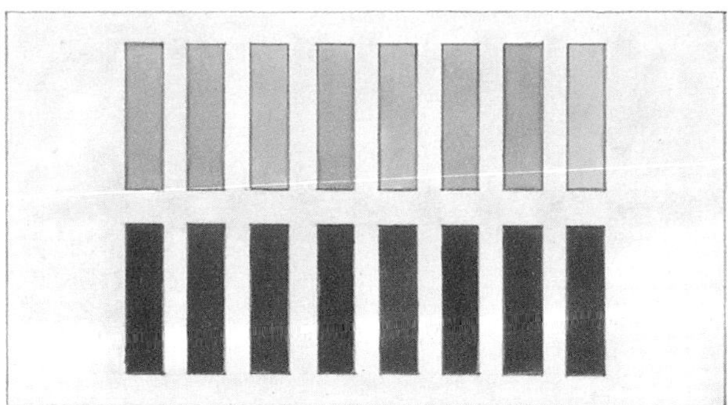

2 *Using the template as a guide, cut eight pieces from fabric A and eight pieces from fabric D. Make sure that you position the template each time so that the marked grain line lies either horizontally or vertically along the straight grain of the fabric.*

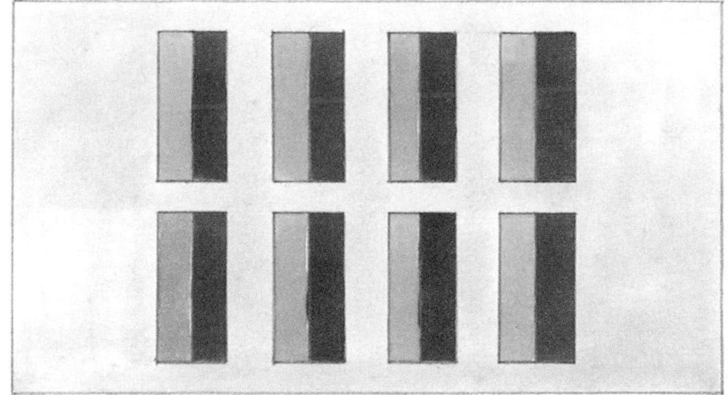

3 *Take one piece of fabric A and one piece of fabric D, and place them right sides together. Stitch a ¼ in. seam along one of the long edges by hand or machine (see page 46, Piecing), and press the seam toward the darker fabric. Repeat with the seven remaining pairs of pieces.*

4 *Take two pairs of patches and place them right sides together so that the edge of fabric A on one piece is against the edge of fabric D on the other. Join this seam and press it to the darker side to form one of the four basic patches for the block. Repeat three times to make the other patches.*

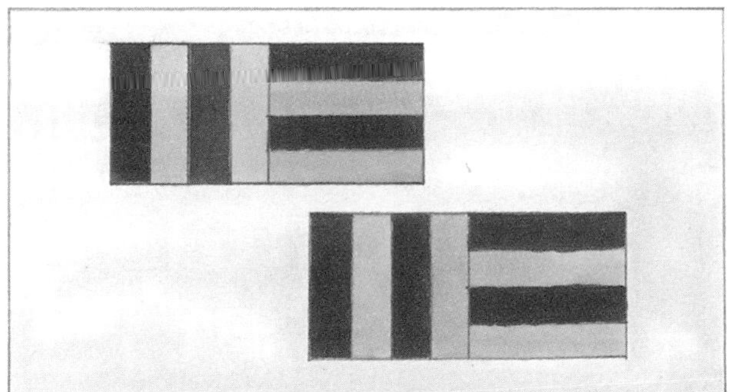

5 *Take one patch and turn it 90° so that the strips are horizontal. Right sides together, join it in the same way to the side of another patch turned so the strips are vertical. Press the seam open. Repeat for the other patches.*

6 *Join the two halves together as shown to complete the blocks, and press the seam open. You now have a complete Rail Fence block.*

As the name implies, nine-patch blocks are divided into nine sections, which are joined first in rows of three; then three rows are joined to form the whole block. Nine-patch blocks are exciting to work with because the larger number of patches offers more variety in the designs. Nine-patch block designs often have a blank square in the center, which can be a focal point for a splash of color or some form of fancy quilted embellishment. We have chosen the Churn Dash block for the second block of our sampler quilt. It is based on an even grid of nine squares, it needs only three templates, and it will give you practice in stitching diagonal seams.

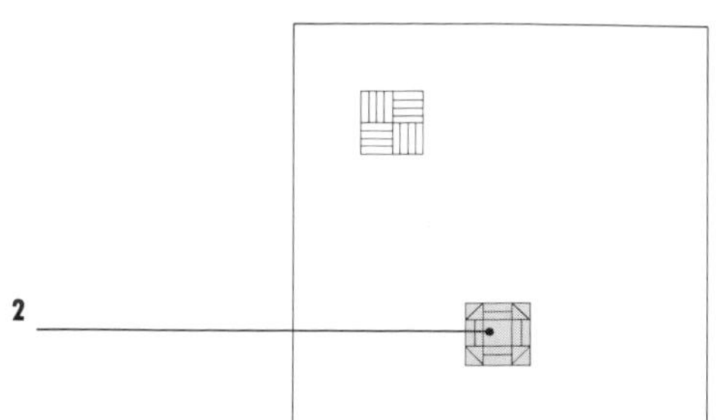

SAMPLER QUILT

2 The Nine-patch block

As with many other blocks, a nine-patch often has several names. Churn Dash and Hole in the Barn Door are sometimes called Wrench, and Jack in the Box is also known as Double Z. Some nine-patch designs, such as Bear's Paw and Hole in the Barn Door, have the block divided slightly differently from the basic nine-patch, in that the central section of the grid is narrower than the outer sections, but many nine-patch designs are based on a grid of nine equal squares.

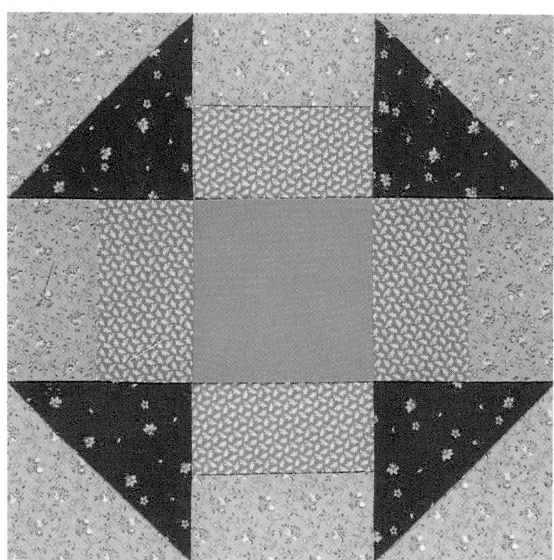

▲ *The finished block, showing an interesting interplay among the different fabrics.*

RECOGNIZING A NINE-PATCH BLOCK

The most regular nine-patch blocks are made up of nine equal squares **a**, *so they are easy to recognize. However, more complex blocks may also be nine-patch designs. The test is whether you can construct them into three straight rows of three blocks, regardless of the widths of the blocks; designs* **b** *and* **c** *are both still nine-patch blocks, even though they look very different from traditional ones.*

Basic nine-patch.

Bear's Paw variation.

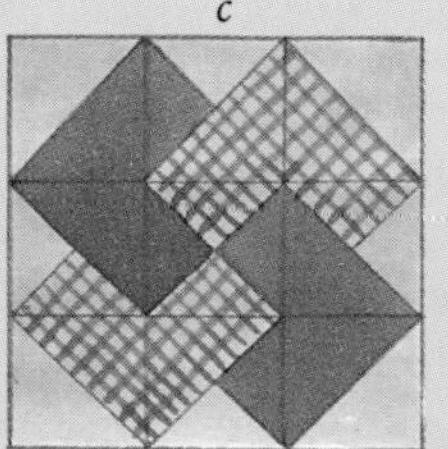

Card Trick design.

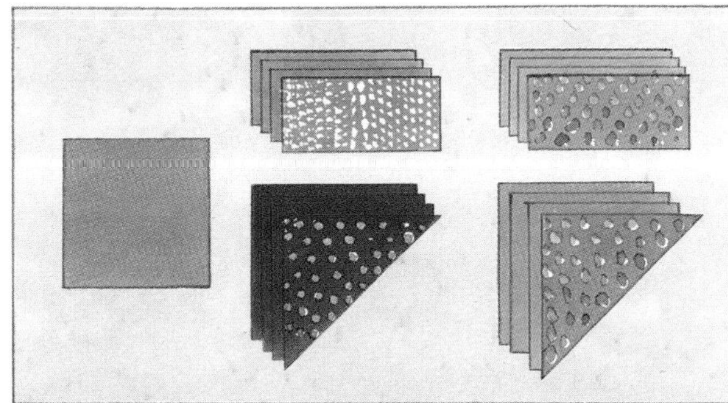

1 *Make templates 2:1, 2:2, and 2:3 on page 66. Using template 2:1 cut one piece from fabric C (see page 44, Cutting fabrics). Using template 2:2, cut four pieces from fabric B and four from fabric D. Using template 2:3, cut four pieces from fabric A and four from fabric D.*

2 *Following the instructions on page 46 (Piecing), join the light green (Fabric D) triangles to the dark pink (Fabric A) triangles along the long edge, right sides together, taking care not to stretch the fabric as you stitch. This gives you four identical square patches, called unit* **a**.

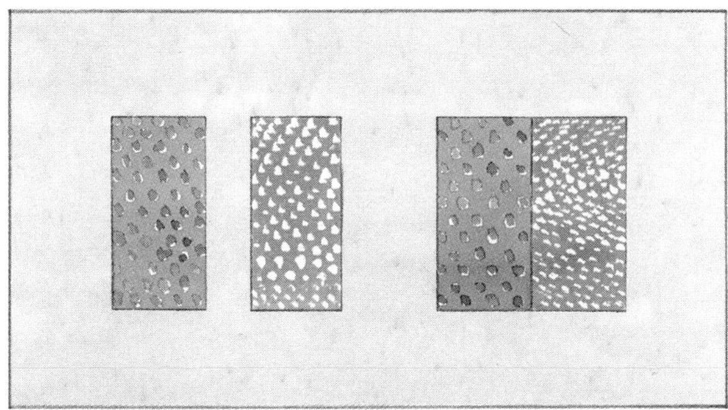

3 *Right sides together join the light green (Fabric D) rectangles to the light pink (Fabric B) rectangles along one long edge. This will give you four more identical square patches, called unit* **b**.

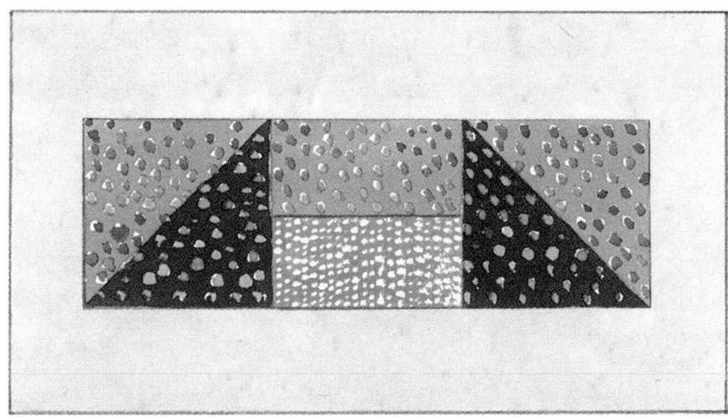

4 *Join two unit* **a** *patches to the edges of one unit* **b** *patch. Position the patches so that the light green triangles and the light green rectangle are all at the top of the new design. Repeat to make two identical strips.*

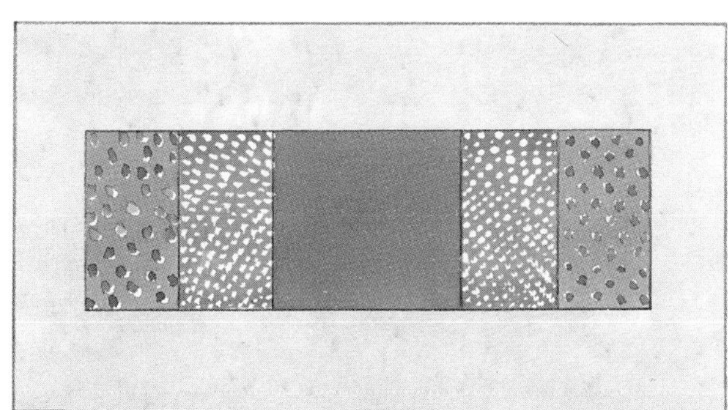

5 *Join the two remaining unit* **b** *patches to the edges of the dark green (Fabric C) square, making sure that the light pink rectangles are next to the square on both sides. This makes the central row of the block.*

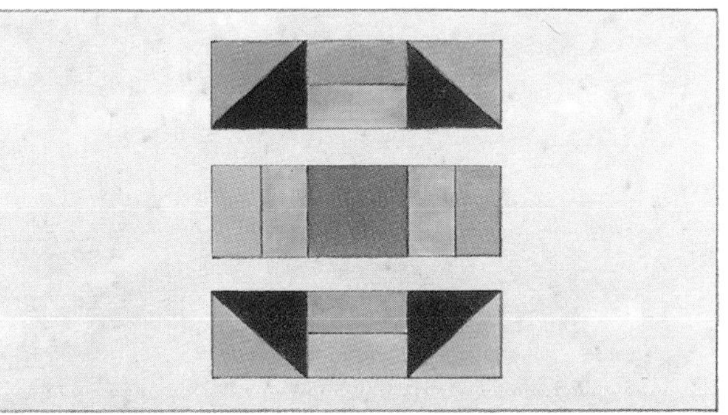

6 *Join the three rows, making sure that the light pink rectangles of the top and bottom strips are next to the green central square. You now have a Churn Dash block.*

3 The Sugar Bowl block

Like the Rail Fence block (see page 72), this block is a four-patch design made in four even, square patches. This one, however, uses two templates and also introduces curved seams. Curved seams introduce exciting new dimensions into quilt patterns, because they take the eye away from the grid structure of the block and allow it to be drawn across the work to follow the curved lines. On page 146 you will find ways in which you can combine Sugar Bowl blocks to make more complex patterns such as Drunkard's Path where, as the name suggests, the curves weave to and fro across the quilt top. Here, though, we are making only one block; the light/dark contrast between the green and pink produces a strong design using just two different fabrics.

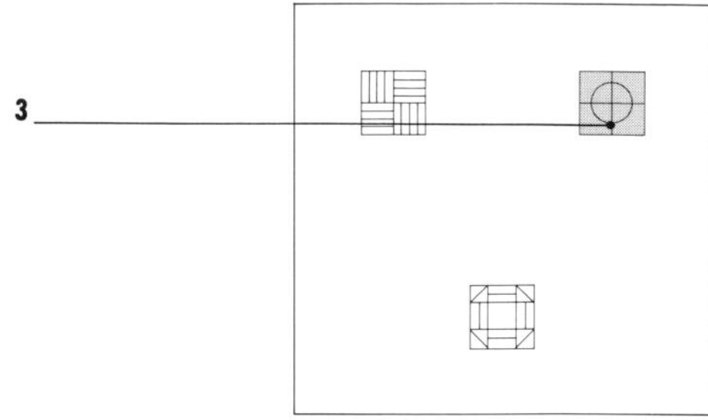

▼ *The finished block, showing a strong contrast between the two fabrics.*

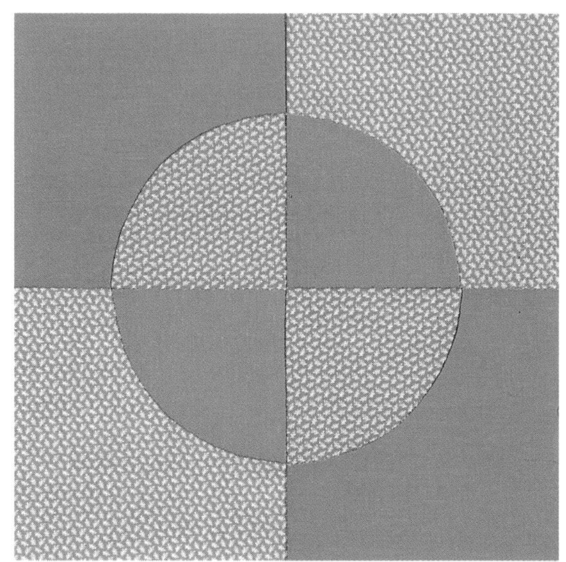

CUTTING CURVED SEAMS

When you are cutting out your fabric it is very important to make sure that any curved edges are smooth. Cut them carefully with scissors, or use a rotary cutter against a strong template. It is important to have a strong template so that you don't cut into the template itself.

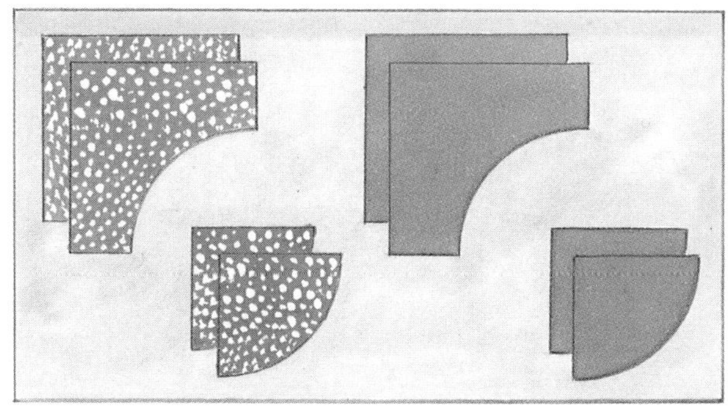

1 *Make templates 3:1 and 3:2 on page 67. Using template 3:1, cut two pieces from fabric B and two from fabric C. Using template 3:2, cut two pieces from fabric B and two from fabric C.*

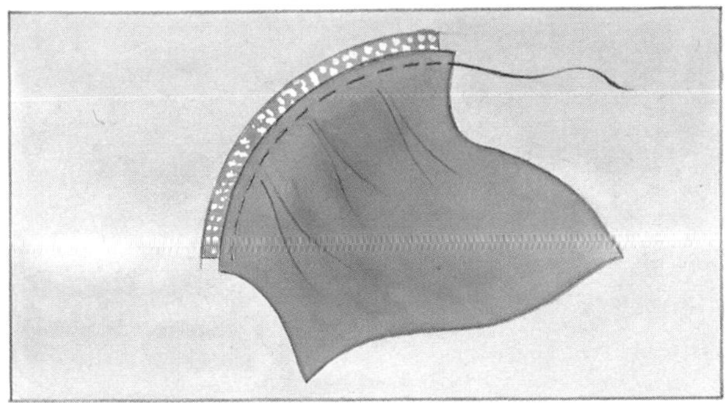

2 *Following the instructions on page 47 for curved seams, stitch the curved edges of the pink (Fabric B) quarter-circles inside the edges of the large green (Fabric C) pieces.*

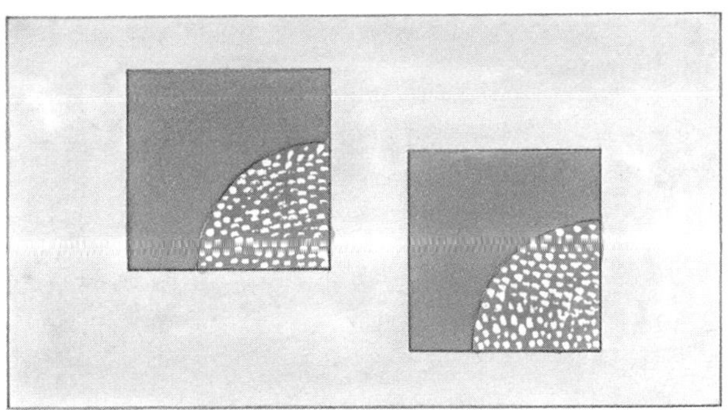

3 *Open out the pieces to the right side. You now have two identical patches, unit* a.

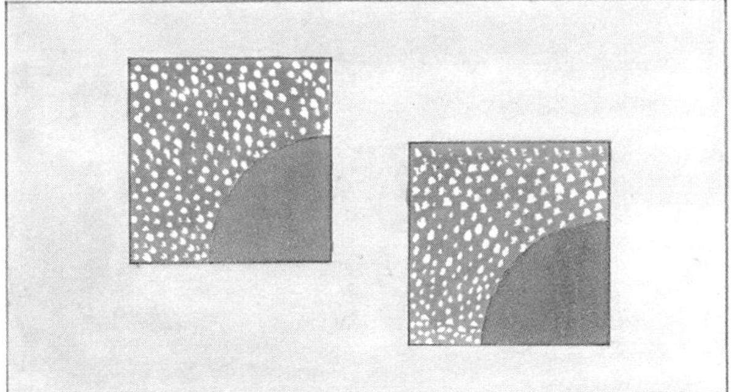

4 *Using the same method, stitch the green (Fabric C) quarter-circles to the curved edges of the large pink (Fabric B) pieces. You now have two more patches, unit* b.

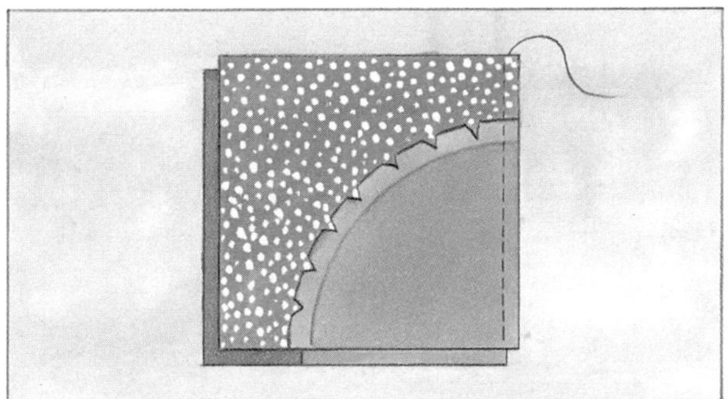

5 *Stitch one unit* a *to one unit* b, *matching the seams carefully so that you get a smooth half-circle.*

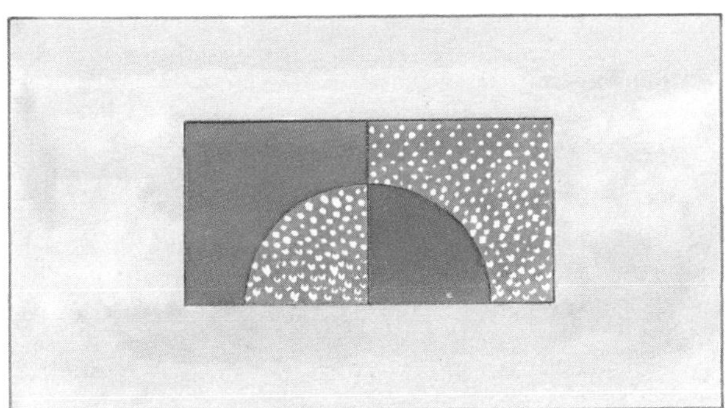

6 *Stitch the other two units* a *and* b *together to form an identical half-block.*

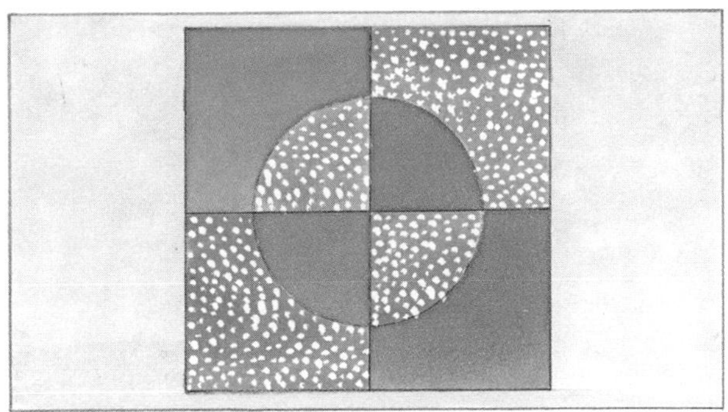

7 *Matching the seams carefully at the edges and in the center, stitch the two half-blocks together so that you have a complete circle in the center of the block.*

4 The Appliqué block

Appliqué can be worked by hand or machine. When you appliqué by machine, it is impossible to hide the stitching completely. You can achieve a low-key effect by turning under the edges of the shapes and applying them with a single line of machine straight stitch, or you can capitalize on the machine stitching and cover the raw edges by stitching around the edges of the shapes with satin stitch or a close zigzag. When you stitch by hand, you can choose whether to make the stitching nearly invisible, or part of the decorative effect by using blanket, feather, or a variety of other embroidery stitches.

On this block we show you how to turn the edges under and baste them before you position the motifs. When you get more proficient, you may prefer to use the quicker turn-as-you-go method – the shapes are simply pinned in place, and you turn under the seam allowance as you stitch around the edges of the shape. Another method involves cutting the required shapes from freezer paper and sticking the edges under by pressing them to the tacky wax layer; the appliqué is stitched to the background fabric, then a slit is cut behind the appliqué to remove the paper.

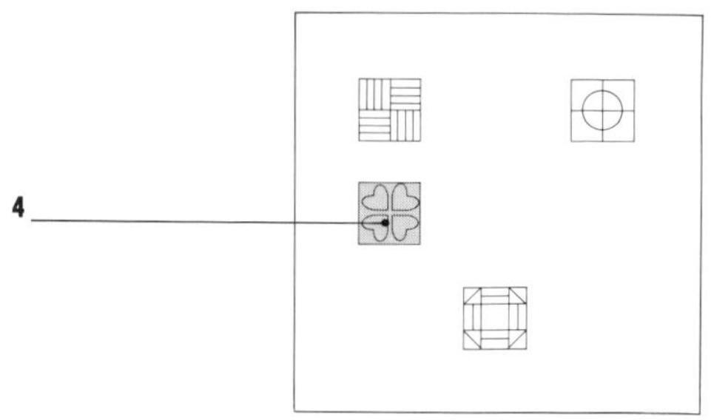

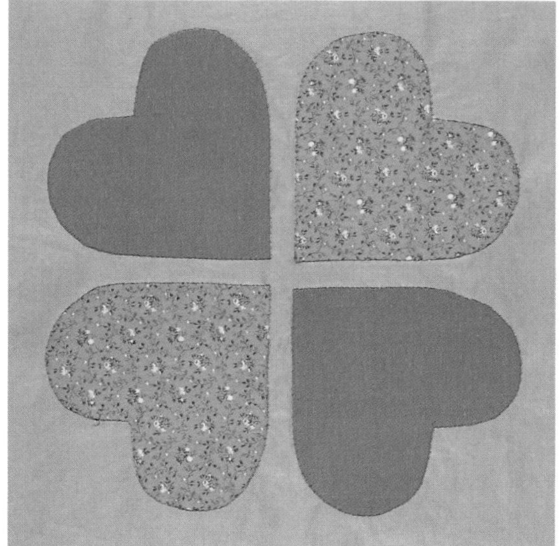

▲ *The completed block, a simple design of hearts in green fabrics set off by the pink background.*

TIP

When you are sewing by hand, your thread can easily become tangled and form small knots. There is nothing more irritating than this, but you can prevent it by running the thread across a lump of beeswax. The coating of wax must be quite light, however, or you may discolor the fabric.

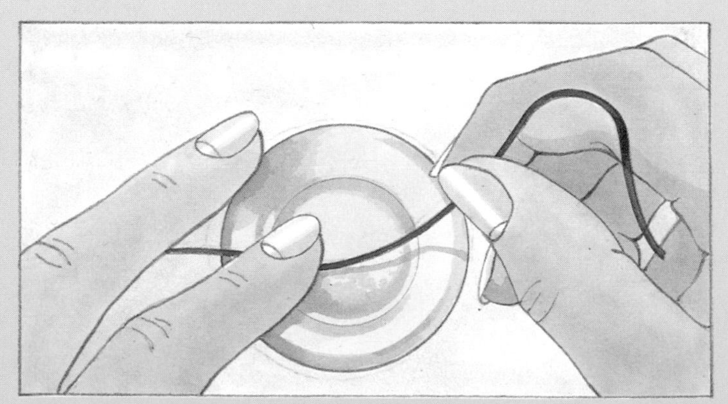

1 *Trace template 4 on page 68, and cut a heart template for the appliqué pieces (see page 42, Making templates).*

2 *Using the template (see page 42, Making templates), cut two hearts from fabric C and two from fabric D (see page 44, Cutting fabrics).*

3 *Fold and baste under $^{1}/_{4}$ in. all around the edges of the heart shapes. Clip to the seam allowance at the top of each heart so that the fabric folds under smoothly. Keep the curves smooth around the edges of each shape.*

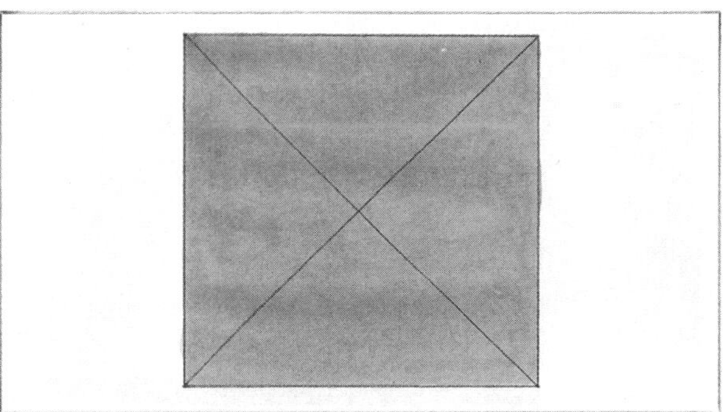

4 *Cut a $12^{1}/_{2}$ in. square from fabric F and fold it lightly across the diagonals, so that you have some guidelines for positioning your appliqué shapes.*

5 *Pin or baste the heart shapes in position on the background fabric so that there are even borders of the pink (Fabric F) square around the edges of the hearts and between them.*

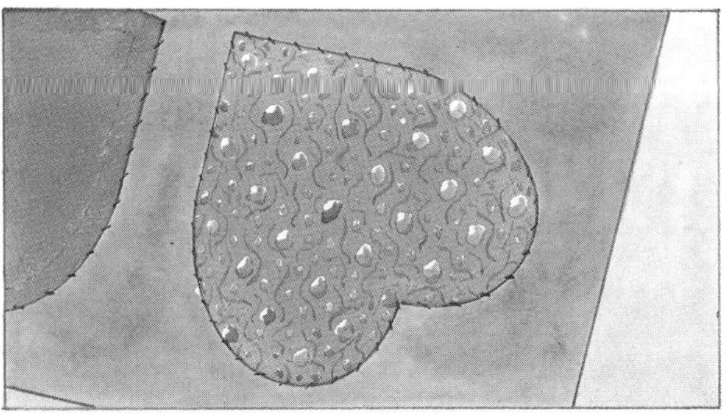

6 *Using green sewing thread, blind-stitch the hearts to the background fabric by taking tiny hemstitches around the edges of the shapes. Remove the pins or basting threads. To reduce bulk you can cut away some of the background fabric behind the heart shapes.*

Log Cabin is one of the most exciting and versatile of all patchwork designs. It can be made in two colors or fifty colors; any fabric can be used; the strips may be any width you choose; and once several blocks are completed, they can be arranged in many different ways to make an endless variety of designs. Even the ways in which the strips are attached can be varied. The Log Cabin designs in the Pattern Library (pages 136-139) show you just a few of the myriad possibilities open to you.

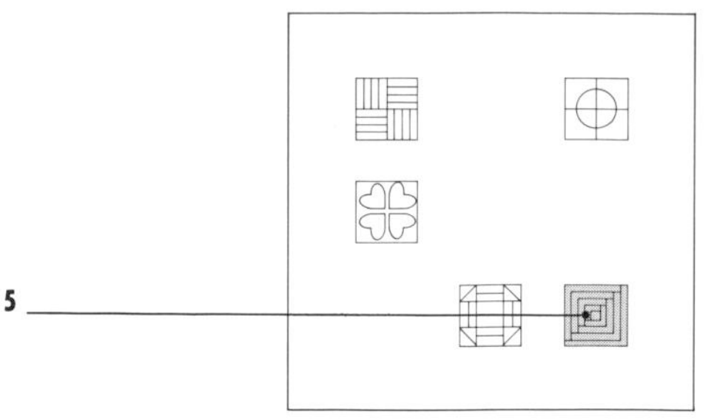

SAMPLER QUILT

5 The Log Cabin block

▼ *The finished Log Cabin block, half dark and half light to represent night and day.*

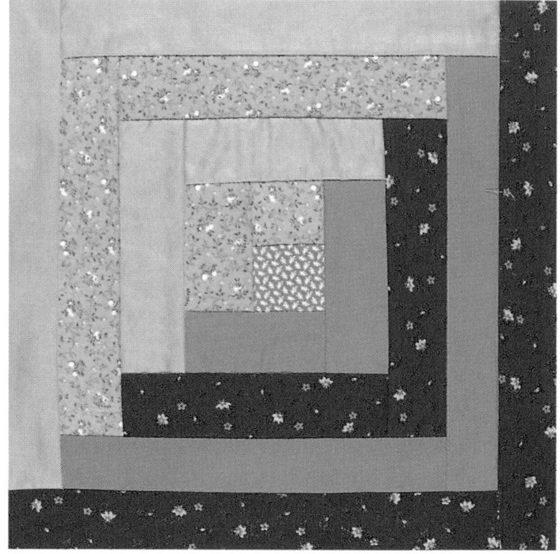

To introduce you to the basic principle of Log Cabin, which is different from other methods of patchwork, we are using a standard block which makes use of five different fabrics.

To make the block, you will need strips of each fabric $1\frac{5}{6}$ in. wide; if you find this measurement difficult to achieve accurately, cut your strips 2 in. wide and take a fraction more than the standard $\frac{1}{4}$ in. for your seam allowance as you stitch each seam. The strips are best cut using a rotary cutter and board (see page 44, Cutting fabrics).

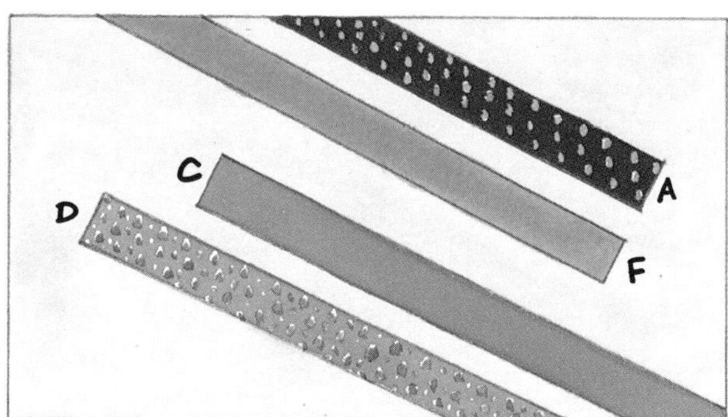

1 *From fabrics A and F, cut strips measuring $1\frac{5}{6}$ in. across; you will need a length of about 14 in. of each fabric, but this doesn't all need to be in one piece. From fabrics C and D, cut strips the same width and a total of 36 in. in length for each. Cut along the grain.*

2 *From fabric G, cut a $12\frac{1}{2}$ in. square. Fold the square in half diagonally and then in half again, and press lightly; unfold it, and you will have your diagonals marked, which will help you to keep the strips straight.*

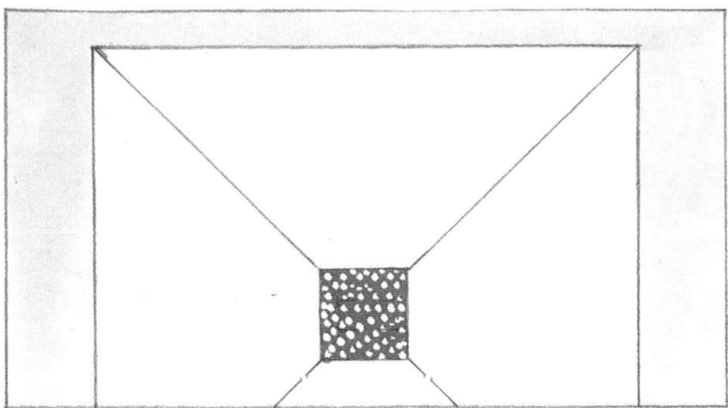

3 *From fabric B cut a $1\frac{5}{6}$ in. square, and pin it in the exact center of the large fabric square, using the pressed lines as a guide for positioning it.*

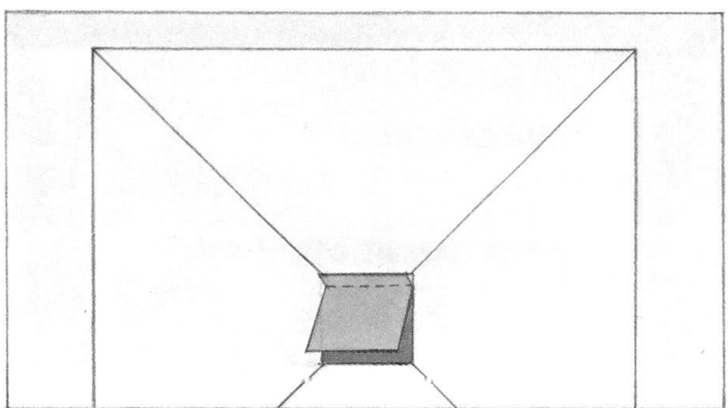

4 *Cut a strip from fabric D the same width as the small square and lay it face down over the square so that the two raw edges align. Stitch a $\frac{1}{4}$ in. seam by hand or machine.*

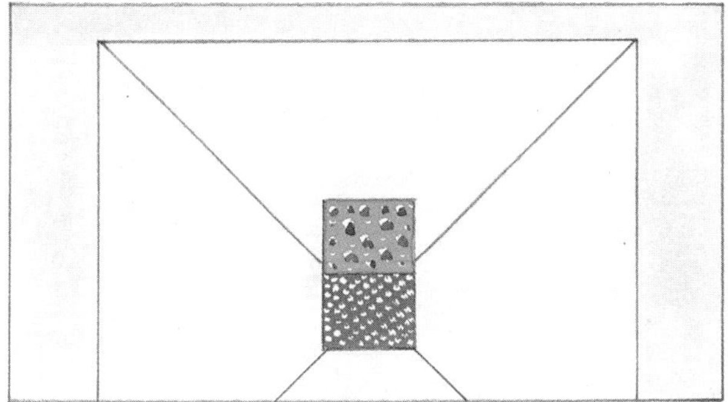

5 *Fold the fabric strip open so that the right side is up, and press the seam.*

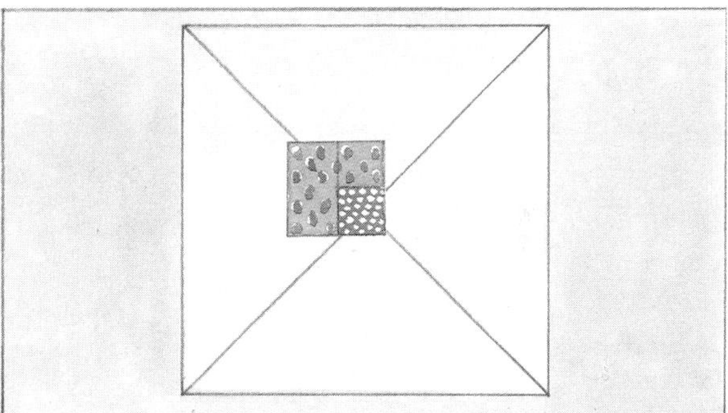

6 *Cut another strip of fabric D, this time long enough to go across the square and the edge of the first strip, and attach to the next edge around in the same way.*

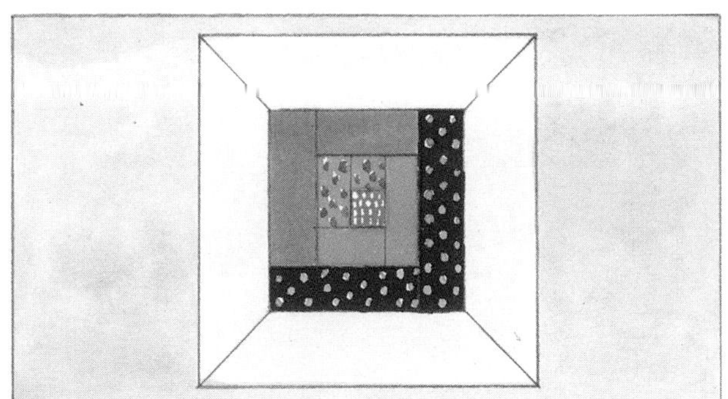

7 *Attach strips of fabric C to the remaining two sides in the same way. Continuing to work around the square in the same direction, add two strips of fabric F and then two strips of fabric A in the same way to make the next round. As you work your way outward on the block, you need longer and longer strips.*

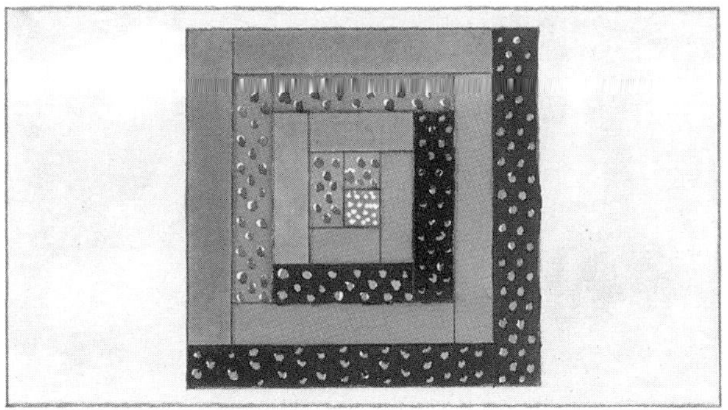

8 *Finish off the block with another round of strips D and C, and a final round of strips F and A. Make sure that you stitch around the block in the same order for every round.*

Strip piecing is a marvelous time-saver that enables you to produce very sophisticated results quickly.

In strip piecing, strips are cut from different fabrics, sometimes in varying widths, and joined together along their lengths before being cut into the required patches. If you don't have a sewing machine it is perfectly possible to do strip piecing by hand, but it is much

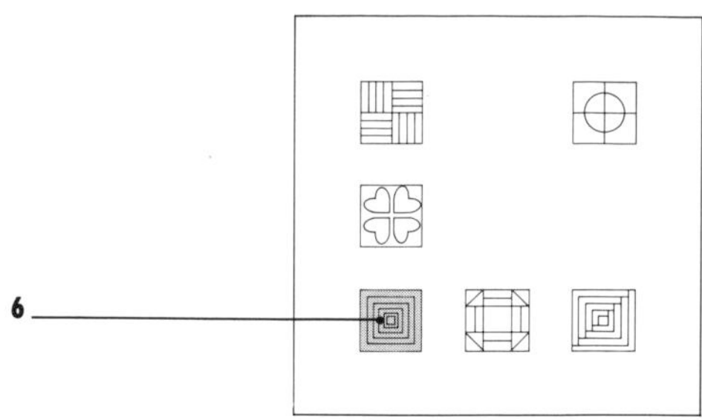

SAMPLER QUILT

6 The Strip-pieced block

faster to do the stitching by machine. Cutting the fabrics with a rotary cutter (see page 44, Cutting fabrics) is very quick and accurate, but if you prefer, the fabrics can be cut in the conventional way with scissors. This block uses even strips of six different fabrics.

If you cut your fabric strips to different widths before they are pieced and reassembled, the finished block has a more random effect.

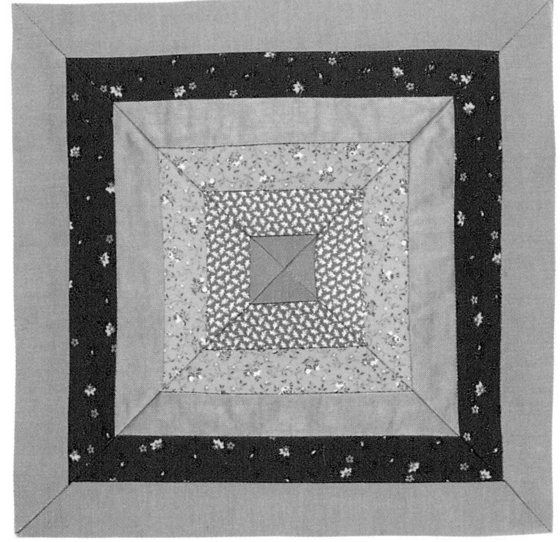

▲ *The finished block. Piecing the strips in this way gives the effect of several squares of fabric inside one another.*

VARIATIONS

String piecing

String piecing evolved as a way of using up long narrow pieces of fabric left over after cutting out garments. These "strings" are often irregularly shaped, but by trimming them into long triangles and sewing them together you can make a new fabric which can then be cut up and used for quilt patches or for garments. Stitch the strings onto a backing of thin fabric using the "face-down, fold-back" method shown on page 80 (the Log Cabin block.)

1 *Cut two strips of fabric, each 28 in. long and $1\frac{1}{2}$ in. wide, from each of fabrics A, B, C, D, E, and F.*

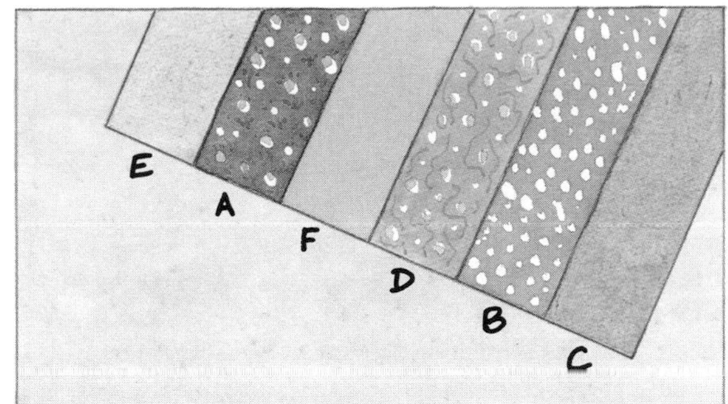

2 *Following the method for piecing (see page 46), join one set of fabric strips along their long edges in the order E, A, F, D, B, C. Do the same with the other set of strips; you now have two identical lengths of strip-pieced fabric.*

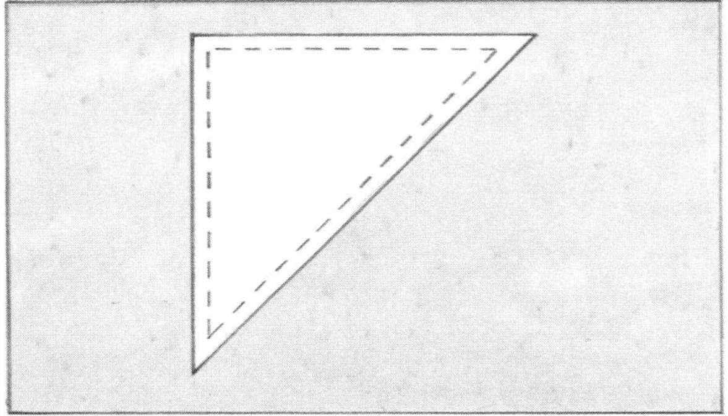

3 *Make a template using template 6 on page 68 (see also page 42, Making templates).*

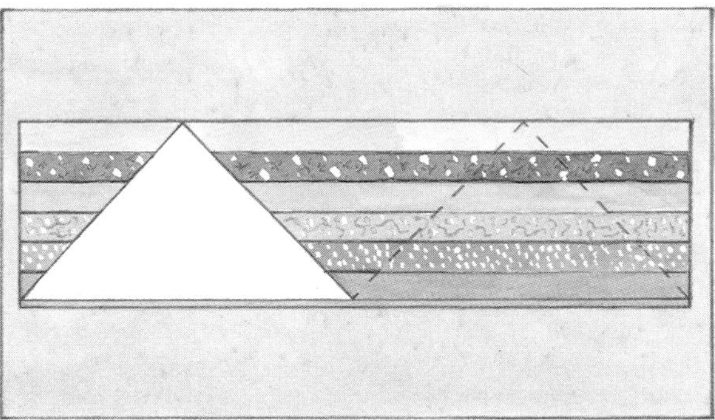

4 *Use the template to cut two triangles from each length of strip-pieced fabric, laying the long edge of the triangle $\frac{1}{4}$ in. in from the raw edge of fabric E each time.*

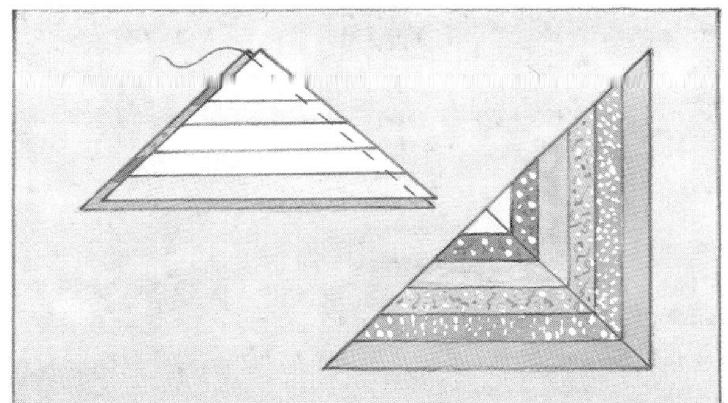

5 *Stitch two of the triangles together along one short seam, matching the fabrics and making sure that the seam lines match exactly. Stitch the other two triangles together in the same way to form two identical half-blocks.*

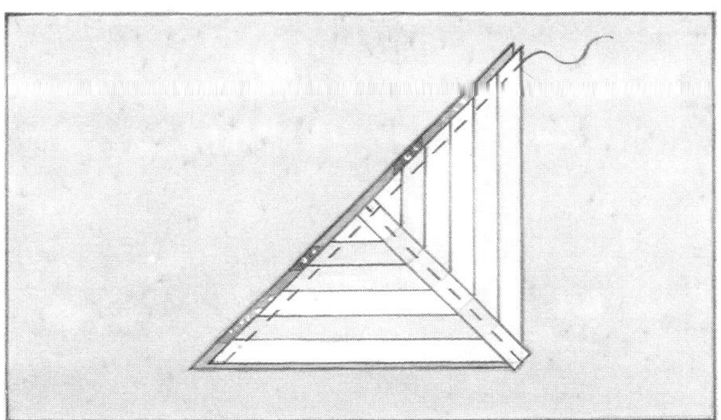

6 *Stitch the two half-blocks together along their long edges, matching the fabrics and the seam lines exactly, to complete the block.*

Diamonds can be used to produce wonderful star shapes simply by stitching them around in a circle. As you can see from the examples on page 132 (Non-block patterns), the stars can become quite spectacular; the Star of Bethlehem pattern is very dramatic and can be made large enough to cover a whole double quilt top. This star is a little more modest, to get you used to using diamonds in a star

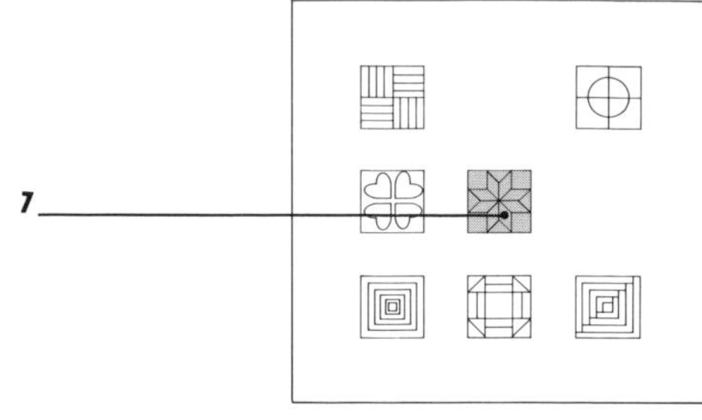

SAMPLER QUILT

7 The Star block

arrangement. When the basic star has been pieced, it is appliquéd by hand to the background fabric to make a block.

The number of points your star has is determined by the acute angle at the tip of the diamond; this star uses 45° diamonds, so the star has eight points (360° divided by 45°). The use of the two pink fabrics, one light and one dark, arranged in pairs, gives a three-dimensional look to the finished star. If you want to make stars with six points, then you need to use 60° diamonds (360°÷6). It is possible to create stars with even more points, but if the angle becomes too fine it is difficult to piece the diamonds accurately, so six-point and eight-point designs tend to be the most popular.

TIP

For the star to look effective, each point must be really sharp and crisp. It is easier to baste sharp points if you trim away some of the excess fabric. Cut across the top of the point and turn it down. Now turn down one side and then the other side.

▼ *The finished block shows a good contrast between dark, light and middle values.*

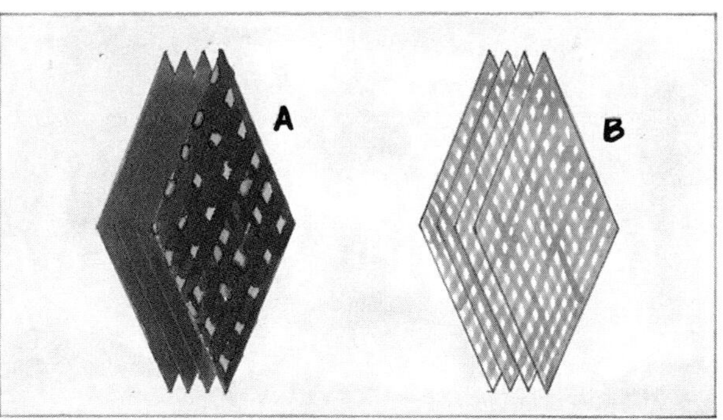

1 *Make template 7 on page 68 (see page 42, Making templates), and use it to cut four pieces from fabric A and four pieces from fabric B.*

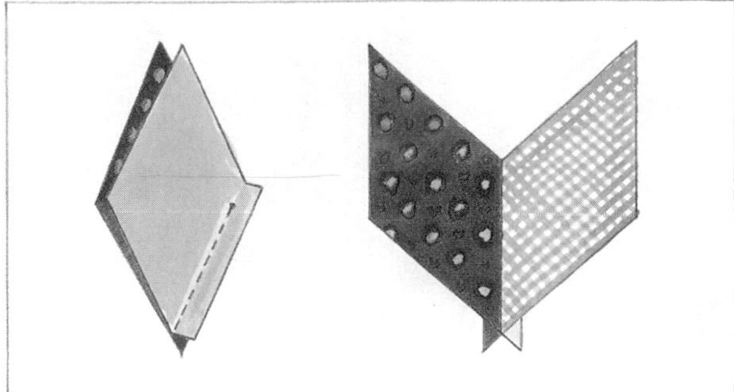

2 *Take one diamond in fabric A and one in fabric B and put them right sides together. Following the instructions on page 46 (Piecing), stitch down one edge so that side* **a** *of the fabric A diamond is joined to side* **b** *of the fabric B diamond.*

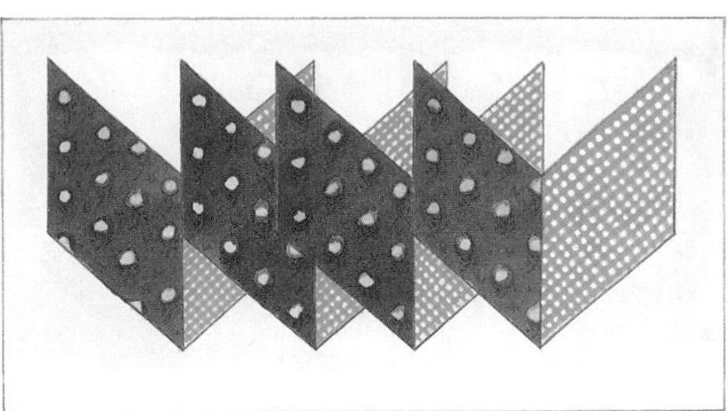

3 *Do the same with the remaining pairs of diamonds so that you now have four identical V-shaped patches. On all the seams, leave the top open for the first $^1/_4$ in.; this will make it easier to turn under the seam allowances later.*

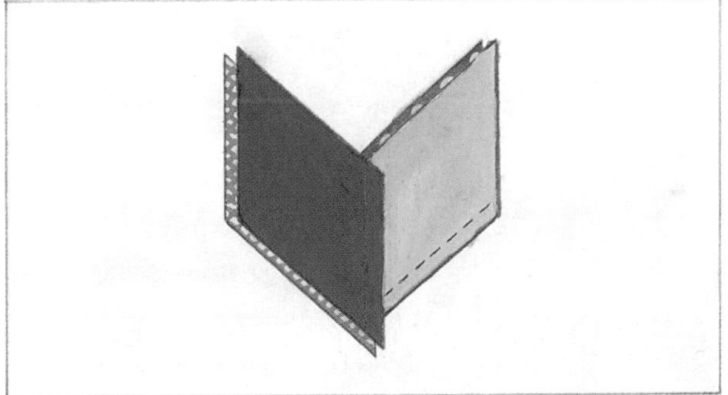

4 *Place two of the patches right sides together and stitch down the right-hand lower edge to form a half-star. Once again, leave the top $^1/_4$ in. of the seam open.*

5 *Do the same with the remaining two patches; you now have two identical half-stars.*

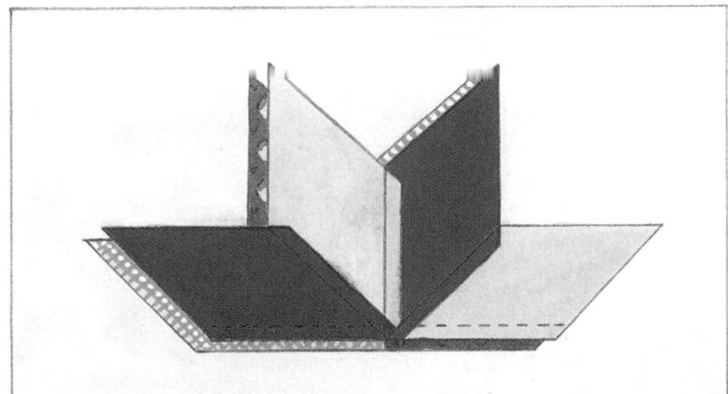

6 *Place the two half-stars right sides together and stitch a straight seam across them; follow the suggestions in the Tip box on page 47 to make sure that all the points meet accurately. Leave this seam open for $^1/_4$ in. at each end.*

7 *Tack under the $^1/_4$ in. seam allowances on the edges of the star. Following the instructions on page 78 (Appliqué block), stitch the star by hand onto the center of a $12^1/_2$ in. square of fabric E. You now have an eight-point star block for your quilt top.*

This delicate block, made in two basic pieces, is a variation on the traditional pattern known as Flying Geese, which always features a pattern of right-angled triangles arranged in the same direction. The "geese" can be made to fly all around the block, or entirely in one direction across it, or around a border (see page 150, Pieced border patterns). Here, one gaggle flies south and the other gaggle north!

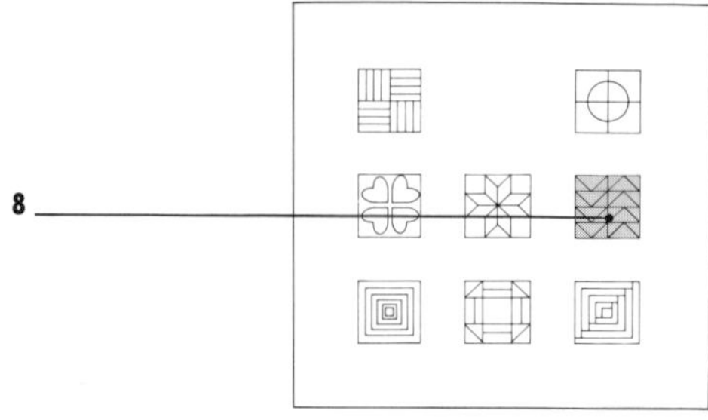

SAMPLER QUILT

8 The Flying Geese block

▼ *The finished block, showing foursomes of "geese" flying in different directions.*

This is the most complex block for your sampler quilt, and you need to be very accurate when you are making the templates (see page 42) and cutting out the fabric (see page 44). A quilter's ruler for right-angled triangles will come in handy for cutting your shapes.

USING A QUILTER'S MAT

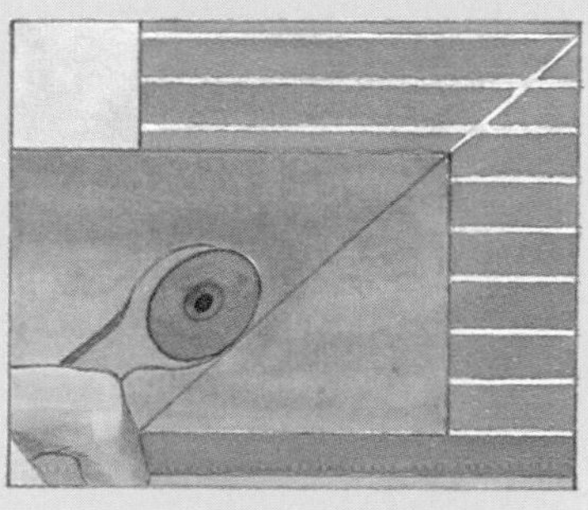

Cutting a strip of fabric will be much more accurate if you cut it with a rotary cutter and a quilter's ruler or a rotary cutter and a mat used for cutting triangles. Cut a strip of fabric the width of one of the perpendicular edges of the small triangles, then use the 45°angle guide to cut the triangles across it. Repeat for the larger triangles, using the larger template and a wider strip of fabric.

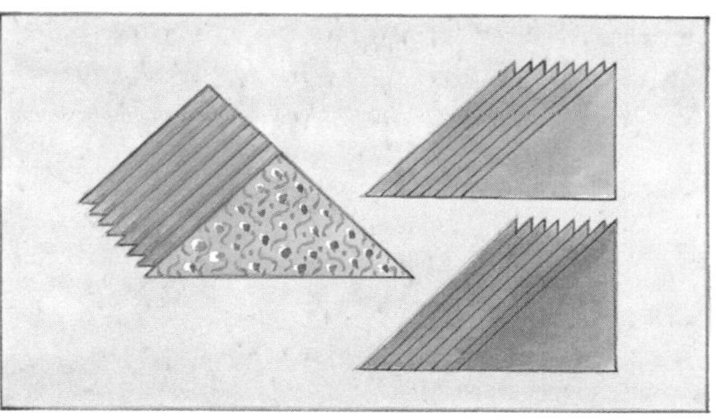

1 *Make triangular templates 8:1 and 8:2 on page 69. Using template 8:1, cut eight shapes from fabric D. Using template 8:2, cut 16 shapes from fabric F.*

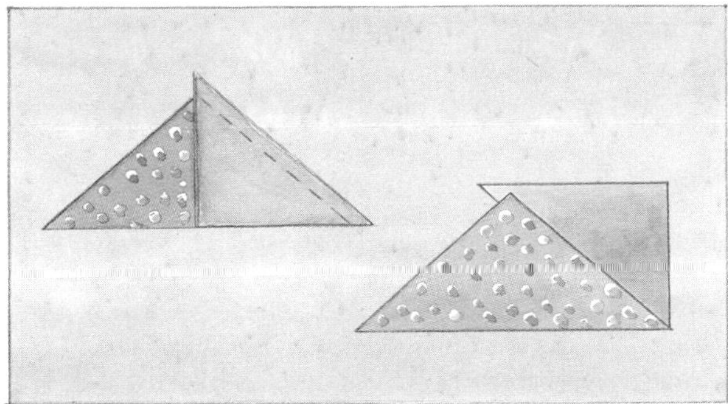

2 Following the instructions for piecing on page 46, stitch the long side of one pink (Fabric F) triangle to the right-hand diagonal of one green (Fabric D) triangle. Repeat the procedure for the other green (Fabric D) triangles, and press all the seams.

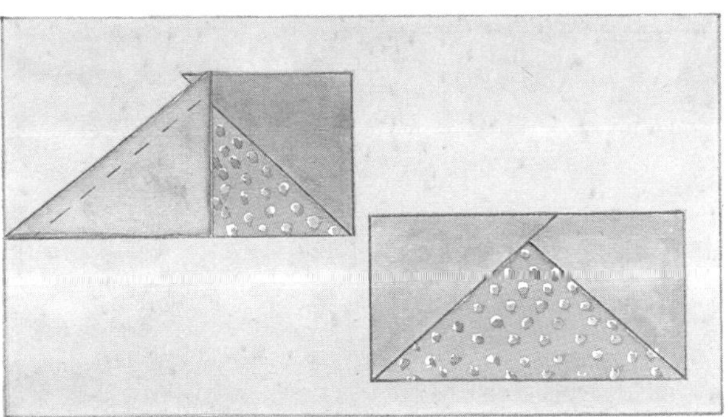

3 Stitch the long side of one pink (Fabric F) triangle to the other diagonal of each green (Fabric D) triangle. You now have eight identical rectangles.

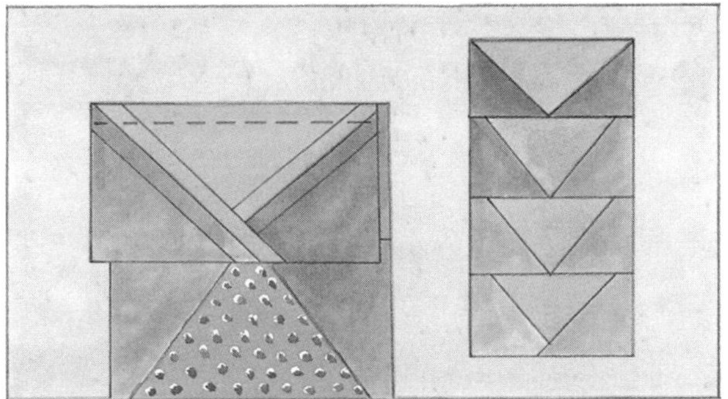

4 Stitch the rectangles together in two groups of four, making sure that the green triangles point in the same direction in each group. Stitch the seams so that the point of one triangle just touches the base of the next.

5 From fabric A, cut three strips ¾ in. wide and 12 in. long, and two strips ¾ in. wide and 12½ in. long.

6 Stitch one of the shorter strips between the half-blocks, taking a ¼ in. seam on each side and making sure that the green triangles point in different directions in each half. Stitch the other two short strips to the outside edges of the rectangles.

7 Stitch the longer strips to the top and bottom of the block, again taking ¼ in. seams. You now have a complete Flying Geese block.

9 The Reverse appliqué block

This block introduces a new technique, reverse appliqué. Instead of stitching fabric shapes on top of a background fabric as you did for the appliqué block earlier, the second fabric is laid underneath the background, which is then cut away in shapes to reveal it.

Just as conventional appliqué gives a slightly puffed or three-dimensional look to the shapes applied onto the flat background fabric, this method gives a slightly puffed look to the top layer of fabric as it is turned and stitched over flat areas of fabric shapes.

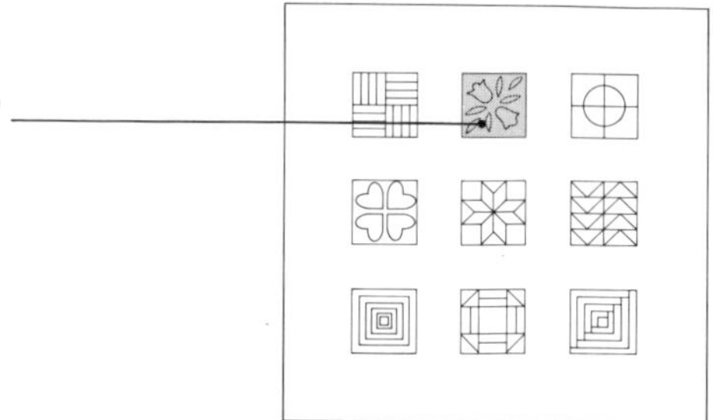

There are many methods of reverse appliqué, and variations within the methods themselves, but this block uses one of the simplest. Use this method for virtually any conventional appliqué designs (see page 134, Appliqué motifs) to vary the final effect.

A well known form of reverse appliqué is that produced by the Indian women of Panama's San Blas Islands. Their traditional dress includes a sleeveless blouse called a mola, with reverse appliqué panels on both front and back. These colorful and intricate panels have semi-naturalistic designs based on plants, people, and creatures, or tales from local folklore. Several layers of different-colored fabrics are used; empty spaces are often filled with lines of plain stitching or embroidery.

▶ *The finished block: the red tulip shapes and dark green leaves produce a pretty pattern on the light green background.*

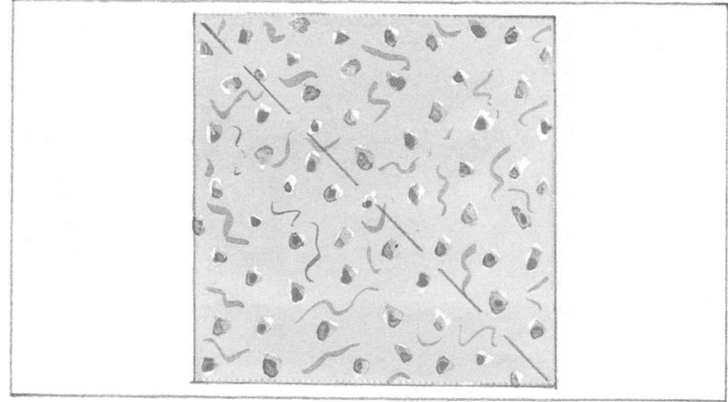

1 *Make templates 9:1 and 9:2 on page 70. From fabric D cut a $12^1/_2$ in. square; this will be your background fabric. Make a soft diagonal fold across the square to divide it into two large triangles; this will help you position the templates accurately on both sides.*

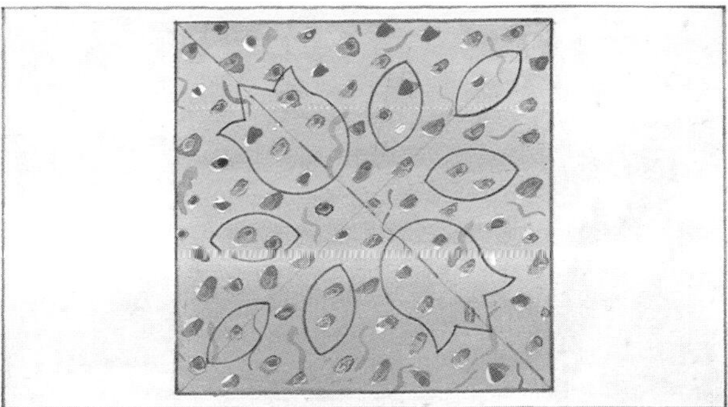

2 *Mark the tulip and leaf shapes on the background square by drawing round with a soft pencil, positioning them so that each diagonal half is a mirror image of the other. Make sure that the shapes are at least ½ in. from the edges of the square.*

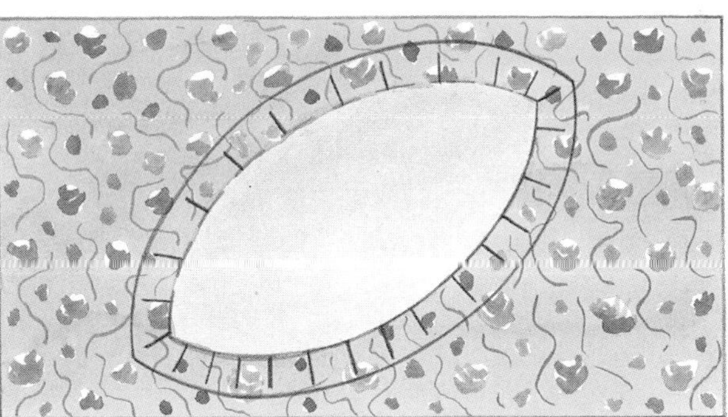

3 *Using small, sharp scissors, cut ¼ in. inside each of the pencil lines and carefully clip any curves; clip into the corners of the shapes also.*

4 *Using the tulip template as a rough guide, cut two shapes from fabric A that are at least ½ in. larger all around than the template.*

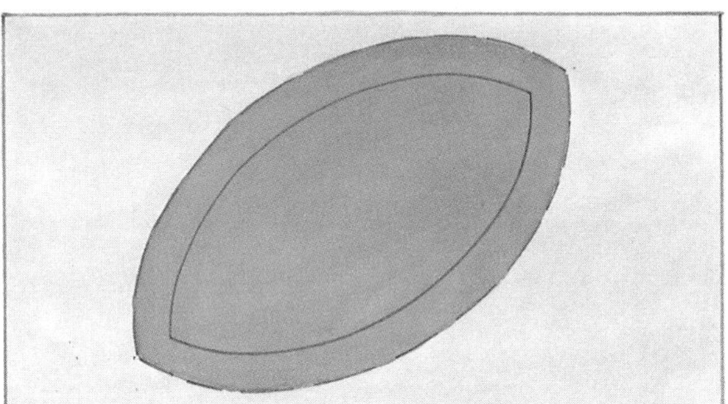

5 *Using the leaf template as a rough guide, cut six shapes from fabric C that are at least ½ in. larger all around than the template.*

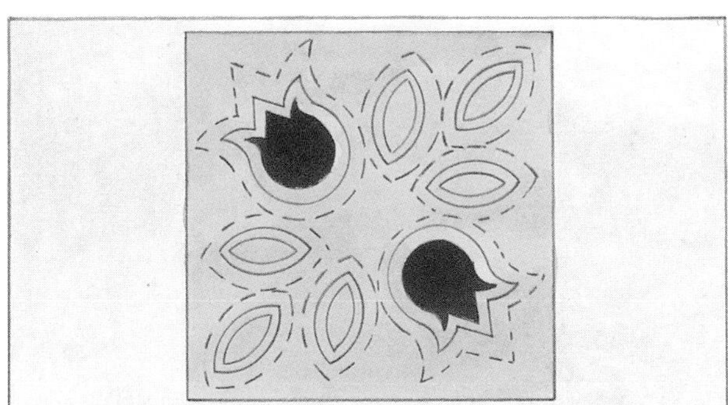

6 *Baste the dark pink (Fabric A) pieces, face up, underneath the tulip-shaped holes in the background fabric. Baste the dark green (Fabric C) pieces behind the leaf-shaped holes in the same way.*

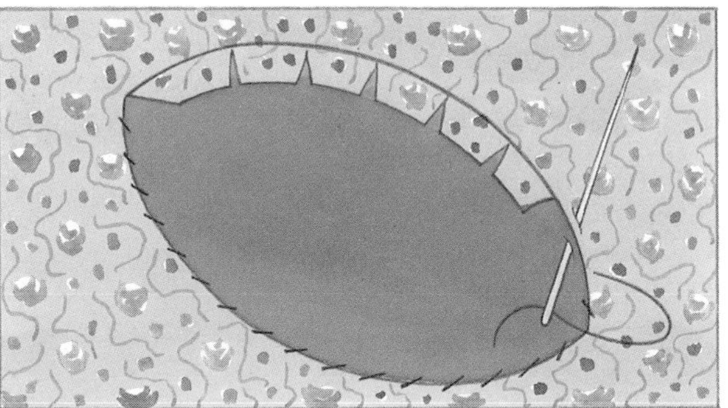

7 *Roll under the raw edges of the background fabric until the pencil line is just hidden, and blind-stitch the background fabric to the colored shapes underneath. Keep the curves of the rolled fabric smooth so that each piece of reverse appliqué makes a pleasing shape.*

You now have nine blocks for your sampler quilt, and it is time to put them together. This stage turns your work from a collection of blocks into a real quilt top, by adding sashing or setting strips between the blocks. Not all quilts made in blocks have sashing in between (see page 38), especially when the quilter wants to create a secondary design by arranging the blocks side by side, but the plain sashing in a neutral color around the different designs of a sampler quilt sets all the blocks off very well and produces a sense of homogeneity.

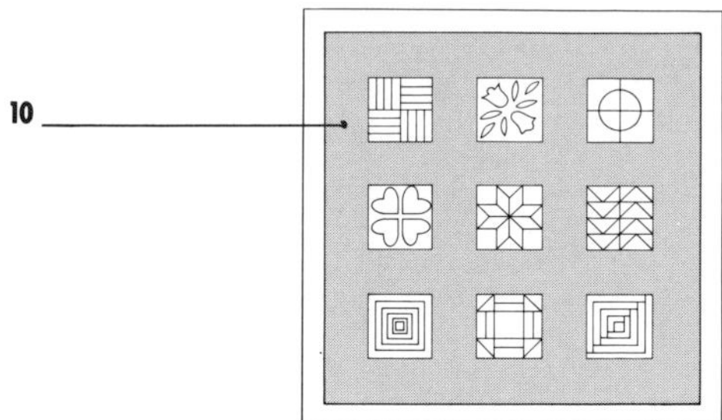

SAMPLER QUILT

10 Setting the blocks

The blocks are arranged in a pattern to give a pleasing balance of shades and colors across the quilt. If you have used different fabrics to make your blocks, lay them on the floor first to see whether you want to adjust the order of the blocks.

▲ *The quilt top begins to take shape; sashing or setting strips of unbleached muslin divide the blocks.*

VARIATIONS

Choosing the sashing

The kind of sashing you decide on depends on the overall effect you want to create. For a quilt with a large number of similar blocks, a narrow sashing could look effective, perhaps blending in with the colors used in the blocks.

If you used mainly solid colors for the blocks, the sashing could be patterned for contrast. Or it could be a much darker, lighter or brighter color to create the effect of a series of bars across the quilt.

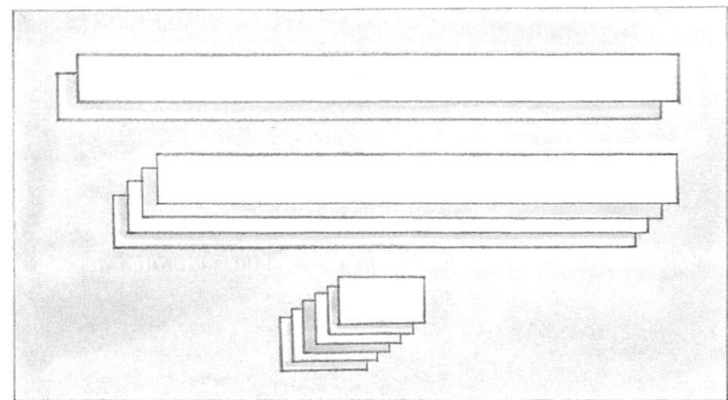

1 *From Fabric G, cut strips in the following measurements:*
six strips $8^1/_2$ in. × $12^1/_2$ in.
four strips $8^1/_2$ in. × $52^1/_2$ in.
two strips $8^1/_2$ in. × $68^1/_2$ in.

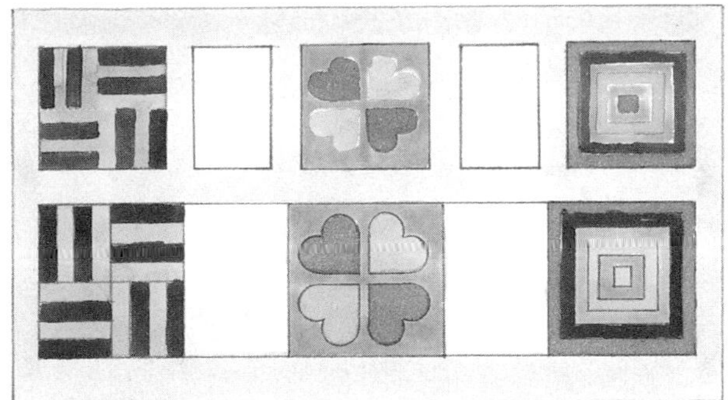

2 *Taking $^1/_4$ in. seams each time, stitch one of the short strips between the Rail Fence block and the appliqué hearts block, and another between the appliqué hearts block and the strip-pieced block.*

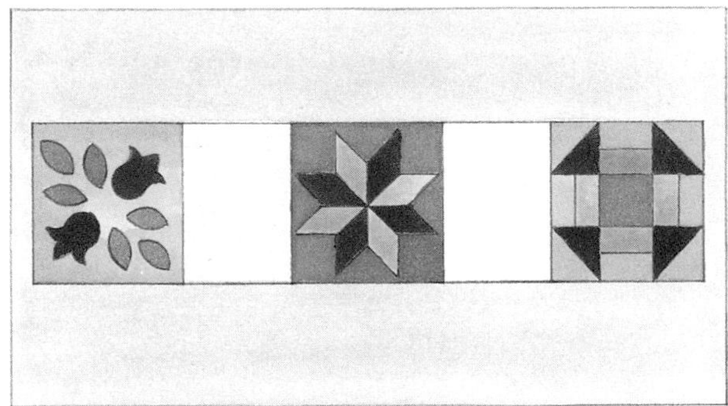

3 *In the same way, make a second row with the reverse appliqué block left, the Diamond Star in the middle, and the Churn Dash block right.*

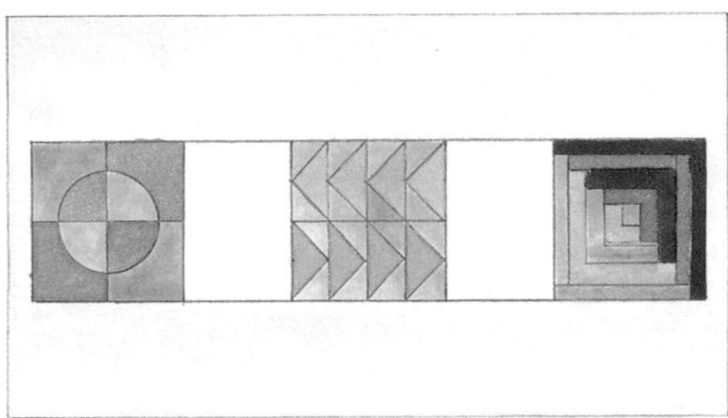

4 *Make a third row in the same way with the Sugar Bowl block left, the Flying Geese in the middle and the Log Cabin block right. Make sure that the Flying Geese fly up and down, and that the dark edges of the Log Cabin are on the outside.*

5 *Stitch the four middle-length strips of muslin to join the rows of blocks and to finish the outside edges of the rows. Make sure that you join the strips in the correct order, so that the Diamond Star is in the center of the quilt top.*

6 *Add the two long strips of muslin to the top and bottom of the quilt top.*

SAMPLER QUILT

11 Adding a border

Adding a simple patchwork border to your quilt top is the final stage before you begin preparations for the quilting itself. This border uses a variation of the method that you used for the Strip-pieced block (see page 80), but on a much larger scale.

The squares in this border are 4 in. wide, so their seams should line up with your block edges. As you attach the border, make sure that the seam lines match; this will make the quilt top look very neat. You will need 72 squares to go around the edge, so you should be able to use the same repeat of the six fabrics twelve times. Keep them in the same order around the quilt edges so that they don't distract the eye.

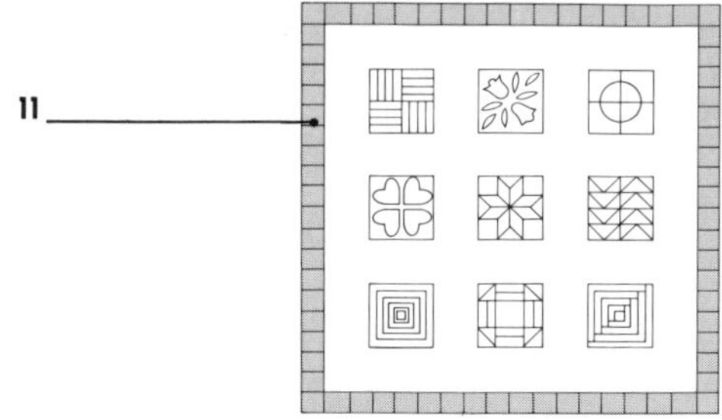

► *The completed quilt top: the patchwork border picks up the fabrics from the block designs.*

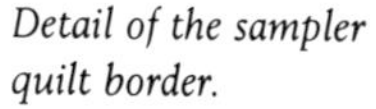

Detail of the sampler quilt border.

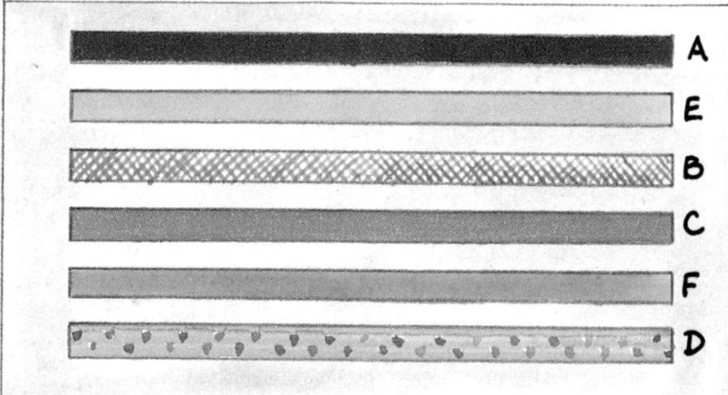

1 *From fabrics A, B, C, D, E, and F, cut strips $4^1/_2$ in. wide. You will need a total length of about 60 in. for each fabric, but this doesn't all have to be in one strip; if it works better with the fabric you have, you could make two pieced strips of 30 in. each as you did for the strip-pieced block.*

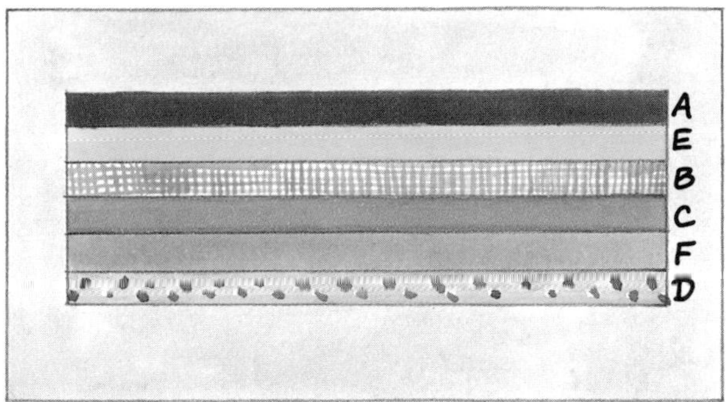

2 *Use a $^1/_4$ in. seam to join the strips in the order A, E, B, C, F, D. This will give you a pieced strip (or two shorter ones) in which each individual strip is 4 in. wide.*

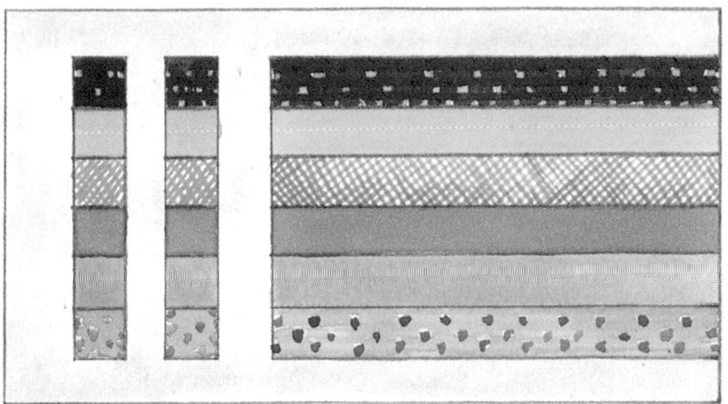

3 *Using a rotary cutter (see page 44, Cutting fabrics), cut strips $4^1/_2$ in. wide across the width of the composite strip.*

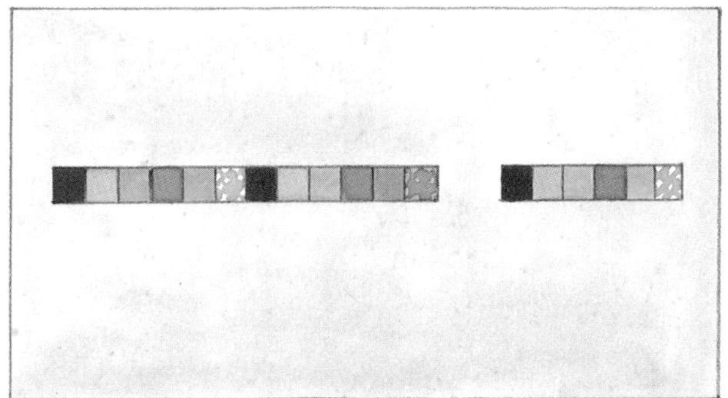

4 *Join these new strips in groups of three to produce four strips containing 18 squares. Keep the squares in the same order each time.*

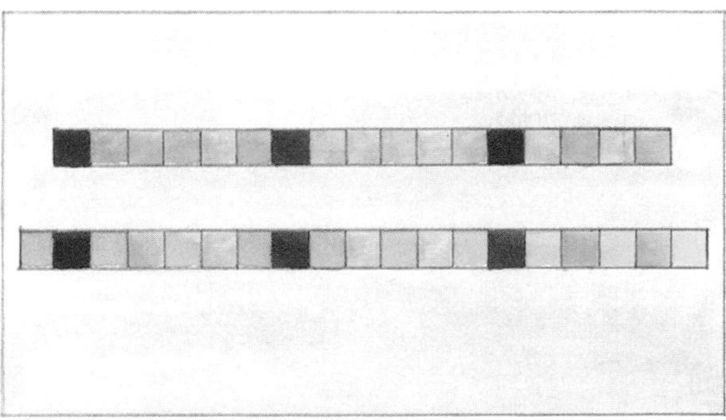

5 *Rip out the seam joining the final square (of fabric D) of two of the strips, and join the extra squares to the beginnings of the other two strips, next to fabric A. This gives you two strips of 17 squares and two of 19.*

6 *Join one of the shorter strips to the top edge of the quilt top, taking a $^1/_4$ in. seam. Join the other short strip to the bottom edge, making sure that the colors are running in the same order around the quilt.*

7 *Join the longer strips to the edges of the quilt, making sure that the colors still run in the same order around the quilt. You are now ready to prepare for quilting.*

The piecing of your quilt top is now complete, and it is time to mark the quilting patterns onto the fabric. It is best to do this before you baste the quilt top to the batting; it is easier to make the marks accurately if you can rest the fabric on a hard surface. Once the batting is in place, the surface becomes spongy. Two traditional patterns have been selected to quilt the sashing; a twisting cable repeat pattern, and a corner flower motif. The cable pattern has a 4 in. repeat, so it fits in exactly three times along the edge of each block and exactly twice across the width of the sashing. The cable ends are finished off neatly by using the templates.

SAMPLER QUILT

12 Marking the quilting patterns

A checkerboard background texture has been chosen for the reverse appliqué block, so that you can practice stitching a texture of this kind. The checkering needs to be marked at this stage, too, but the other blocks don't need any marking as you will be using the seam lines as quilting guides.

There are many methods of marking quilt patterns (see page 48), but here we are using one of the easiest – tracing around a template with a water-soluble-ink pen. This gives you a good clear line to stitch on, and when you have finished, any visible marks can be gently sponged away with cold water.

There are, of course, many other designs which can be used on quilt tops; if you prefer to use alternative designs, there are plenty of ideas in the Pattern Libraries for quilted border patterns (see page 152), individual motifs (see page 134), and background textures (see page 154). Choose your design, scale it up or down to the appropriate size, then follow the instructions in this lesson for marking the designs onto the quilt top.

▲ *The marked quilt top: the lines made by the soluble-ink pen show up clearly on the fabrics.*

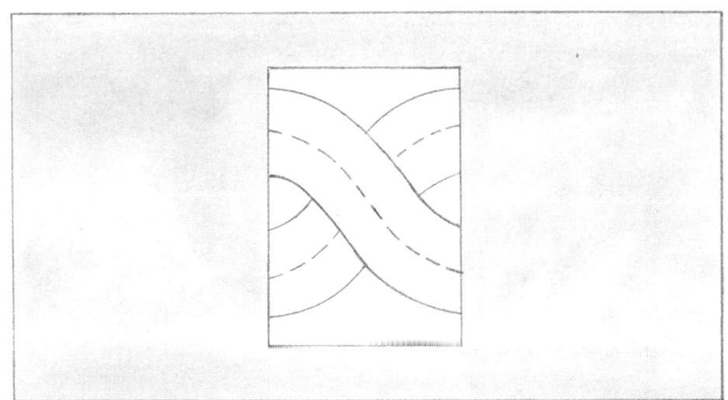

1 *Make templates 12:1, 12:2, and 12:3 on page 71. Either use template plastic or cut them from paper and glue them on cardboard.*

2 *Start in the center of each side and, working outward, mark 11 repeats of template 12:1 down the centers of the sashing bands. Finish each end off neatly with template 12:2. Mark the two long pieces of sashing down the center of the quilt in the same way.*

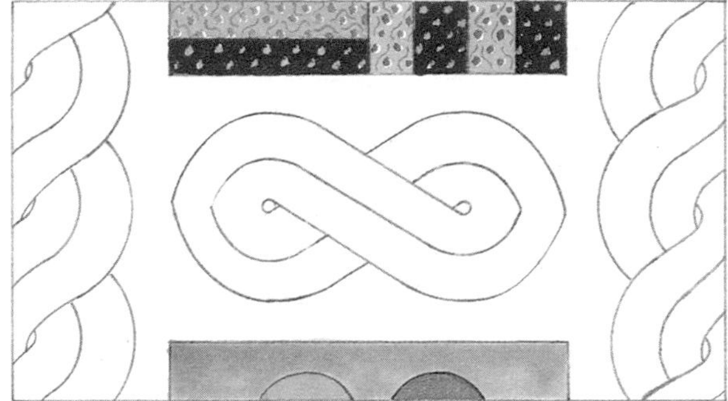

3 *On each short section of sashing, mark template 12:1 once and template 12:2 twice to create six mini-cables.*

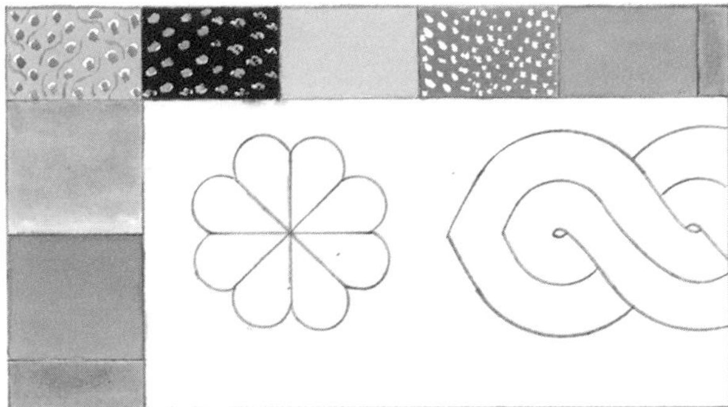

4 *At each corner of the sashing, use template 12:3 to mark a flower motif.*

5 *On the reverse appliqué block, draw the diagonals across the block using a water-soluble-ink pen.*

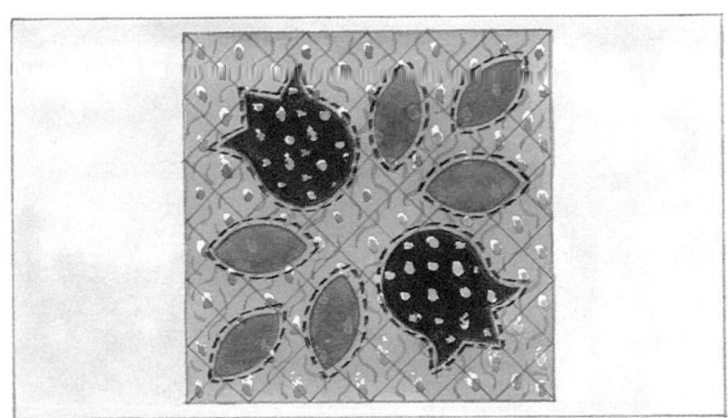

6 *Working outward from these lines in both directions, draw parallel lines 1 in. apart; a quilter's ruler (see page 86) is very useful for this task. Draw the lines outside the appliqué shapes.*

Now you are ready for the final stage, turning your quilt top into a quilt. Your fabric is marked with the quilting patterns, and now needs to be put together with the batting and the backing fabric.

All of the quilting can be worked by hand or by machine (see page 56, Quilting). If you quilt by machine, remember to finish off the threads neatly, ideally by pulling the top thread through to the back of the quilt and knotting it with the bobbin thread. Or, if your sewing machine does a neat reverse stitch, you could work a few stitches in reverse at the end of each quilted line, but this shows on the right side unless you match the thread to the fabric color exactly. Whether you are quilting by hand or machine, choose the colors of thread that you want to use for the quilting either to blend in or to stand out; we have used green on the muslin, and pink and green on the blocks and border, but the patterns on the muslin would also look effective quilted in pink or ecru.

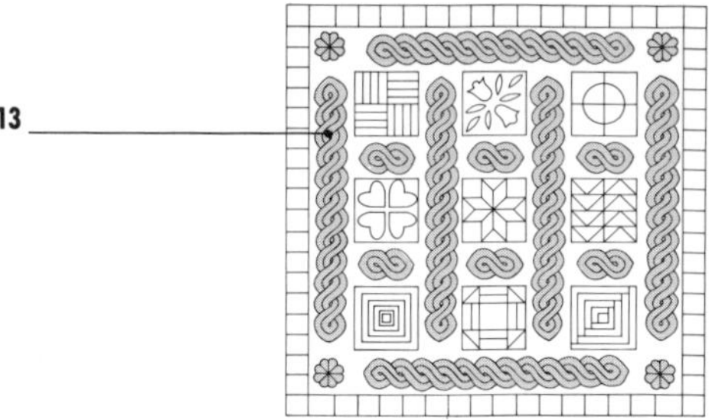

13 Quilting the sampler quilt

► *The quilt top with all the quilting complete.*

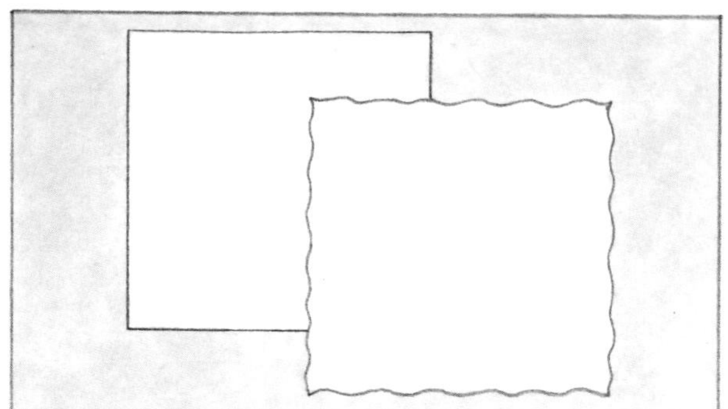

1 *If your batting is not already cut to the exact size, cut it to 78 in. square. Cut a piece of muslin thc same size.*

2 *Following the instructions on page 52, make a sandwich of the muslin, the batting, and the quilt top, and secure the layers together with a grid of basting threads. The muslin and batting should be ¾ in. larger than the quilt top all around.*

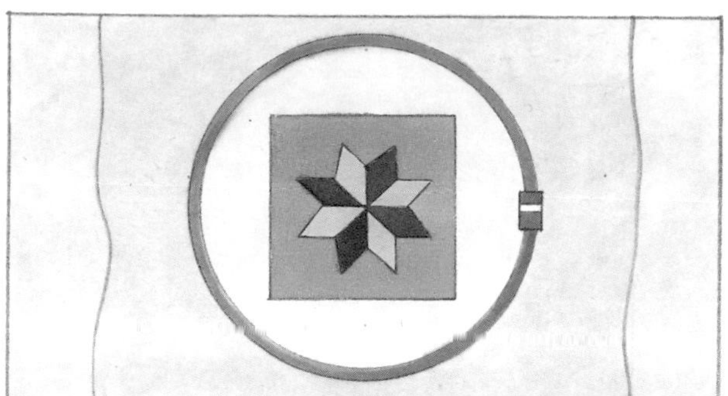

3 *Secure the quilt to the frame as shown on page 54. Unless you are using a full-size frame, work on one area of the quilt at a time, quilting from the center out so that you minimize the risk of the fabric puckering. This applies to both hand and machine quilting.*

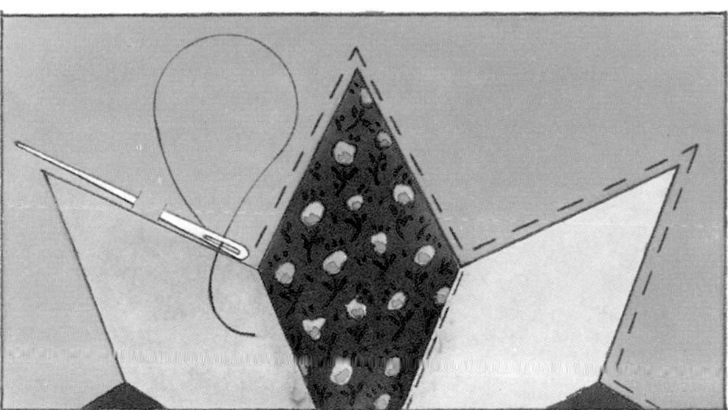

4 *Following the instructions on page 58 for quilting in the ditch, quilt the Flying Geese, Rail Fence, Log Cabin, Diamond Star, Strip-pieced, and Churn Dash blocks. Quilt just outside the edges of the appliquéd Diamond Star shape.*

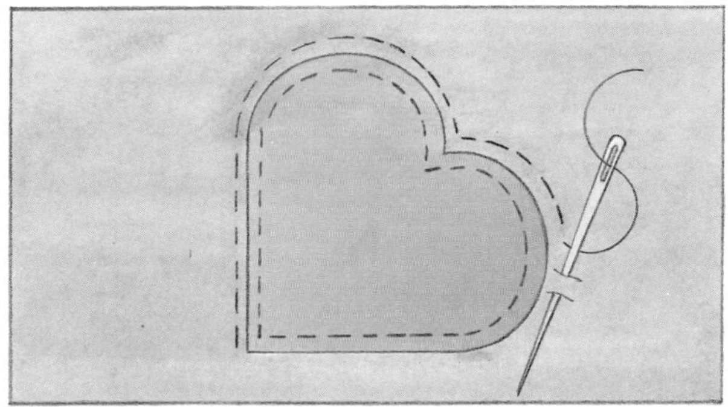

5 *Following the instructions on page 58 for outline quilting, quilt the Sugar Bowl block. Stitch inside the appliqué hearts in the same way, and work a row of quilting stitches 1/4 in. outside the design as well.*

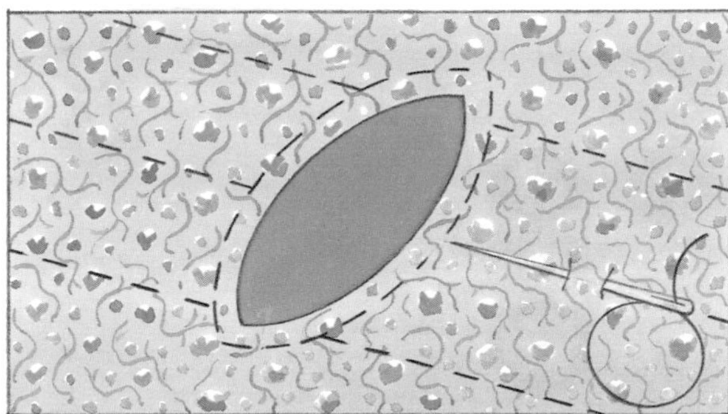

6 *Quilt the checkerboard design around the reverse appliqué block, stitching a line 1/4 in. outside each leaf and flower and stopping each diagonal row on that line.*

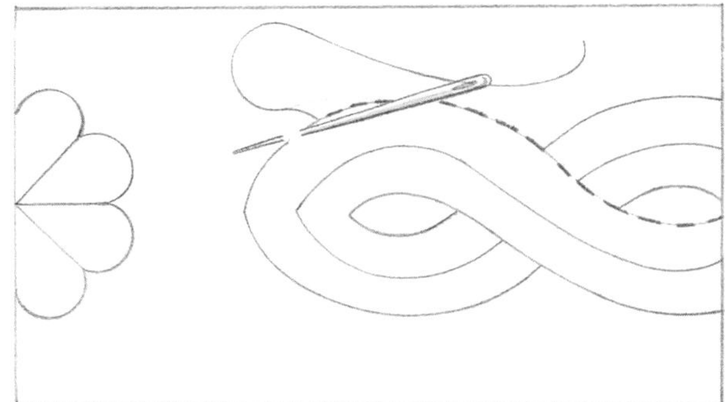

7 *Quilt the cable designs first, and then the corner motifs on the sashing.*

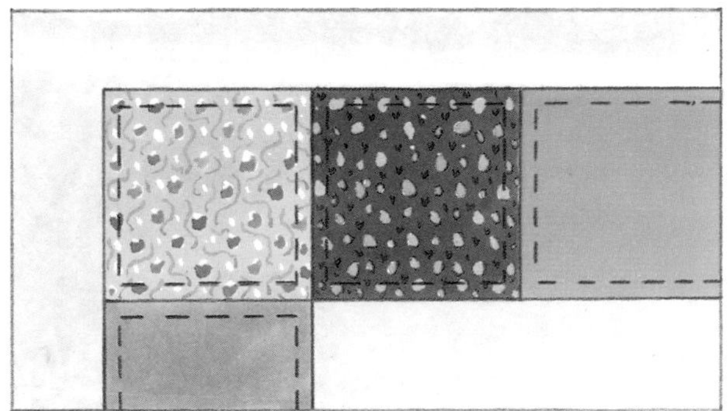

8 *Quilt the border squares either "in the ditch" (see page 58) or 1/4 in. inside each patch. With a damp cloth, sponge away any blue marks remaining from the soluble-ink pen; your quilt is now almost finished.*

You have now reached the final stage of your sampler quilt: binding the raw edges. There are many different ways of binding a quilt (see page 60), and the binding can be plain, patterned, or pieced. Plain quilts are sometimes finished with shaped edges, such as scallops or rows of triangle shapes. Piped edges or ruffles, either single or double, can also look effective for some quilts. In this case, though, the sampler quilt is quite ornate, and an elaborate binding might have detracted from it, so we have chosen a simple binding worked in the same fabric that you used for the sashing and the backing. This gives a neat but unobtrusive finish. The squared corners are easier to work than mitered ones, but if you prefer the effect of mitered corners, as many quilters do, follow the instructions below.

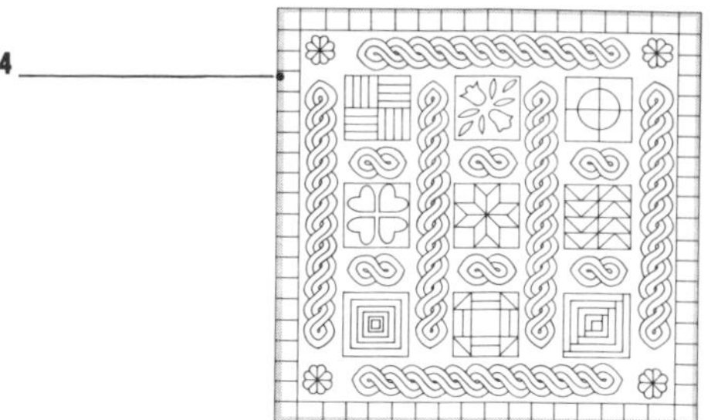

SAMPLER QUILT

14 Binding the sampler quilt

Be sure to add your name and date to the quilt for posterity. You might even include the reason for making the quilt, for example, to celebrate a wedding or to remember a friend of many years. Embroider the data on the quilt top in the sashing or inside a block. Or, if your sewing machine can form letters, sew the details into the backing fabric before it is joined to the quilt top and batting.

▲ *The finished quilt, with all the raw edges neatly concealed inside a muslin binding.*

MITERED CORNERS

To miter the corners of your binding, cut four strips $78^1/_2$ in. long, and join them in a large circle by making seams at each end as shown left. The tip of the seam should be $^1/_4$ in. from the end of the strip, and the angle should be an exact right angle. Trim the seams down each side and cut away the tips, then press each length of binding in half lengthwise to mark the fold line. Attach the binding in the same way as for straight binding (see page 60), but machine stitch it all around the quilt edge before turning it to the back.

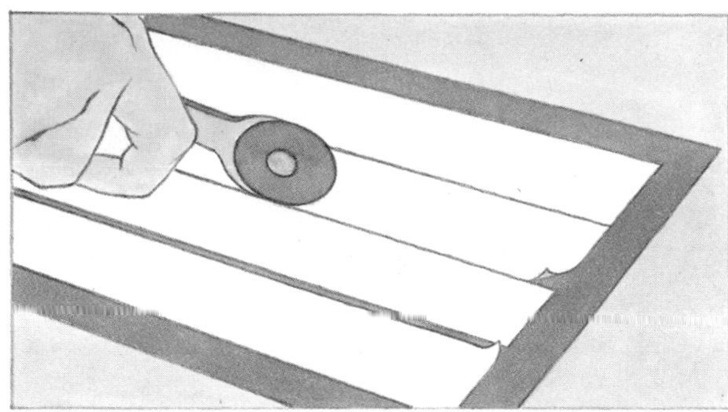

1 *From the muslin (fabric G), cut four strips 79 in. × $2^1/_2$ in. You will find it most accurate to use the rotary cutter and board for this; first cut a piece 79 in. × 10 in., then cut this wide strip into four narrow ones.*

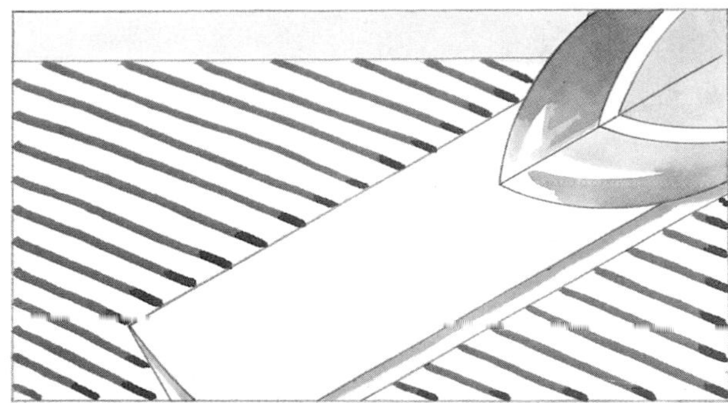

2 *Fold each of the strips in half lengthwise and press; this will give you a good fold line when you turn the strips over the quilt edges.*

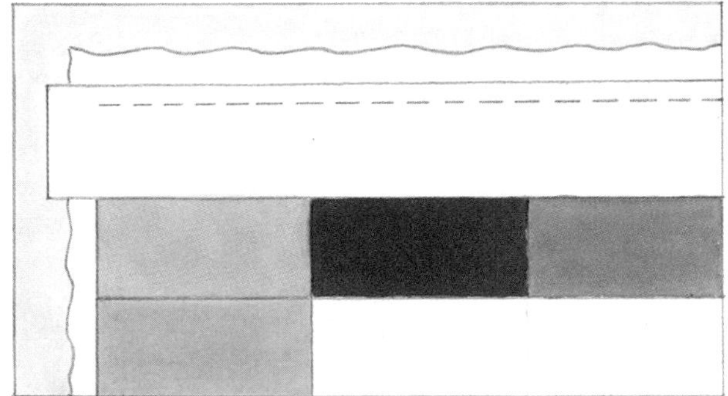

3 *Open up one of the strips and place it face down on one side of the quilt, so that the raw edge aligns with the raw edge of the border (not the raw edge of the backing). Stitch a seam $^1/_4$ in. from the edge, by hand or machine. Repeat along the opposite quilt edge.*

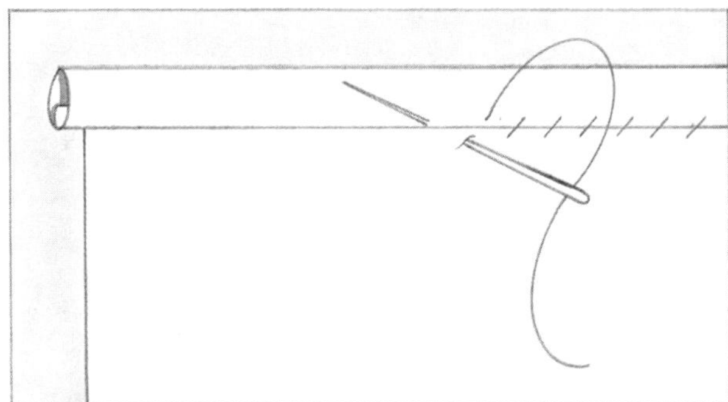

4 *Fold the strips over the raw edges to the back of the quilt. Turn under $^1/_4$ in. and hem by hand to the muslin backing to give a neat finish.*

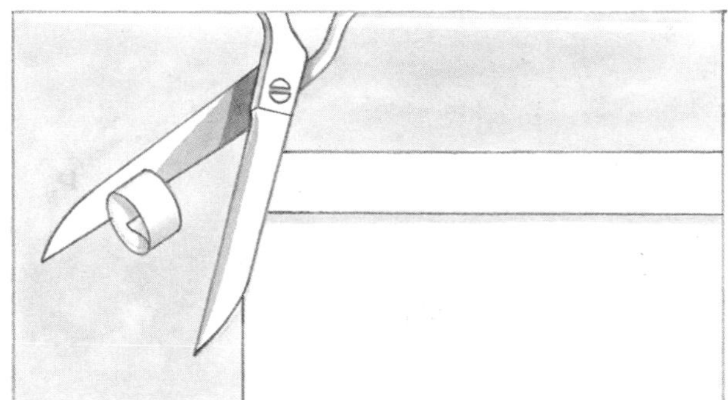

5 *Trim the ends of the strips so that they align with the edges of the backing fabric.*

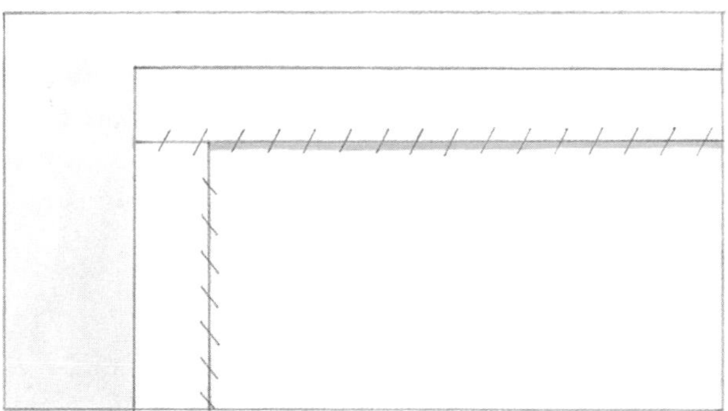

6 *Use the remaining two strips to bind the top and bottom of the quilt in the same way, tucking the raw ends in at the corners and stitching them in place.*

4

Extending your skills

Wholecloth quilting is worked on one body of fabric. No piecing is involved, and the decorative patterns are made entirely by the lines of quilting stitches rather than the patchwork designs.

Medallions are the main motifs used in wholecloth quilts. The medallion provides the main visual focus, usually forming a spectacular centerpiece. Some medallion designs have histories and traditions. Heart shapes and lovers' knots, for instance, were traditionally stitched only on quilts meant for engaged or newlywed couples.

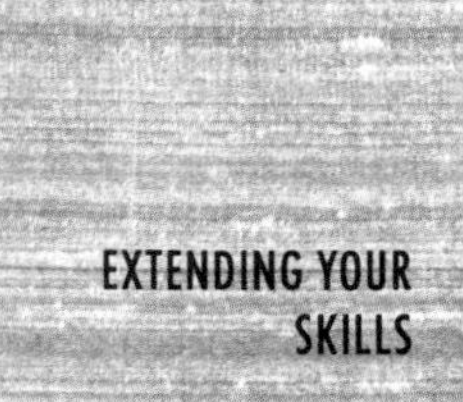

Wholecloth pillow

Many medallion designs were inspired by everyday objects – leaves, flowers, cords, fans, shells. Feather designs, in many different shapes, were especially popular. For this project, we have used a modern stylized flower shape which adds an attractive texture to the glazed cotton pillow top.

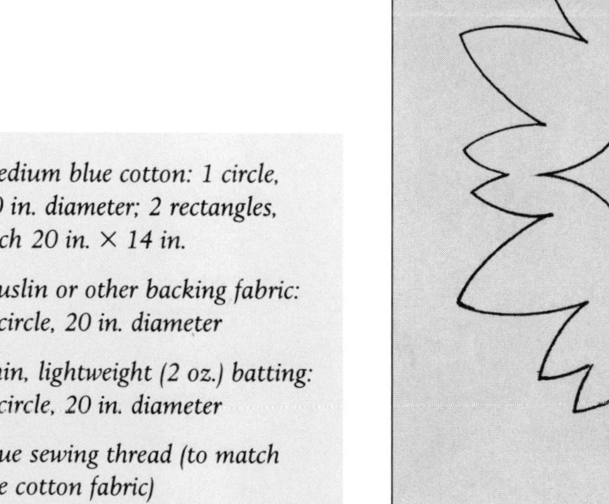

MATERIALS

- *Medium blue cotton: 1 circle, 20 in. diameter; 2 rectangles, each 20 in. × 14 in.*
- *Muslin or other backing fabric: 1 circle, 20 in. diameter*
- *Thin, lightweight (2 oz.) batting: 1 circle, 20 in. diameter*
- *Blue sewing thread (to match the cotton fabric)*
- *Blue quilting thread (darker than the cotton fabric)*

14 in.

14 in.

▲ *Chart for the Flower design.*

1 *Enlarge the chart for the flower to the correct size (see page 40). Remember to put in the center dot. This will help you to position the design in the center of the fabric.*

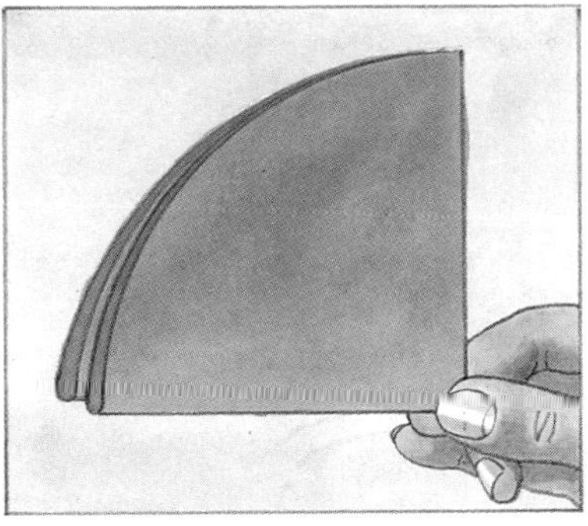

2 *Fold the blue circle in half, then in half again. Mark the center point on the right side with a dot, using a fading-ink pen (see page 29).*

3 *Transfer the flower design to the right side of the blue cotton circle (see page 48), aligning the dot on the chart with the dot in the center of the fabric.*

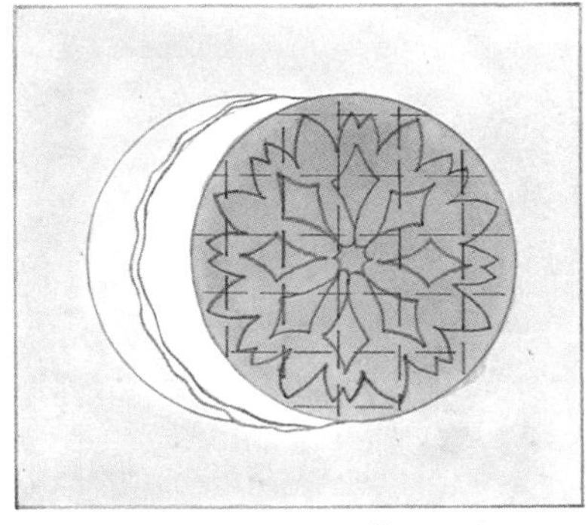

4 *Lay the muslin on a flat surface and put the circle of batting on top, then the marked fabric, right side up. Baste the layers together with a grid of horizontal and vertical stitches (see page 52).*

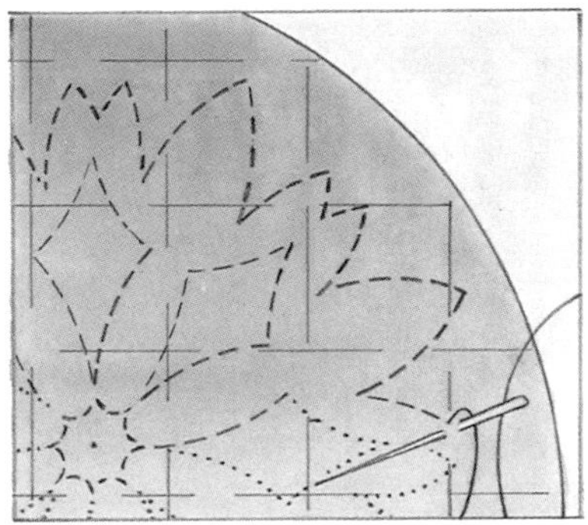

5 *Using the blue quilting thread, quilt the design (see page 56). Begin in the center and work out to prevent puckering. When your quilting is complete, remove the basting threads.*

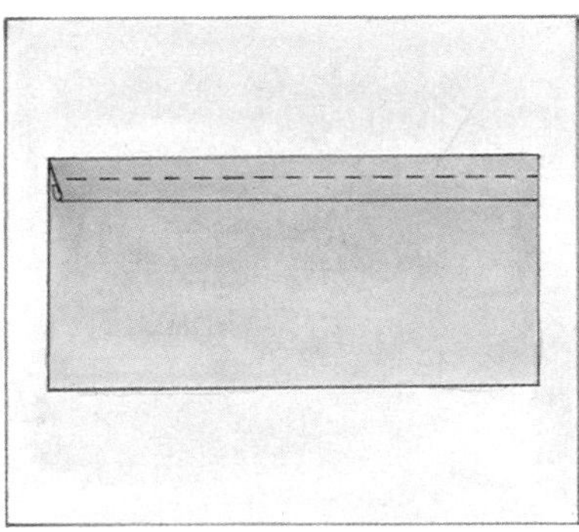

6 *Press and stitch a small double seam on one long edge of each rectangle.*

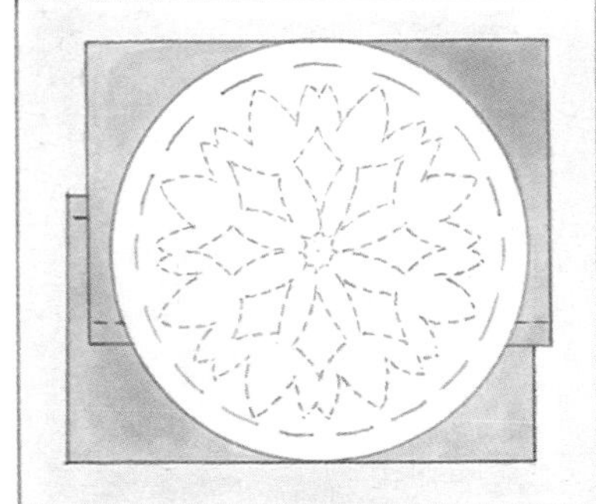

7 *Place the rectangles face up on a flat surface. Place the quilted medallion face down on top so that the seamed edges overlap and the sides are level with the edges of the circle. Baste around 1 in. from raw edges.*

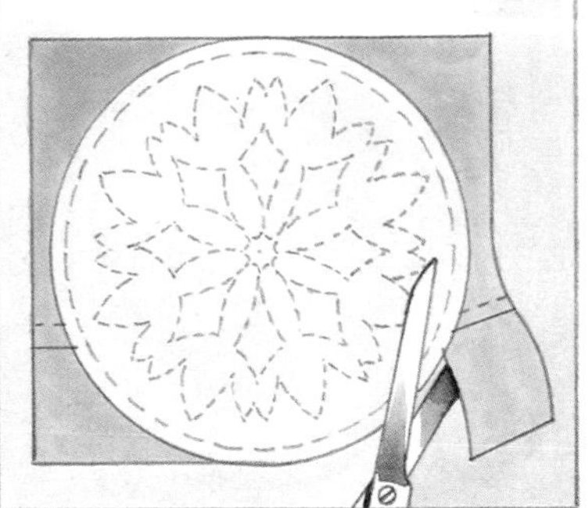

8 *Stitch around the edge twice by machine for strength. Remove the basting. Trim the seam to ¼ in.; trim the excess fabric from the pillow back. Be careful not to cut through the stitching of the seam line. Clip seam.*

9 *Turn the pillow cover right side out and press the backs carefully. Don't press the quilted areas. If the front of the cover is creased, hold a hot steam iron a few inches above the quilting for a few seconds.*

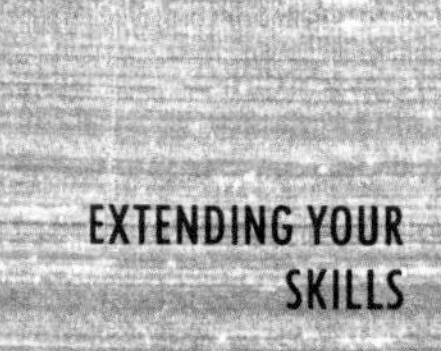

Amish lap quilt

The Amish people follow a simple and industrious way of life. Their stress on simplicity is noticeable in the plain, sometimes stark beauty of their quilts. Many Amish quilts are made from hand-dyed cottons in bright colors; black pieces are added, giving more intensity to the surrounding colors. The Amish sometimes use block patterns, but more usually a large central design is surrounded by one or two borders; quilting with contrasting threads shows off the exquisite patterns in the stitches. The colors used in the oldest Amish quilts, from Pennsylvania, are usually in the cool part of the spectrum. We have used these colors in this simple patchwork design called, among other things, Roman Stripes.

MATERIALS

- *Cotton: $\frac{1}{4}$ yd. × 60 in. of each of 6 colors – pale pink, dark pink, mauve, purple, pale blue, dark blue*
- *Black cotton: $1\frac{1}{2}$ yd. × 60 in.; 6 ft. 2 in. × 4 ft. 2 in.*
- *Thin batting: 6 ft. × 4 ft.*
- *Muslin: 6 ft. × 4 ft.*
- *Matching sewing thread*
- *Right-angle triangle template with shorter sides of 12 in.*

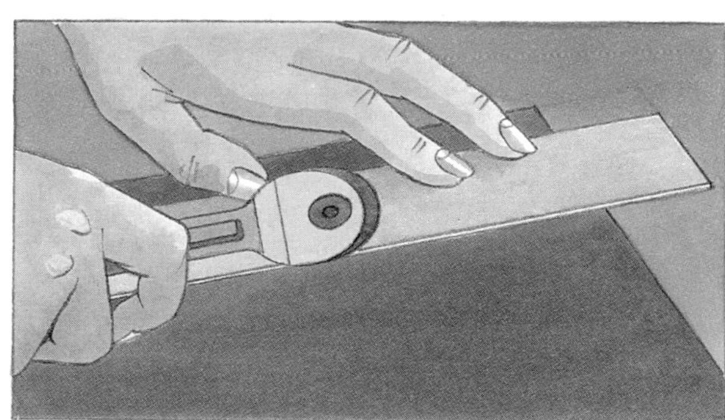

1 *Use a rotary cutter to cut the colored cotton lengthwise into 2 in. strips (see page 44).*

2 *Stitch the strips of fabric together along the long edges to make four wide strips. Work in this order each time – purple, light pink, dark blue, mauve, dark pink, light blue. Use ¼ in. seam allowance.*

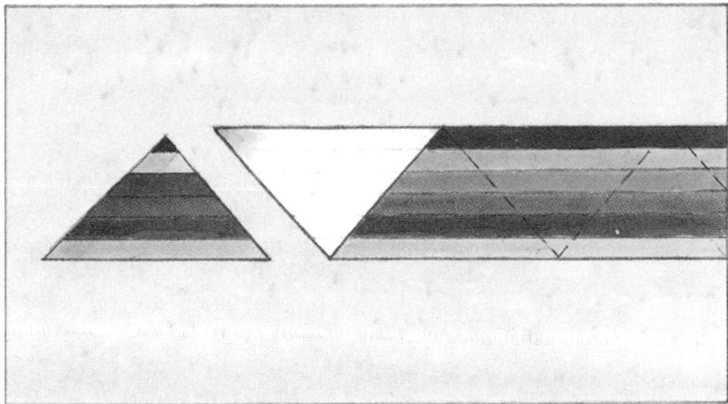

3 *Position the template so that the 90° point is on one edge of one wide strip and the long edge is along the other. Use a rotary cutter to cut a triangle from the strip-pieced fabric. Turn the template around and cut another triangle. Continue in this way until you have cut 24 triangles, 12 in each direction.*

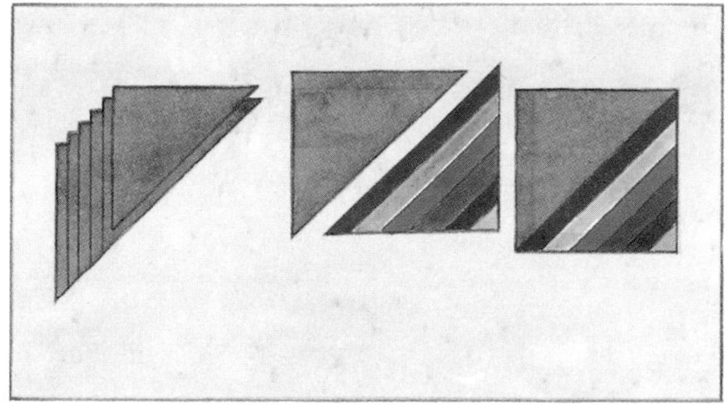

4 *Use the same template to cut 24 triangles from the black fabric. Place the short sides of the template along the grain. With right sides together, join the long edge of a black triangle to the long edge of a strip-pieced triangle. Repeat to form 24 blocks.*

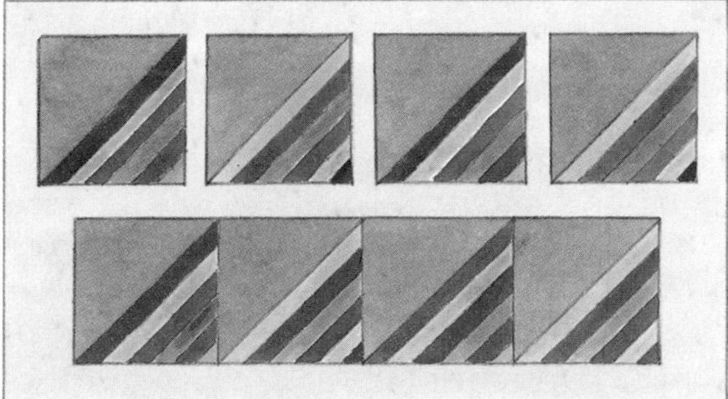

5 *If necessary, trim the blocks slightly to square them up. Follow the layout shown in the photograph to join the blocks in four rows of six, then join the rows together to form the quilt top.*

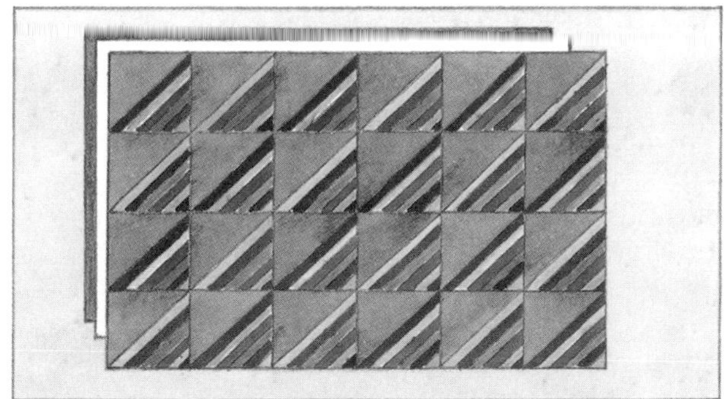

6 *Layer the muslin, the batting, and the quilt top (see page 52). Baste the layers together. Stitch by hand or machine along the seam lines between the blocks and between the triangles. Remove the basting threads.*

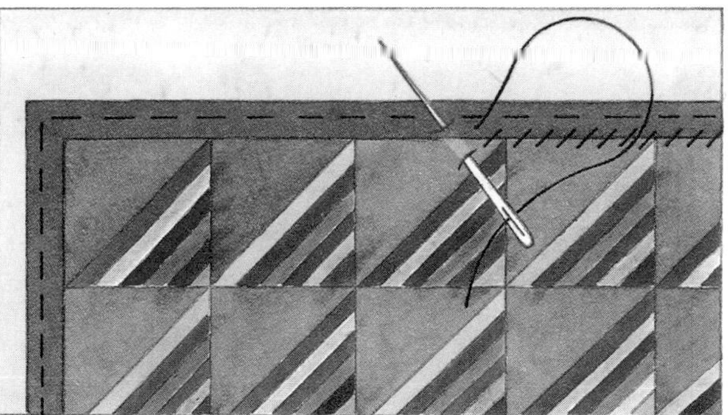

7 *Place the quilted patchwork on the backing fabric, wrong sides together. Turn over each edge of backing fabric ¼ in., then ¼ in. again. Baste backing over the edges of the patchwork; slipstitch into place. Remove basting threads.*

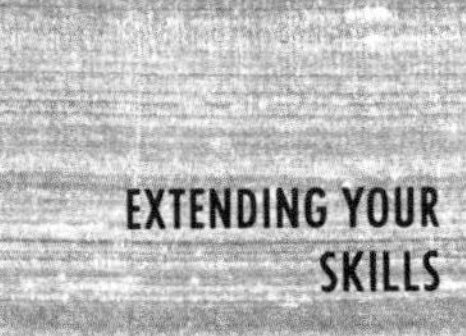

English patchwork

English patchwork is pieced work that is produced by stitching together pieces of fabric that have been basted onto paper shapes. It is very time-consuming, so is not the best method for traditional block patterns which can be stitched far more quickly by the conventional method. It is, however, very useful for shapes which cannot easily be joined with long straight seams, such as hexagons, diamond stars, octagons, and patterns such as Tumbling Blocks or Baby's Blocks (see page 125).

To assemble the pieces for English patchwork, cut the paper shapes from paper such as typing paper, then cut corresponding fabric shapes, with a ¼ in. seam allowance all around. The fabric is then basted over the paper, turning the raw edges to the back, and the shapes are overcast together to build up the pattern. Here, the paper shapes are left in place to stiffen the decoration, but normally they are removed when the basting threads are taken out.

For an eye-catching variation, sew six hexagons instead of seven and make a wreath decoration by leaving out the middle shape.

- *Cotton fabrics with Christmas motifs: 7 pieces, each no less than 6 in. square*
- *Thin card*
- *Sheet of typing paper*
- *Green or red sewing thread*
- *Ribbon or braid: 6 in. length*
- *Small amount of stuffing*

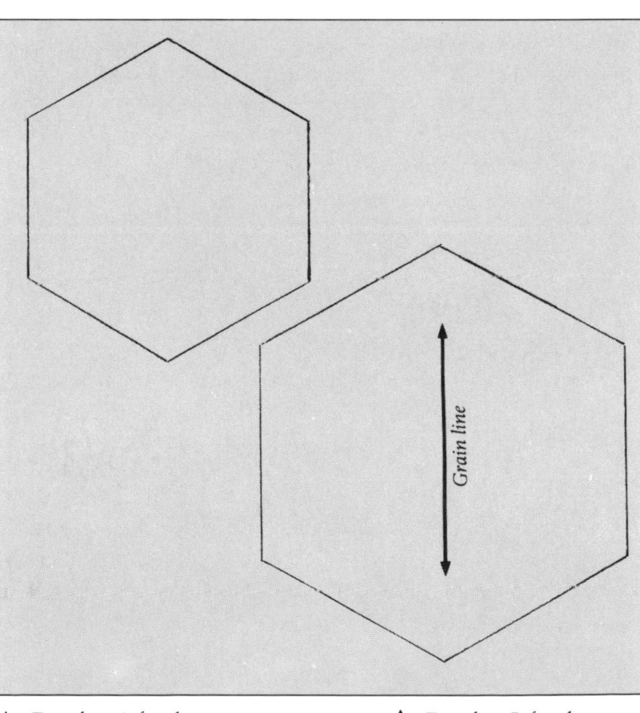

▲ *Template A for the paper shapes.*

▲ *Template B for the fabric shapes.*

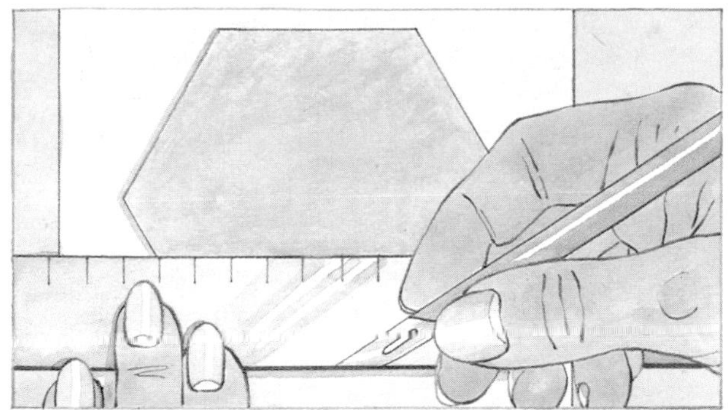

1 *Trace the templates onto thin cardboard, and cut them out very accurately. Mark the grain line onto template B. Cut two shapes from each fabric using template B. Using template A, cut 14 paper shapes.*

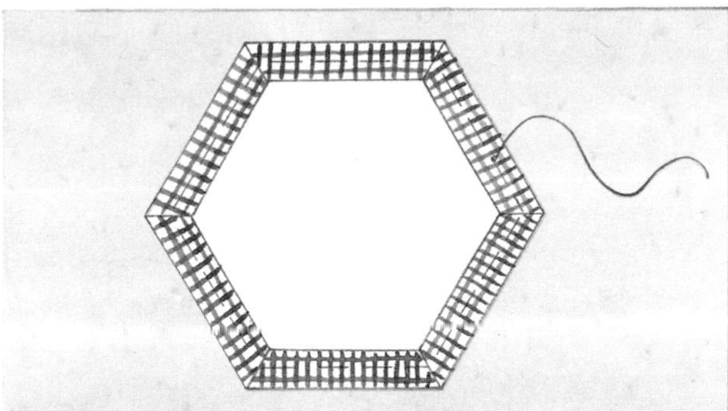

2 *Baste each piece of fabric to a paper shape, stitching down the 1/4 in. overlap all around. Tie a knot in the end of your basting thread and start stitching with the knot on the right side; this will make it easier to remove the basting.*

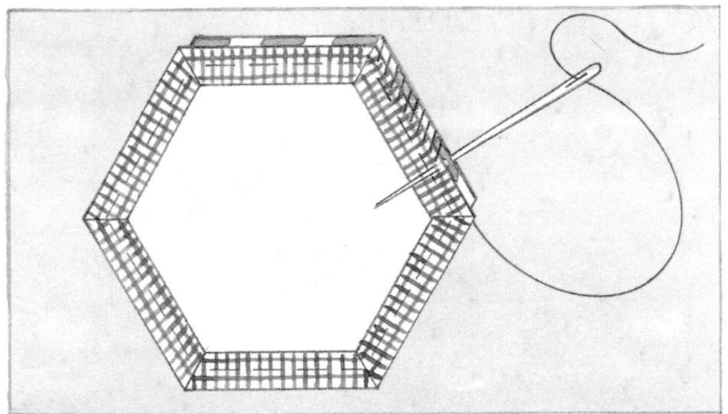

3 *When all your shapes are basted, take two hexagons of different fabrics and place them right sides together. Stitch them together along one side, overcasting with close, firm stitches. Start and finish the thread securely.*

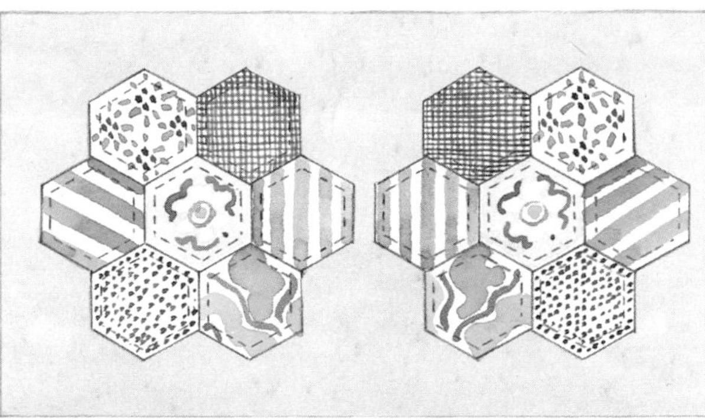

4 *Continue joining hexagons to form a rosette of six different hexagons around a central one; make sure that all the seams between them are stitched. Join the other hexagons in the same way to form a mirror image rosette.*

5 *Place the rosettes, paper sides together, with the same fabric hexagons backing each other at the top, and blind stitch around the edges of the rosettes. Stitch the ends of the hanging loop into the seam at each side of the top hexagon, and leave two or three sides open for stuffing.*

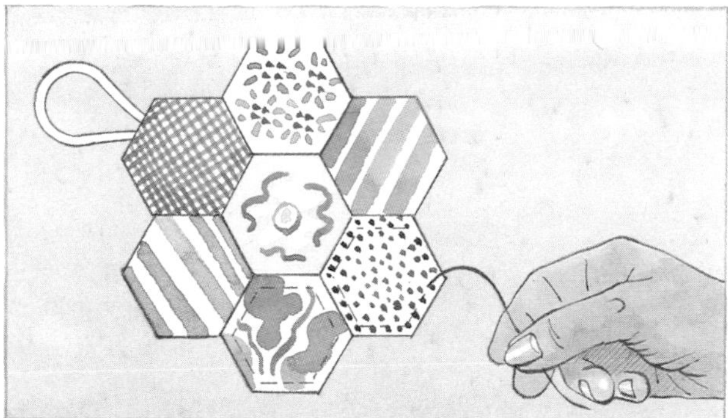

6 *Pad the shape gently with a small amount of the stuffing, and close up the final edges of the rosette. Don't over-stuff, or the shape of the decoration will be distorted. Remove the basting threads.*

This striking patchwork is a type of appliqué. The patches of fabric are laid onto a background, and the raw edges are covered with a length of binding. The final result resembles a stained glass window; the binding makes lines between the fabric pieces in the same way that leading separates panes of colored glass.

If all the lines in the patchwork design are straight, any kind of binding can be used for the "leading," If any of the lines are curved, you will need to use bias binding so that the tape can be shaped to follow the curves. You can use commercial bias binding or cut strips of fabric on the bias; the latter is useful when you want a particular color or size of bias binding.

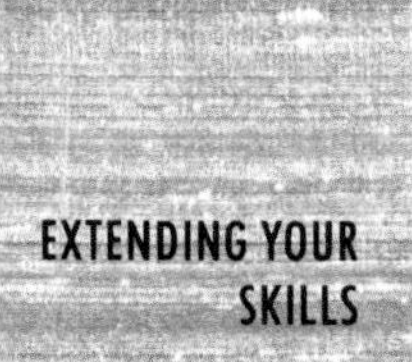

Stained glass wallhanging

This project uses the traditional black binding over bright, jewel-tone fabrics.

MATERIALS

- *Pale green cotton: 30 in. square*
- *Muslin (or other backing fabric): 30 in. square*
- *Thin batting: 30 in. square*
- *Bright pink cotton: 18 in. square*
- *Bright purple cotton: 18 in. square*
- *Bright jade green cotton: 14 in. square*
- *Medium jade green cotton: 14 in. square*
- *1 in. wide black bias binding: 16 yd.*
- *Black sewing thread*

▲ *Chart for flowers and leaves.*

1 *Enlarge the chart to the correct size (see page 40). Go over it with dark felt-tip pen and trace it onto the right side of the pale green fabric. The lines will be covered by the bias binding.*

2 *Use the enlarged drawing to cut templates for the flower and leaf shapes. Cut one flower from each of the purple and pink fabrics and two half-leaves from the two green fabrics.*

3 *Lay out the fabric pieces in the correct position on the pale green fabric. Baste them into place.*

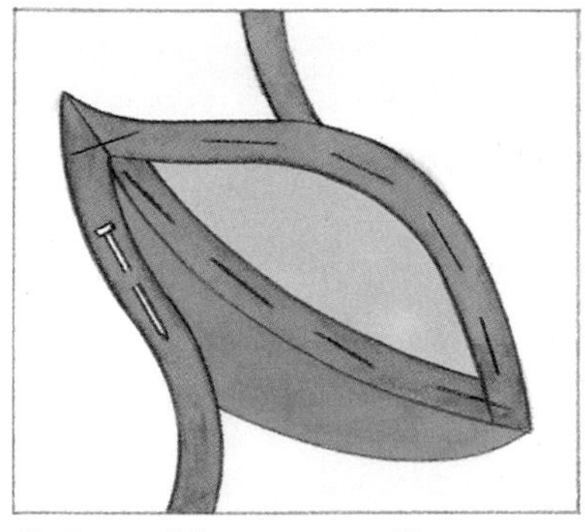

4 *Pin and baste pieces of bias binding, with the edges folded under, along all the lines of the design. Make sure that raw ends are covered by the next piece of binding.*

5 *Lay the batting on top of the backing fabric, and the flower design, face up, on top. Baste the layers together with a grid of vertical and horizontal stitches (see page 52).*

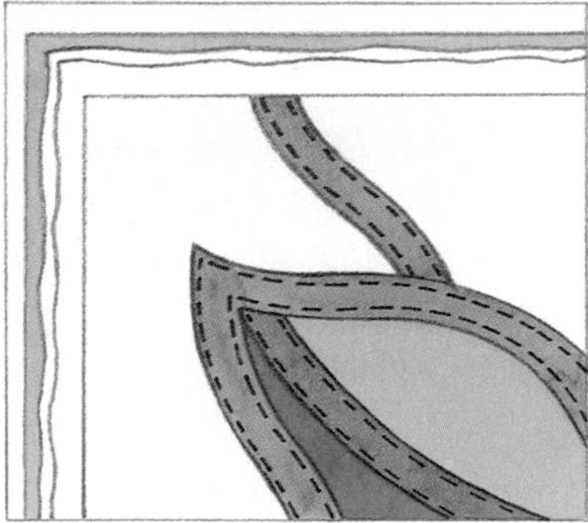

6 *Machine stitch along both edges of each strip of bias binding. Stitch the inside edge of each curve first; this prevents the binding from stretching out of shape.*

7 *Remove basting threads. Add a small circle of black fabric to the center of the flower to cover the raw ends of bias binding. Turn under and hand stitch.*

8 *Bind the raw edges of the square with more black bias binding.*

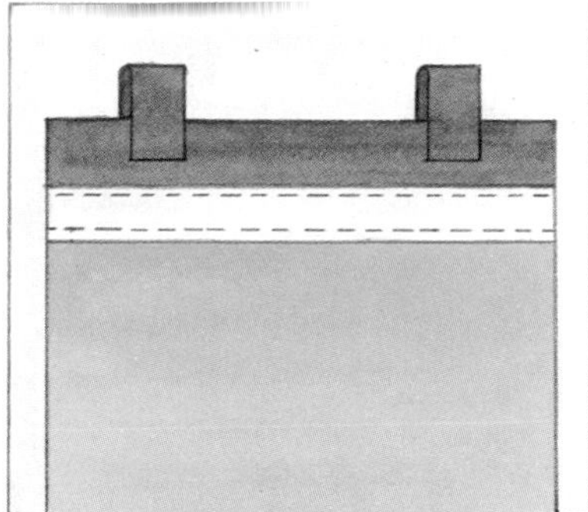

9 *Attach tape loops or a casing made from bias binding to the back of the project for hanging.*

Cathedral window patchwork is an unusual technique. It is neither pieced, appliquéd, nor quilted. It requires no batting, as the thickness comes from folding squares of fabric over on themselves. The finished result is rather three-dimensional in effect, with an overall design which is highly textured.

The base squares are usually made in plain colors, with the "windows" cut from prints.

EXTENDING YOUR SKILLS

Cathedral window

Interesting effects can be achieved by reversing this idea; use a small print for the frames and either a plain color, a large print, or a single motif in the windows. The shape and size of the panels lend themselves perfectly to this herb pillow design and provide an easy introduction to this technique. The potpourri or scented herbs will gradually release their fragrance into a room or drawer.

MATERIALS

- *Pink cotton: 4 squares, each $10\frac{1}{2}$ in. × $10\frac{1}{2}$ in.*
- *Pink print cotton: $\frac{1}{2}$ yd.*
- *Pink sewing thread to match*
- *Potpourri or scented herbs to stuff pillow*

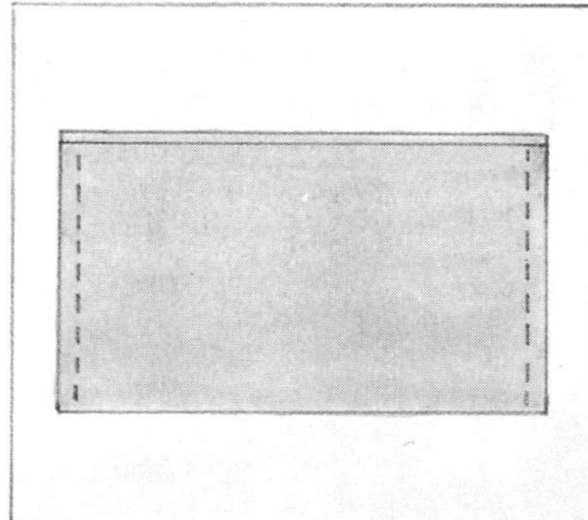

1 *Fold one square in half, wrong sides together, and stitch a $\frac{1}{4}$ in. seam along both short edges. Repeat the process for the other squares.*

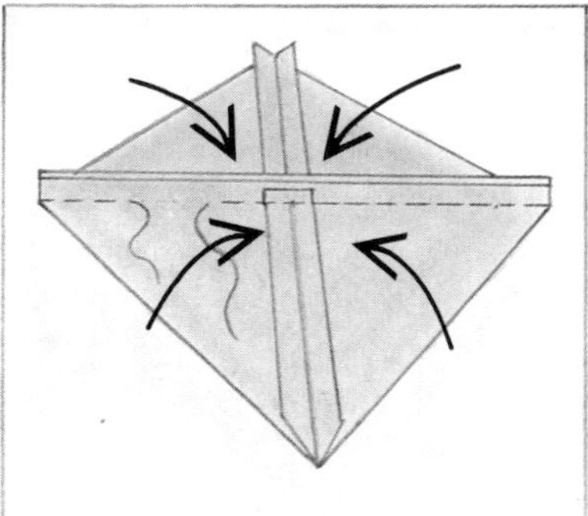

2 *On each square, pin together the tops of the seams and then pin the remaining raw edges together along the top. Leaving an opening for turning, stitch a $\frac{1}{4}$ in. seam.*

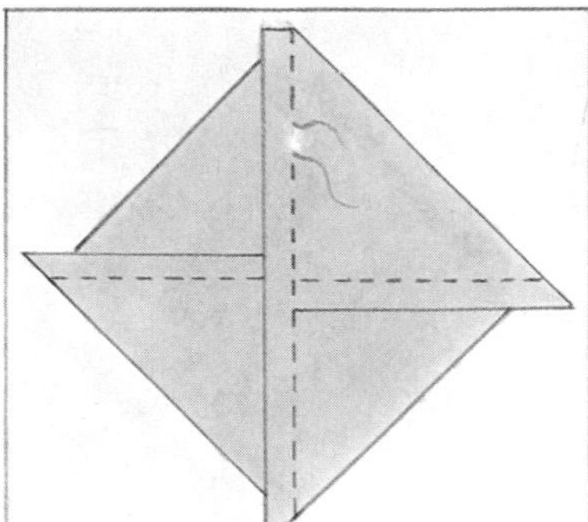

3 *Clip the excess fabric diagonally at each of the corners. This will make the shapes lie flat after they are turned right side out.*

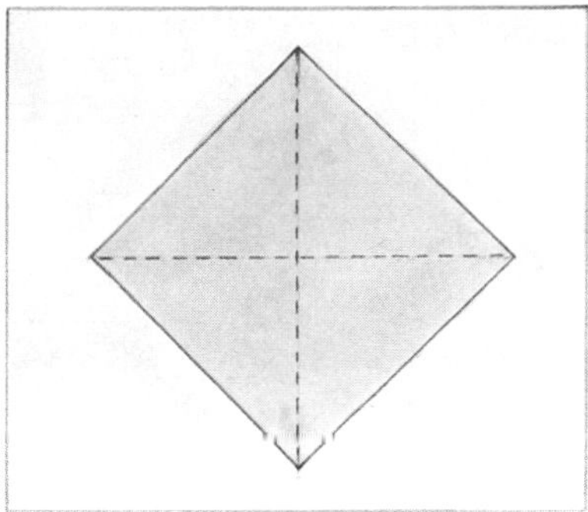

4 *Turn the seamed squares to the right side. Use the tip of a bodkin to push out the corners. Press into square shapes. The opening will be hidden when the pillow is finished.*

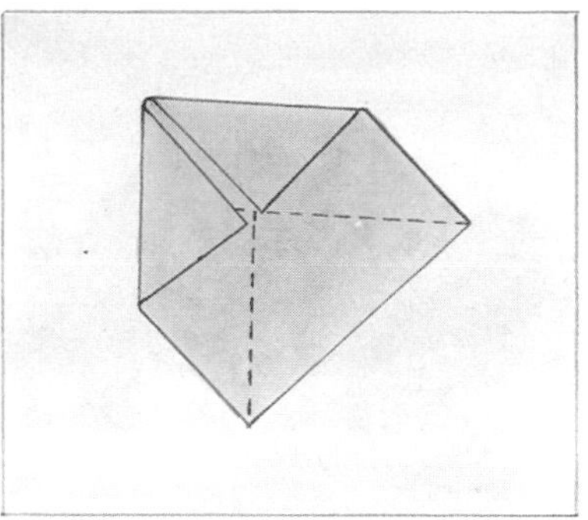

5 *Lay one square flat with the seams on top, then bring all four corners to the center. Press firmly. Repeat for the remaining squares.*

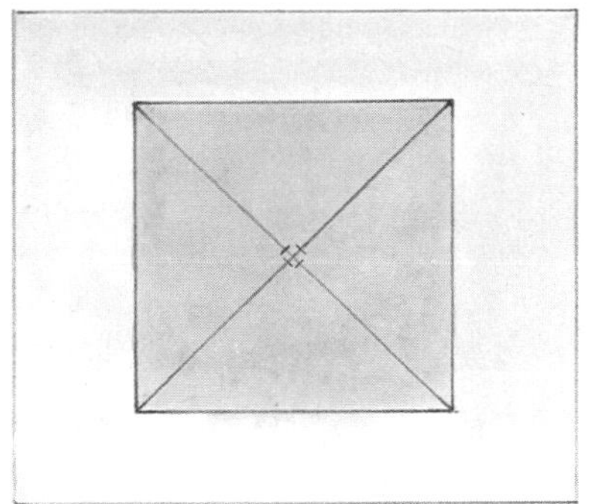

6 *Catch the corners of each square to the center with very small stitches through to the back.*

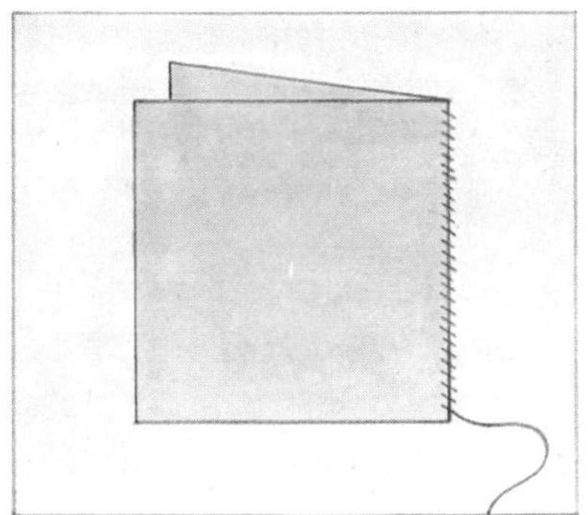

7 *Put two squares together so that the folded sides are facing each other; overcast down one side. Repeat for the other pair of squares, then stitch the pairs together in the same way.*

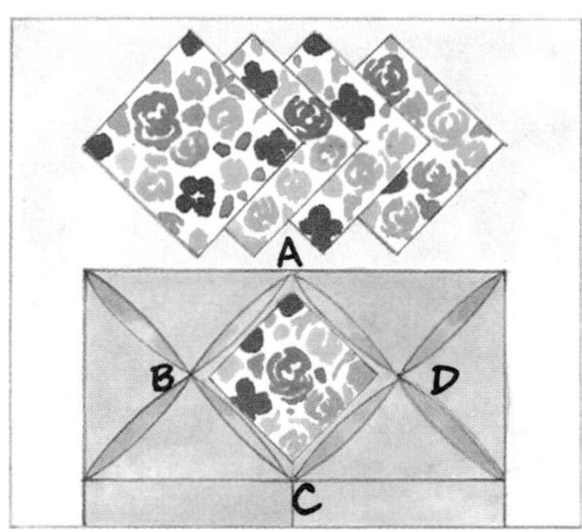

8 *Cut four squares of printed fabric a little smaller than the square made by points A, B, C, and D. Pin them inside the lines made by the folds on each side of the shape.*

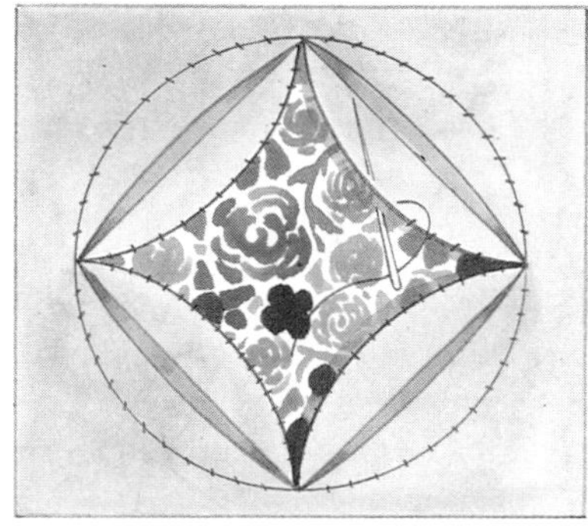

9 *Roll the edges of the "windows" over the edges of the print squares. Stitch the edges down, catching the corners together with two small stitches. Roll and catch the edges just outside the windows.*

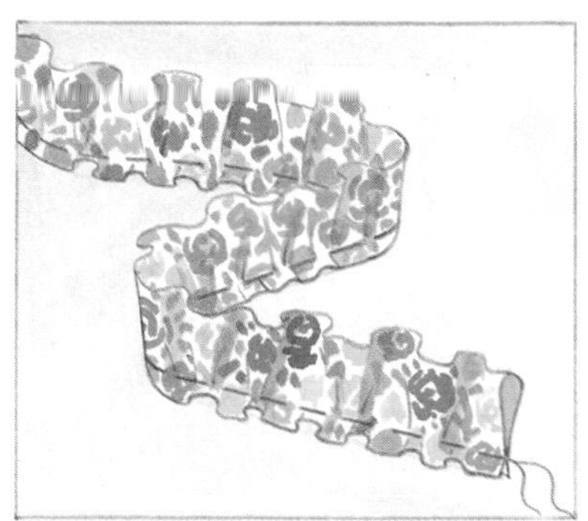

10 *From the print fabric, cut a length 3¼ in. × the complete width. Fold it lengthwise and press fold. Run a gathering thread along the bottom ¼ in. from the raw edges, and pull gently to make a folded ruffle.*

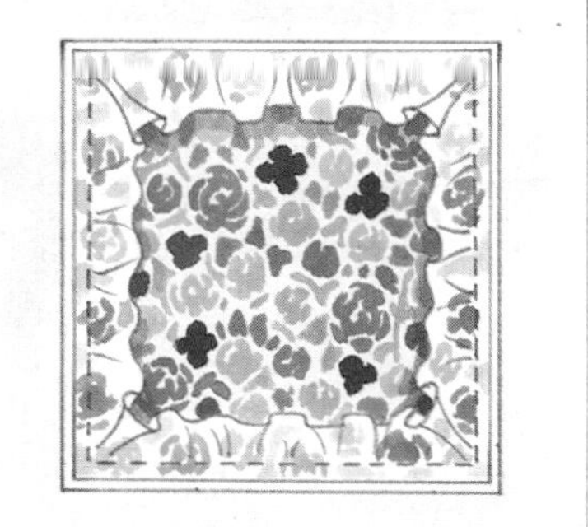

11 *Cut a square of print fabric the same size as your patchwork square plus ¼ in. all around. Pin the ruffle to the pillow top, right sides together. Stitch with a ¼ in. seam all around, then press ruffle out.*

12 *Place the patchwork square on the print backing square, wrong sides together. Slipstitch three edges, then stuff gently with potpourri. Slipstitch the final edge closed.*

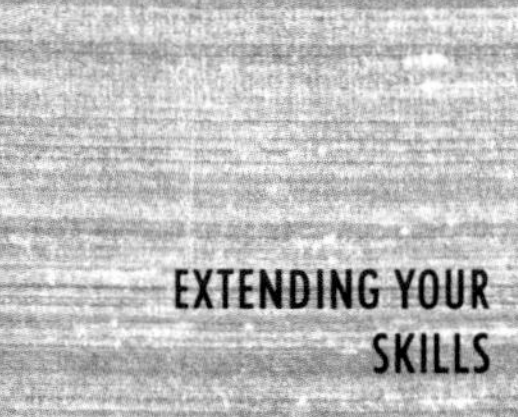

Folded star

Folded patchwork has several variations. The technique used here is also called Somerset patchwork and can be used for items like pillows, cards, and wallhangings. Folded patchwork of this kind is not suitable for bed quilts, however, as there are raw edges inside the folds which would tend to fray with frequent washing. Another folded technique, Prairie Points, is constructed so that the raw edges are sealed; because of this extra protection, it is particularly recommended for items that have to be washed.

This project uses two print fabrics in Christmas colors. The circles are arranged so that a red star appears in the design. If you fold your fabric so that the same motif shows each time, you can create a secondary patern within the star. Use unusual fabrics to vary the design.

For appliqué shapes with extra dimension, use small pieces of folded patchwork to make trees or flowers; bind the edges and attach to a background. This patchwork is usually constructed from the center out, but for flowers and trees you can begin at the outside.

- *Muslin, or other foundation fabric: 5 in. × 5 in.*
- *Red Christmas print cotton: $\frac{1}{8}$ yd.*
- *Green Christmas print cotton: $\frac{1}{8}$ yd.*
- *Matching sewing thread*
- *Glue*
- *White card or mat board with round opening approximately $3\frac{3}{4}$ in. diameter*
- *Red frame, approximately $4\frac{1}{2}$ in. square*

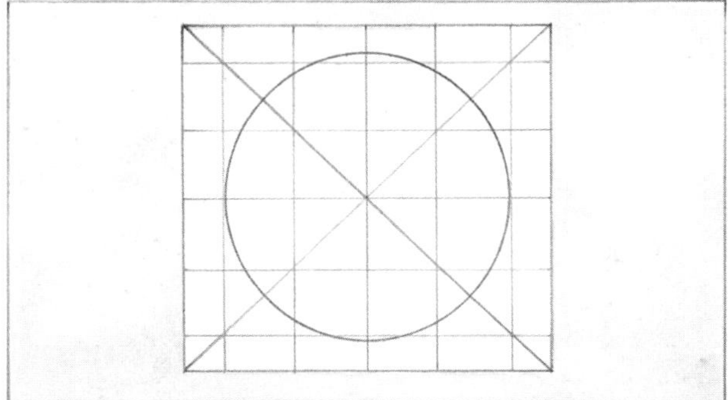

1 *On the square of foundation fabric, draw in diagonals from corner to corner. From the center outward, draw a grid of 1 in. squares – a quilter's ruler (see page 84) is useful for drawing parallel lines. In the center of the grid, draw a circle the same size as the one on the card.*

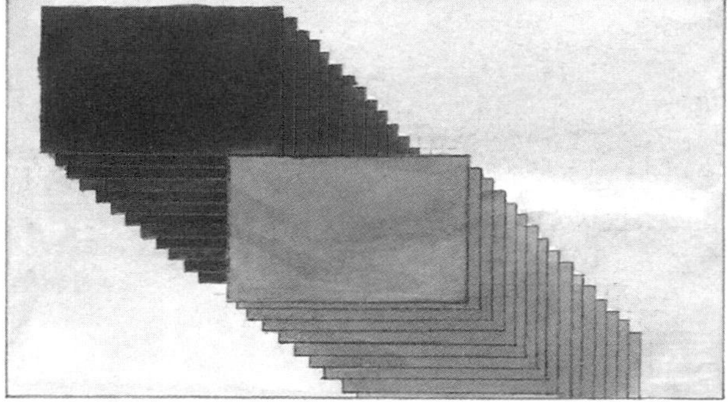

2 *From the red fabric cut 12 rectangles each measuring $1\frac{1}{2}$ in. × $2\frac{1}{2}$ in. From the green fabric, cut 16 rectangles the same size. For accuracy and speed, use a rotary cutter (see page 45).*

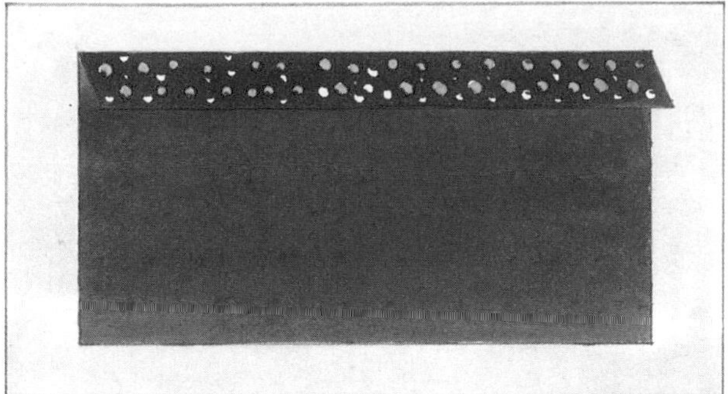

3 *Fold and press under* $^1/_4$ *in. along one long edge of each one of the rectangles.*

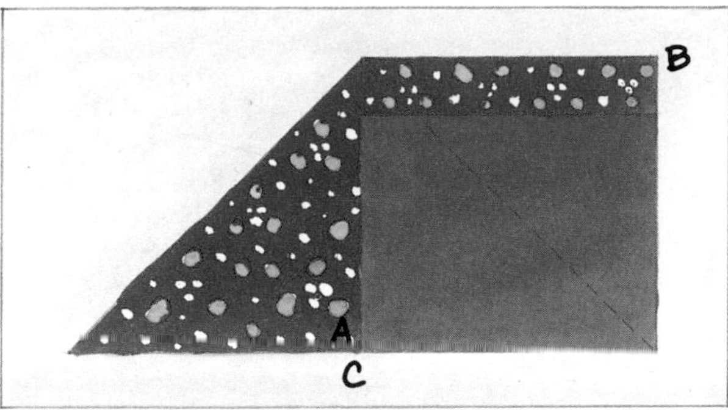

4 *Fold and press points A and B to point C on all pieces, placing wrong sides together as shown. You now have 28 folded triangles; 12 red and 16 green. All show the right side of the fabric on both sides.*

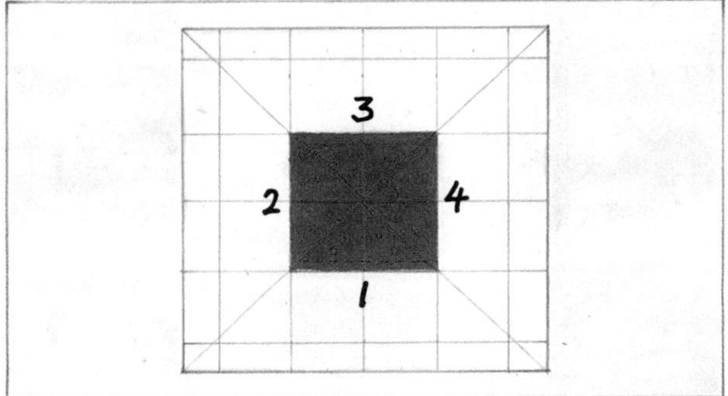

5 *Lay 4 red triangles down on the center of the foundation square, folds up as shown. Use the guidelines to help you position them accurately. Secure each point with an invisible stitch; stitch to the foundation with running stitches around the edges.*

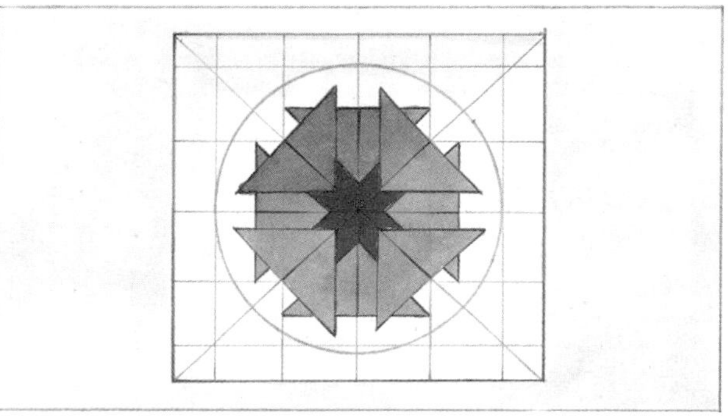

6 *Lay 4 green triangles, points in, over the first 4 red ones. Overlap evenly all around, but position the green triangles further out than the red row. Use running stitch around the long edges as before. Work another row of 4 green triangles in the same way.*

7 *Now add a row of 8 red triangles, positioned in alternating layers as before. Finish off with a row of 8 green triangles to complete the star.*

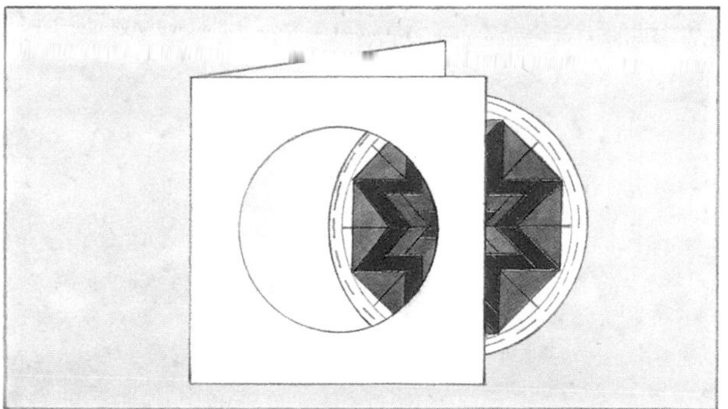

8 *Baste, then stitch just outside the circle on the foundation fabric, and cut out the completed star and circle. Glue around the edges of the star shape. Place the star behind the opening in the card or mat, making sure that it is accurately centered. Place in frame.*

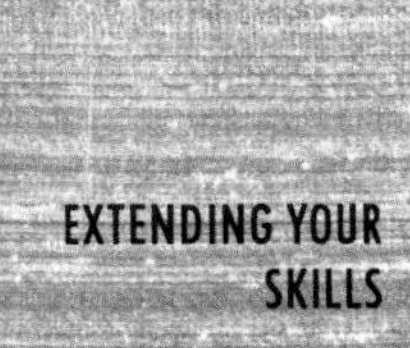
EXTENDING YOUR SKILLS

Trapunto table mat

Trapunto quilting, like conventional quilting, uses a layer of padding, but in trapunto only certain areas are padded rather than the whole of the item. The top layer of fabric is tacked to a firm backing layer, then the chosen areas are stitched to form hollow pockets. These are then lightly stuffed, producing an intriguing three-dimensional effect.

The project here uses a fabric-painted design, but you could just as easily use a printed fabric or one of the specially printed panels. Work the stitching by hand or by machine; machine stitching is much quicker if you have large areas to cover. If you stitch by hand, use a firm backstitch in a strong thread so that the stitching gives a definite outline to the pockets.

MATERIALS

- *Pale yellow cotton: 18 in. square*
- *Muslin or other backing fabric: 2 squares, each 18 in. × 18 in.*
- *Fabric paints: medium and dark yellow; medium and dark orange; medium and dark moss green. (You can purchase colors separately or mix your own.)*
- *Brushes*
- *Yellow sewing thread (to match yellow fabric)*
- *Stuffing*

▲ *Actual size chart for the table mat design.*

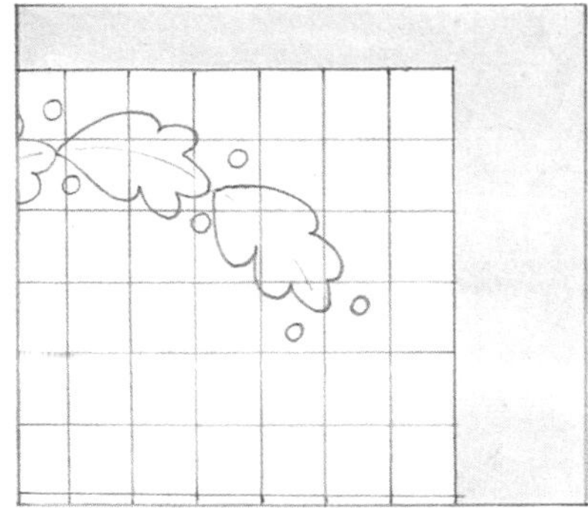

1 *Draw a circle 5½ in. in diameter and arrange leaf and berry shapes around it. Go over the design lines with black felt-tip pen.*

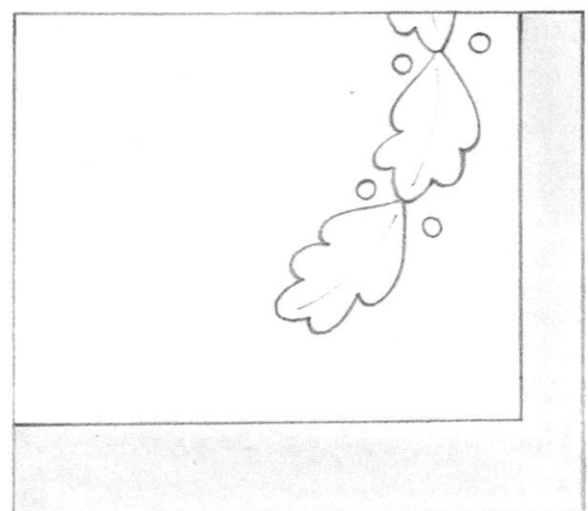

2 *Place the yellow fabric, right side up, over the design and trace the main lines using a matching crayon or silverpoint (see page 49).*

3 *Use the yellow, green, and orange fabric paints to color in the leaves and berries; alternate yellow leaves and green leaves.*

4 *With slightly darker shades of the same colors, add veins to the leaves and details to berries. When the paint is dry, set the colors according to the manufacturer's directions.*

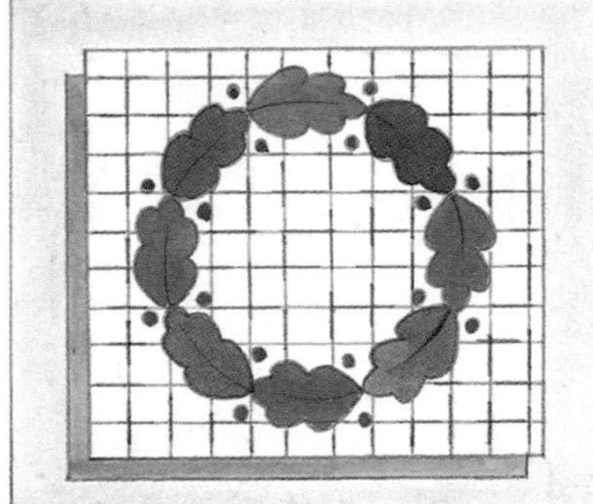

5 *Place the painted panel over one square of the backing fabric, wrong sides together, matching edges. Baste with a grid of horizontal and vertical stitches (see page 52).*

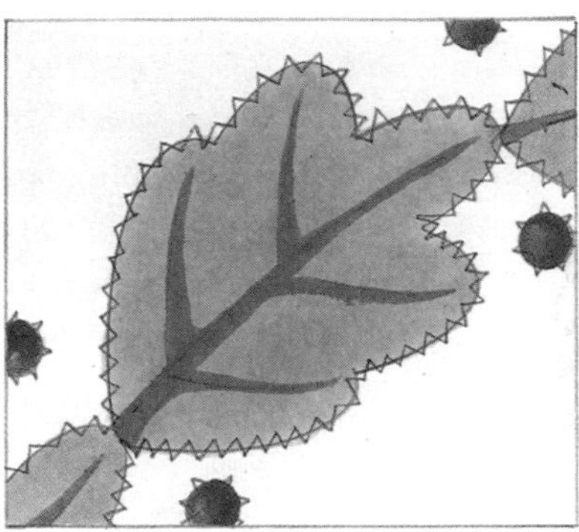

6 *Outline the leaves and berries with machine zigzag or straight stitch; use backstitch if stitching by hand.*

7 *Behind each pocket formed by the stitched outline, cut a small (½ in. - ¾ in. long) slit in the backing fabric. Be very careful not to cut through the top fabric.*

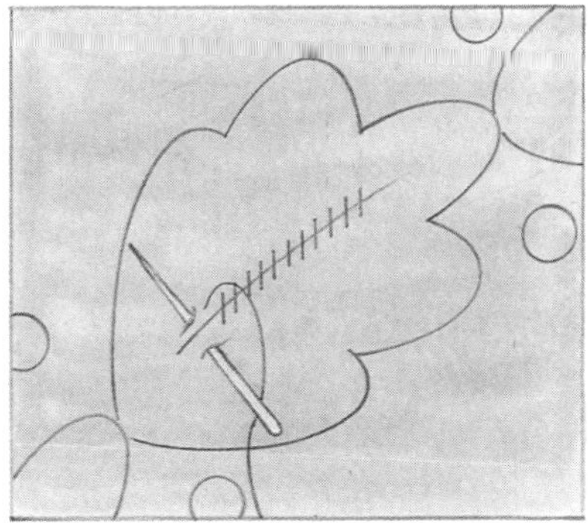

8 *Use a small amount of stuffing to pad each stitched pocket, checking your progress from the front. Don't overstuff or the fabric will distort. Close the slits in the backing fabric with small overcast stitch.*

9 *Baste the second square of backing fabric to the back of the mat, wrong sides together. Fold raw edges to the inside; close with two rows of topstitching around outside edges.*

Italian, or corded, quilting involves stitching two layers of fabric together in a decorative pattern of lines and channels. When the stitching is complete, the channels are threaded with cord or thick wool. This raises the top fabric and produces a textured pattern. Italian quilting is excellent for strong linear designs like this Celtic knot, worked on silk for a skirt pocket. The stitching and quilting are completed

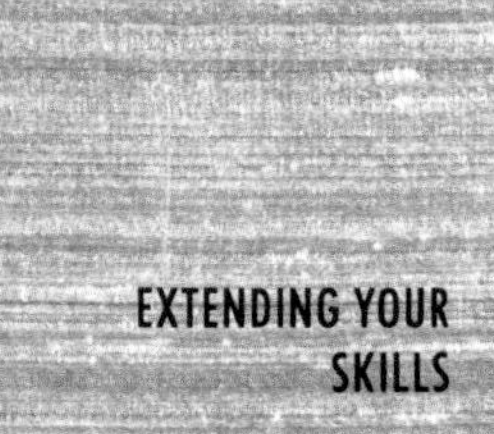

EXTENDING YOUR SKILLS

Corded pocket

before the pocket is attached to the garment. (For a ready-made garment, remove the pocket to embellish it, then stitch in place again.) This design is worked on a pocket for an evening skirt, but would also work smaller to decorate a shirt pocket.

MATERIALS

- *Silk fabric: about 2 in. larger all around than pocket pattern piece*
- *Firmly woven silk for backing: same size as above*
- *Fine cotton cord: 2 yd.*
- *Cotton or silk thread to match silk fabric*
- *Large-eyed tapestry needle*

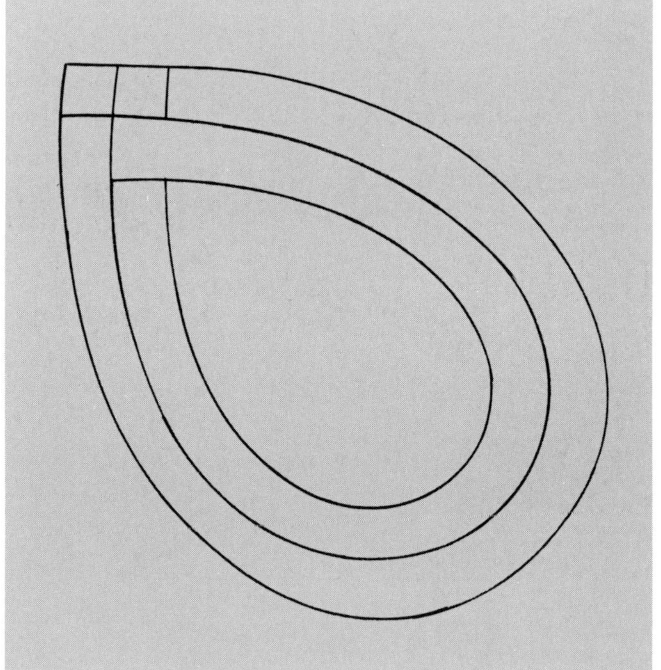

▲ *One quarter of the Celtic Knot pattern, actual size for tracing.*

1 *Trace each quarter of the pattern (opposite below) on the same piece of paper. Turn the paper and reposition it carefully for each quarter.*

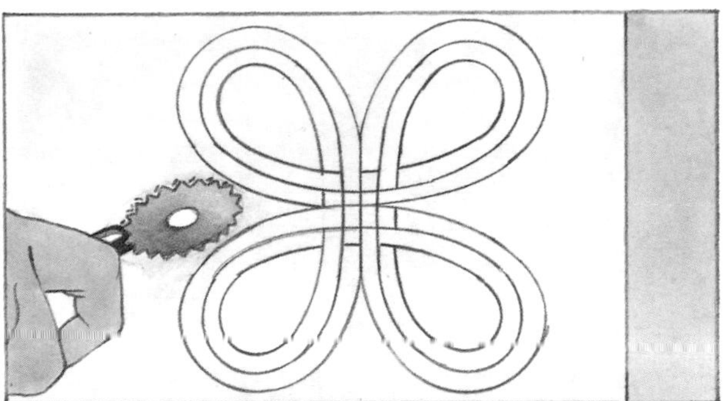

2 *Transfer the design to the right side of the silk fabric, using the tracing or prick and pounce method (see page 49). Allow at least 1 in. of plain fabric around the outside edge of the design.*

3 *Place the silk on top of the backing fabric, wrong sides together. Baste together with a grid of horizontal and vertical stitches (see page 53).*

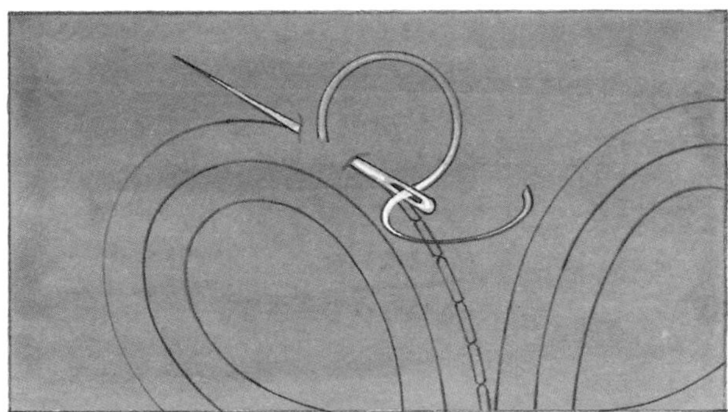

4 *Using backstitch and three strands of cotton or silk thread, stitch along all the lines of the design to form channels. When the stitching is complete, press the design with a warm steam iron.*

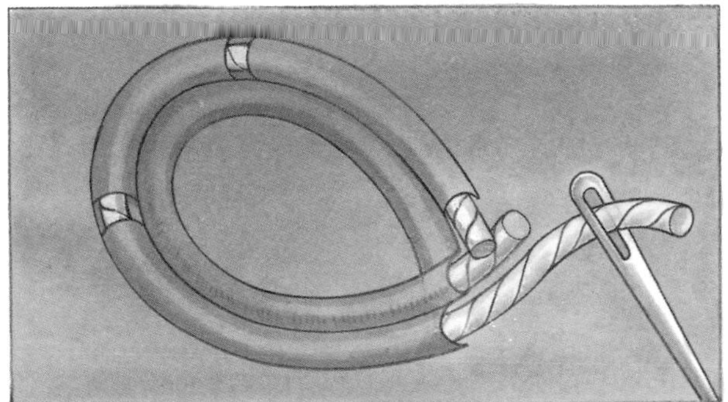

5 *Thread the tapestry needle with a length of cord. Take the needle through the backing fabric at the beginning of one channel. Thread all the channels with cord, taking the needle out of the backing fabric at the end of each channel. Along tight curves, you may need to take the needle in and out of backing fabric several times.*

6 *When the design is completely corded, lay it face down on a soft cloth and press it on the wrong side with a warm steam iron. Center the pocket pattern over the design, cut out, and continue making the garment.*

Sashiko quilting is a traditional Japanese technique. The stitching is worked in bold threads; the thickness depends on the thickness of the fabric. The stitches are longer than for ordinary quilting. Stitch length for sashiko is about twice as long on the front as on the back. The designs are usually geometric repeats. This silk evening bag illustrates the use of several different designs inside straight

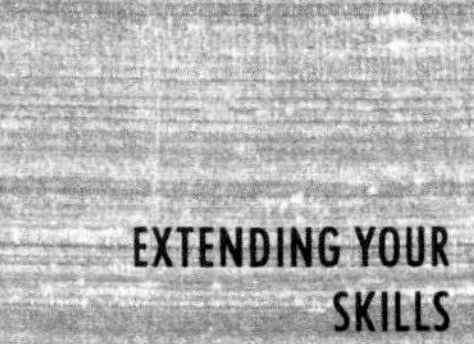

EXTENDING YOUR SKILLS

Sashiko bag

outlines. Sashiko work can be flat or padded; this project is gently padded with a thin layer of batting to give it extra texture.

Because the stitches are designed to show, it is important to make them look as even and attractive as possible. On straight lines, pick up as many stitches as possible on your needle so that you get into an even rocking rhythm; on curves it will only be practical to pick up one or two stitches to keep the curve smooth. Try to sew the same number of stitches per inch throughout the design and make sure that they don't overlap.

MATERIALS

- *Jade green silk: two pieces, $21\frac{1}{2}$ in. × $7\frac{1}{2}$ in. each; $3\frac{1}{2}$ in. × 5 in. rectangle; 3 in. × 3 in. square*
- *Thin (2oz) polyester or silk batting: 21 in. × 7 in.*
- *Iron-on interfacing (light)*
- *Gold thread*
- *Small gold beads*
- *Green silk thread to match*
- *Green sewing thread to match*
- *Thin gold or jade cord*
- *Thick gold or jade cord for handle*

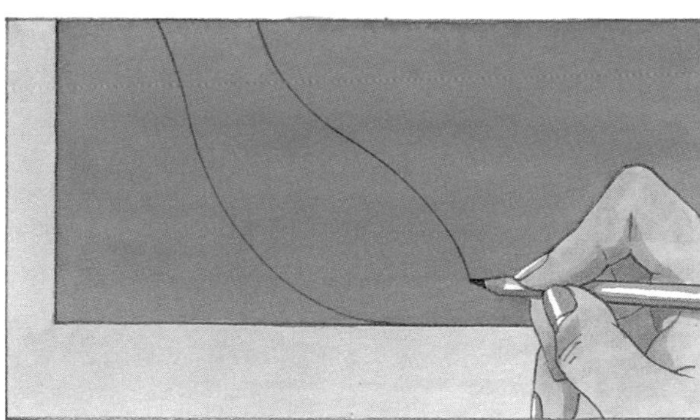

1 *Enlarge the chart to the correct size (see page 40). Using a crayon slightly darker than the silk, or a silverpoint (see page 49), transfer the design onto the right side of one of the large pieces of silk.*

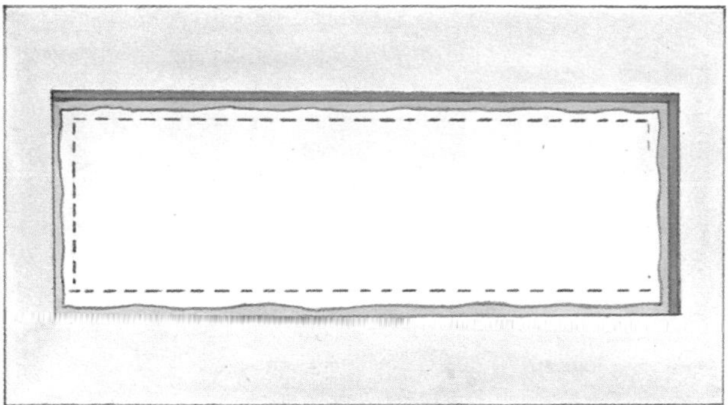

2 *Place the silk pieces right sides together and pin the batting in the center of the top piece. Machine stitch around the rectangle, leaving one short side open for turning. Clip across the corners and remove the pins.*

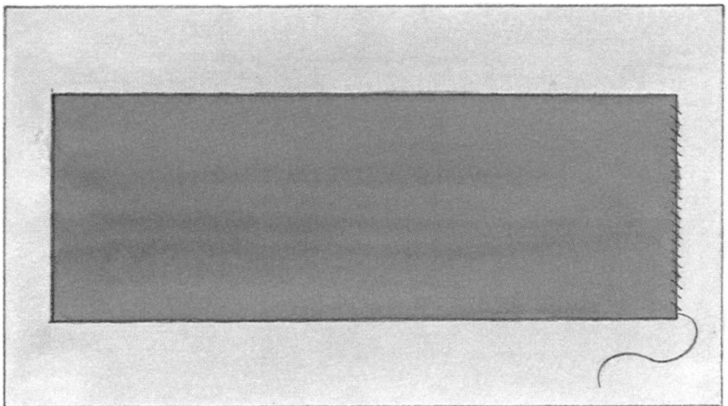

3 *Turn right side out and slipstitch the open end, turning under 1/4 in. of each piece of fabric to make a rectangle 7 in. × 21 in.*

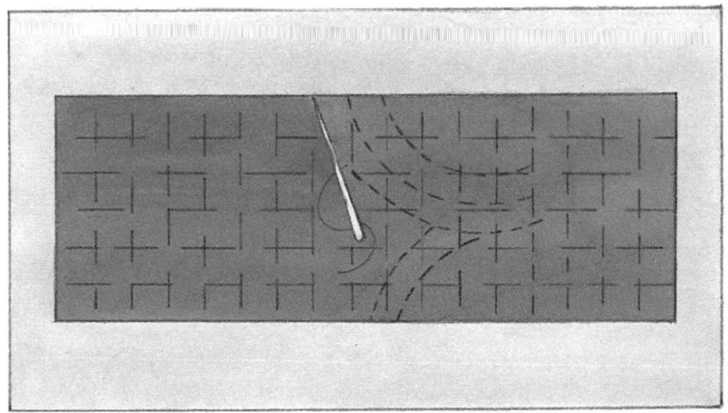

4 *Baste the layers with a grid of horizontal and vertical stitches (see page 53). Using the gold thread, make sashiko running stitches along all the lines of the design. Begin each thread with a small knot pulled into the lining.*

19 1/2 in.

6 1/2 in.

▲ *Chart for the evening bag.*

Back of sashiko evening bag.

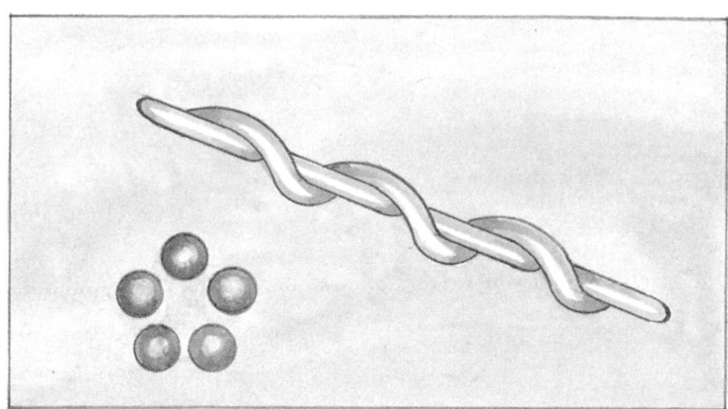

5 *Using the gold thread, whip a line of stitches through the running stitches that divide each pattern block; this gives a solid gold line. Add several gold beads where indicated on the chart.*

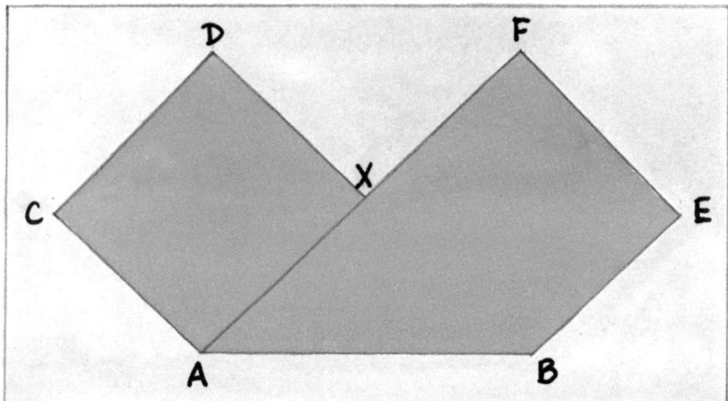

6 *Lay the quilted rectangle face down; fold along line AB to make the shape shown.*

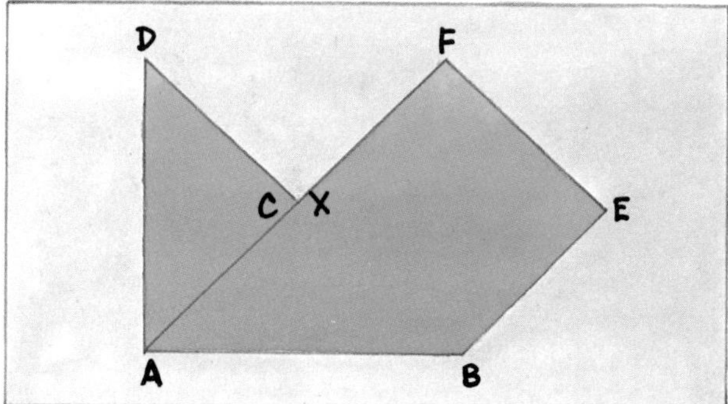

7 *Fold corner C to point X; turn the piece over. Fold corner E to point X. Pin the edges together where they meet so that the bag keeps its shape.*

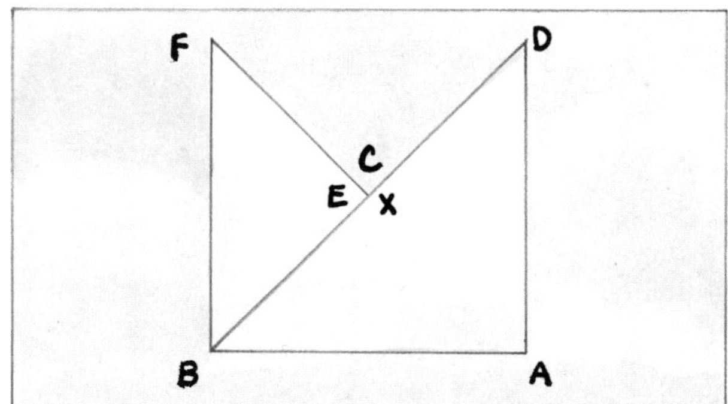

8 *Turn the bag inside out and slipstitch from corner A to point CX and from corner B to point EX.*

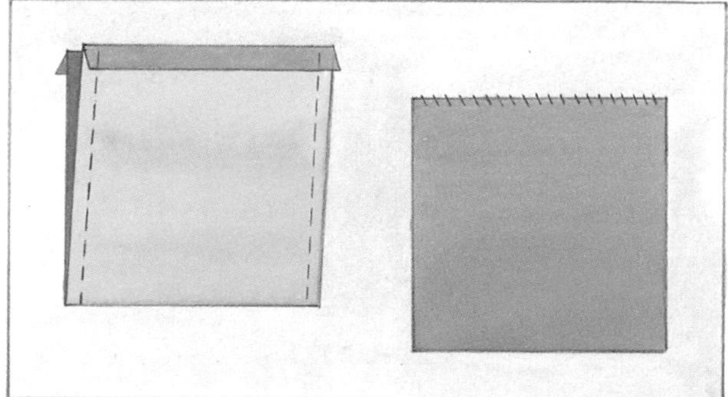

9 *Add iron-on interfacing to back of two small green silk pieces. Fold the rectangular piece in half across its width, right sides together, and sew together with a $^1/_4$ in. seam allowance. Clip the corners and turn right side out. Slipstitch the open ends closed to make a 2 $^1/_2$ in. square.*

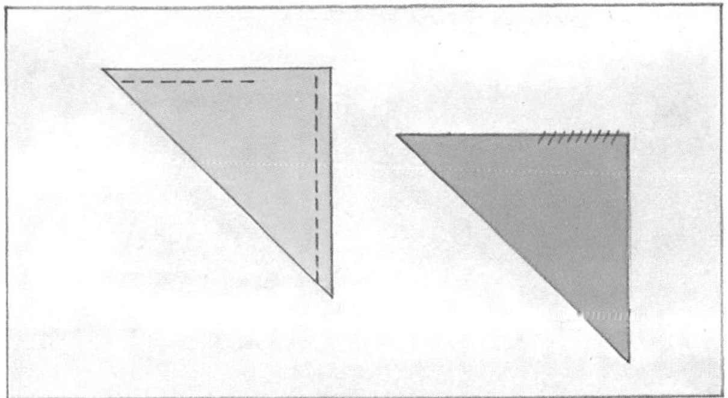

10 *Fold the square of silk diagonally, right sides together, and stitch ¼ in. seams along two sides, leaving a small opening for turning. Clip corners, turn right side out and slipstitch the opening closed.*

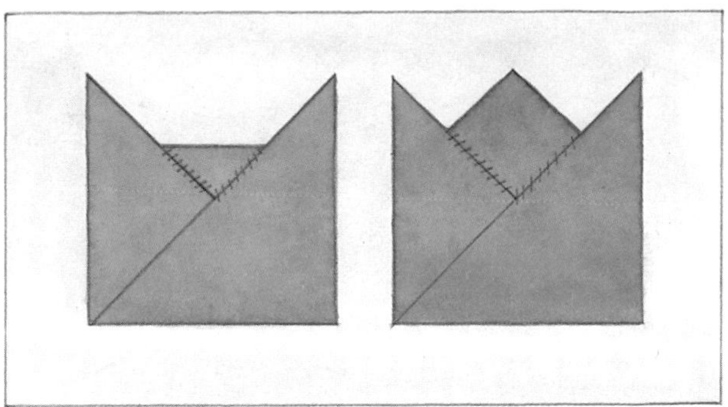

11 *Slipstitch the triangular piece into the V shape at the front of the bag and the square piece into the V at the back, working the stitches neatly from the inside of the bag.*

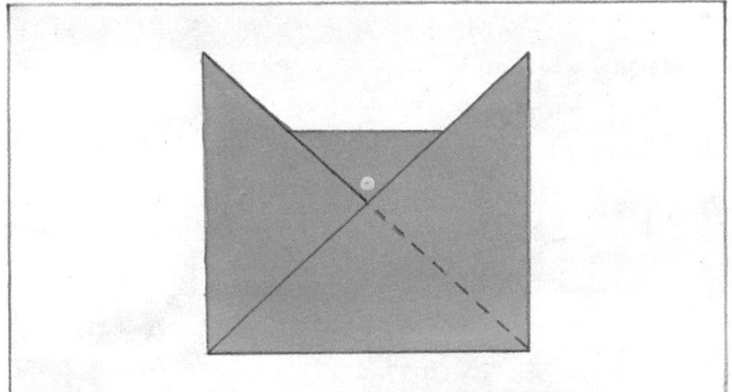

12 *Fold the top half of the square over the front of the bag and add a snap or other closure underneath the flap.*

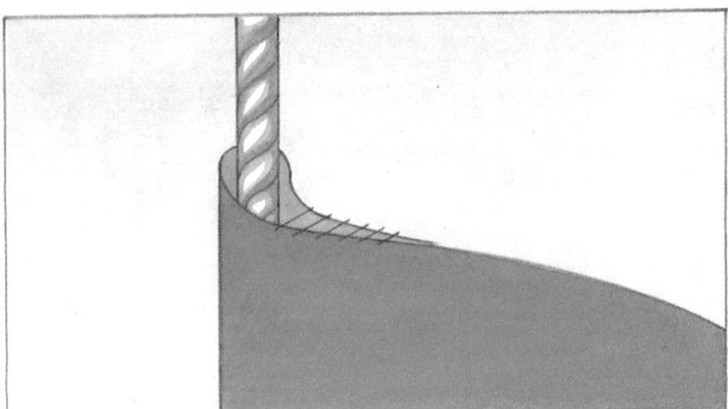

13 *Cut a length of thick cord for the handle; stitch the raw ends invisibly to the points of the bag sides. If the cord is bulky, wrap the end in the point of the bag, then stitch the diagonal sides together to hide it.*

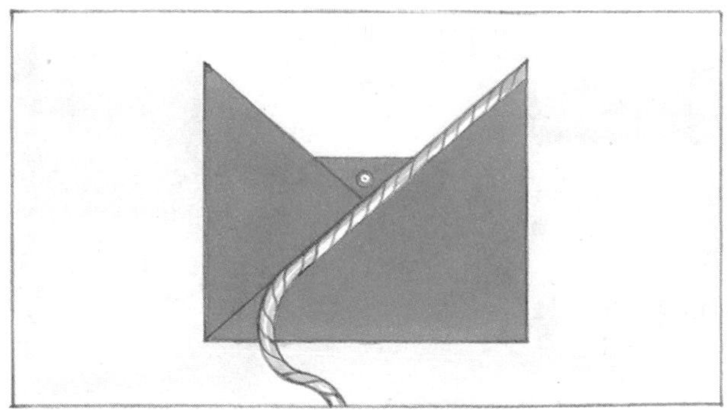

14 *Add thin cord to the seam lines on the front and back of the bag, using invisible slipstitches.*

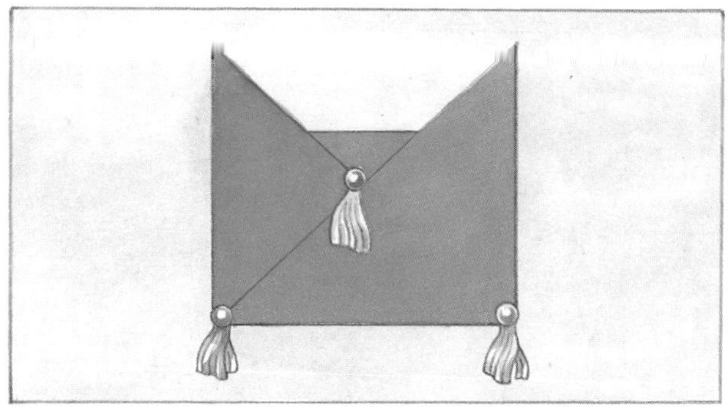

15 *Make three tassels from the gold thread and the green thread; stitch them to the bottom corners of the bag and the tip of the front flap.*

5

Pattern library

Using the library

This section shows many popular piecing and quilting patterns, both traditional and modern. The Pattern Library is divided into types of patterns to make it easy to use. For example, nine-patch block designs are all together, as are Log Cabin designs, quilted motifs, pieced borders, block and sashing combinations, and so on.

You can use the patterns here in several ways. You might want to choose an alternative design for one of the sections in the sampler quilt. Or, incorporate the designs here into projects found elsewhere. Or, you can use the designs for your own projects. Mix and match the patterns to create your own unique designs.

Top: Fans variation block

Right: Strip-pieced quilt and border

Left: Sunflower Star

Bottom left: Star Blocks with Sawtooth border

Below: Tumbling Blocks with Baby Blocks

Four-patch blocks

Four-patch block designs range from very simple patterns to very complex ones. In some designs, such as Flyfoot *and* Oh Susannah*, all of the quarters in the block are identical; each quarter is stitched in the same relationship to the center of the block. Some designs, such as* King's X*, use quarters made as mirror images; others, such as* Double Four Patch*, use two quarters made up in one arrangement and two in another.*

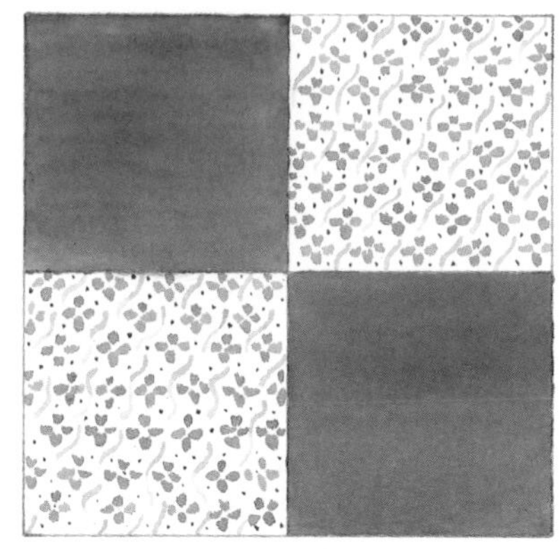

Simple Four Patch

Double Four Patch

Rail Fence

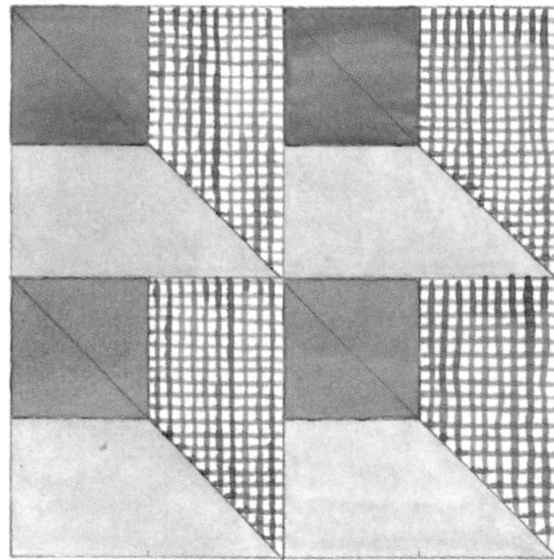

Attic Windows

Four-patch with pinwheels and wholecloth

Pinwheel

Oh Susannah

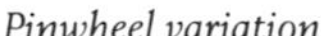

Pinwheel variation

Nine Patch in Four Patch

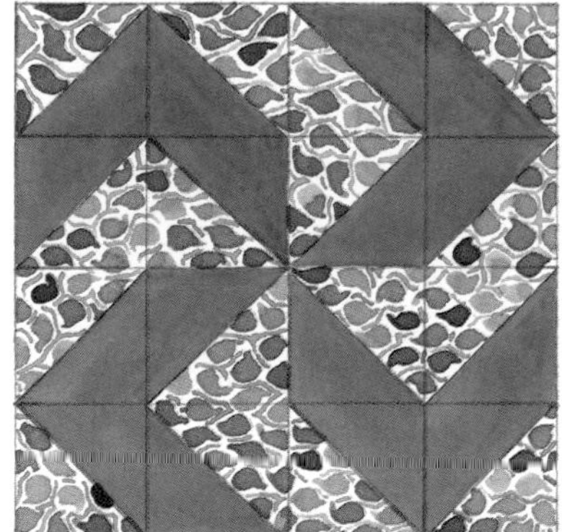

Flyfoot

Double 2

Sawtoothed Square

Ribbon

Star

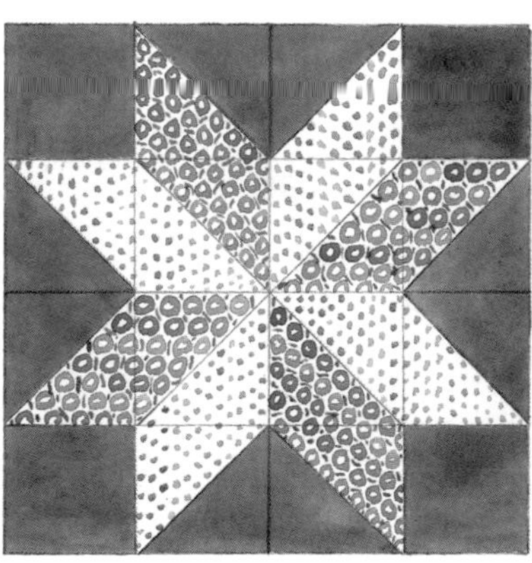

Eight Star Flower

King's X

Nine-patch blocks

Because nine-patch blocks use more pieces, the possibilities for design variations are greater, and you can create some very complex effects. Nine-patch blocks are rarely made with each patch identical. In some designs, such as Rolling Stone *and* Corner Nine Patch, *the middle patch is a plain square of fabric. In the* Nine-Patch Variation, *the middle patch is pieced so that it provides a visual focus for the block. Many nine-patch designs build up a complex pattern across the patches, such as* Jacob's Ladder. Maple Leaf *is another example of a simple picture built from regular patches.*

Basic Nine Patch

Nine Patch variation

Corner Nine Patch

Bear's Paw

Double-patch blocks with wholecloth blocks

Ohio Star

Star variation

54-40 or Fight

Jacob's Ladder

Cross and Crown

Maple Leaf

Card Trick

Churn Dash

Rolling Stone

Irregular blocks

Irregular blocks are less straightforward to piece. Some require curved seams or set-in seams, such as Covered Bridge *and* Fruit Basket. *In others, the piecing is all in straight seams, but the patches are quite complex; for example,* Pine Tree, Pieced Tulip *and* School House. *If you are making one of these blocks, look carefully at the piecing required. Break down the design into its component patches, and try to do most of the piecing in straight seams.*

Many of the irregular block designs use a combination of piecing and appliqué. Grandmother's Fan, Dresden Plate, *and their variations – some of the most popular block designs – are pieced first, then appliquéd onto a background square. The* Carolina Lily *design is pieced in patches, but the fine stems are then appliquéd onto the block (see page 78). These designs still make square blocks when they are finished, so they can be substituted for any of the blocks in the sampler quilt or any project that calls for a block design.*

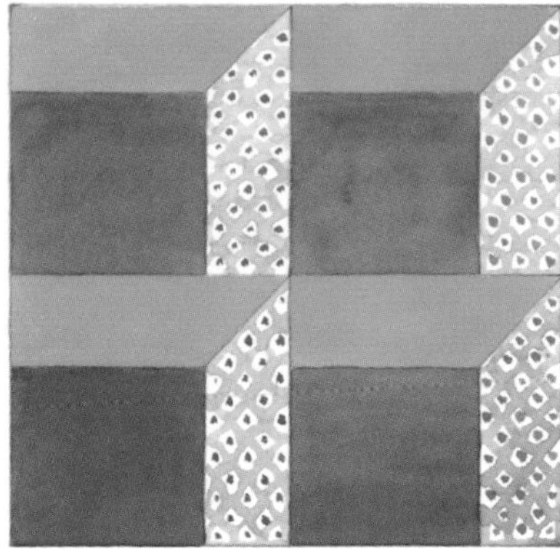

Attic Windows

Attic Windows variation

Four Crown

Sailboat

School House

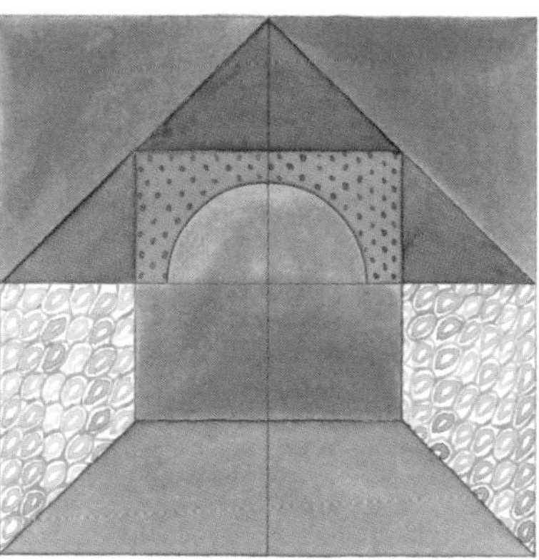

Covered Bridge

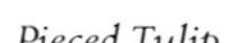

Pieced Tulip

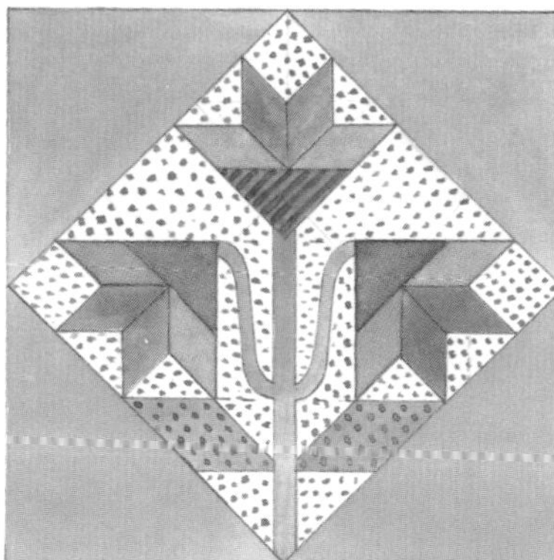

Carolina Lily

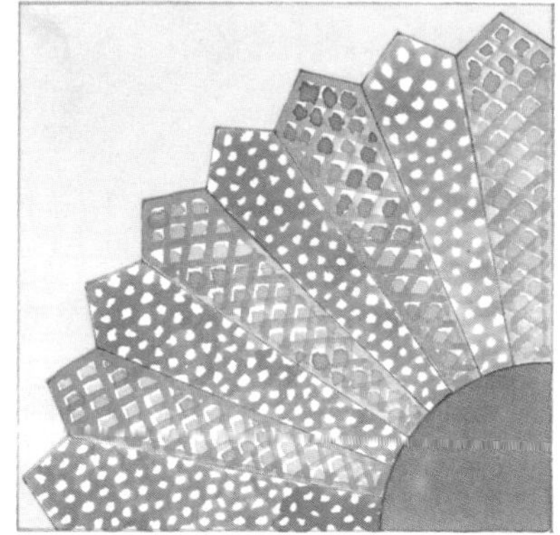

Dresden Plate

Fruit Basket

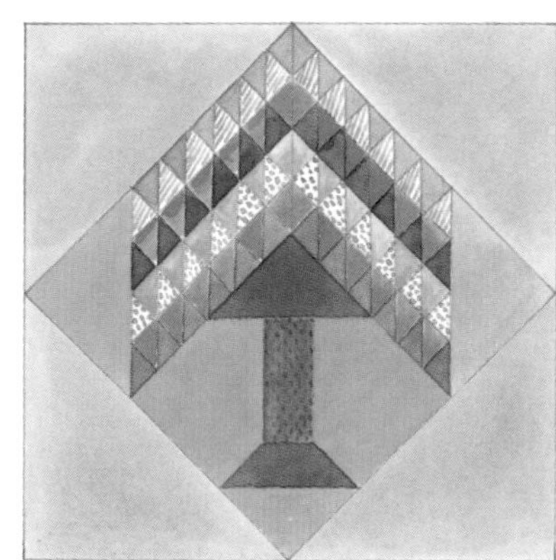

Tree of Life

Pine Tree

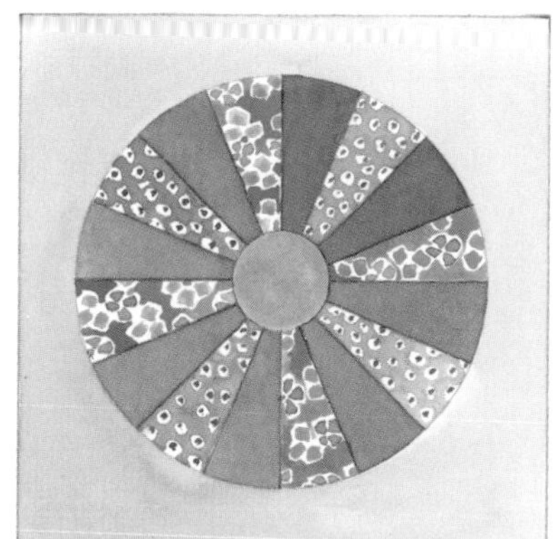

Grandmother's Fan

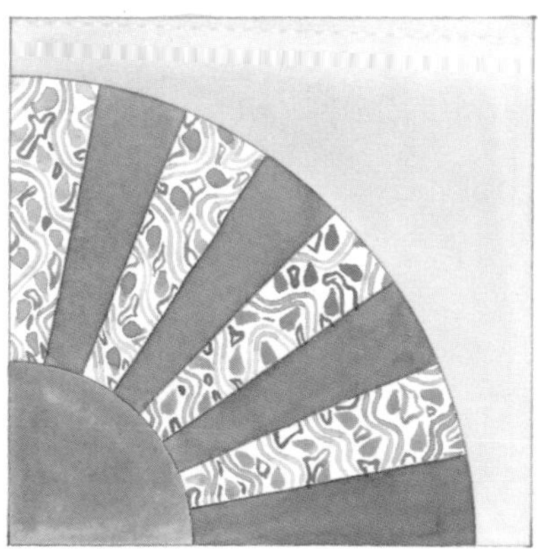

Grandmother's Fan detail

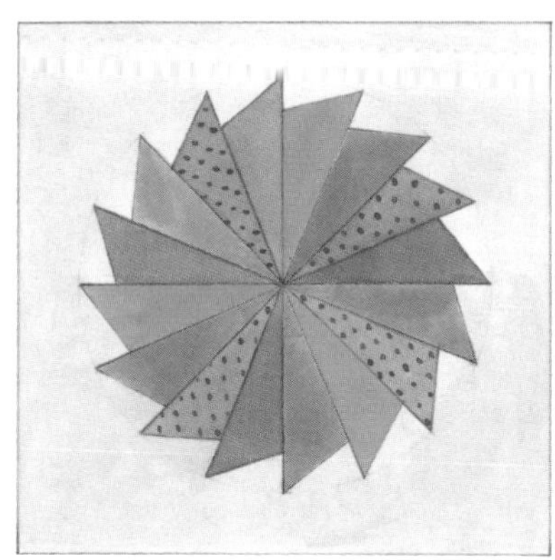

Milady's Fan

Non-block designs

The pieced designs on these pages create fascinating shapes which can be used for whole quilts or appliquéd to a plain background. Spectacular star shapes, such as Lone Star *and* Broken Star *can be built from the 45° diamond shapes shown. 60° diamonds can be used to piece hexagons. If you make partial star or hexagon motifs from triangles, the quilt can then be pieced in strips and the strips joined by machine, an easier approach than the traditional English patchwork method (see page 106). Triangles can also be used to build up large pieced areas.* 1000 Pyramids *use 65° triangles.*

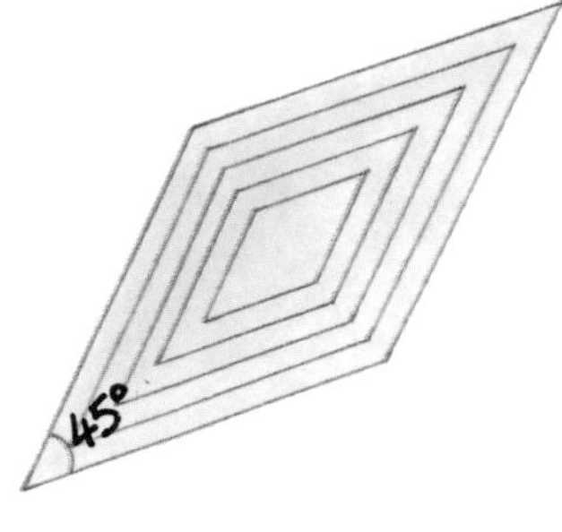

Template for Lone Star

Lone Star

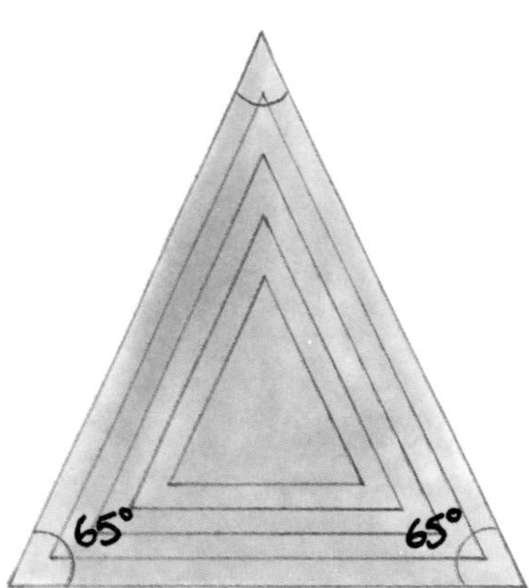

Template for 1000 Pyramids

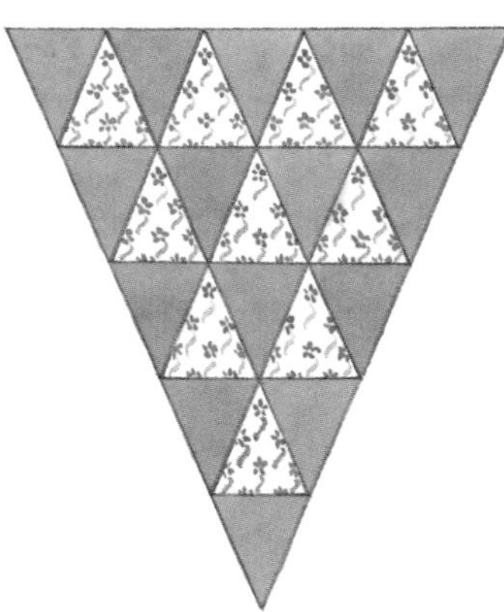

1000 Pyramids

Central non-block design with Flying Geese border

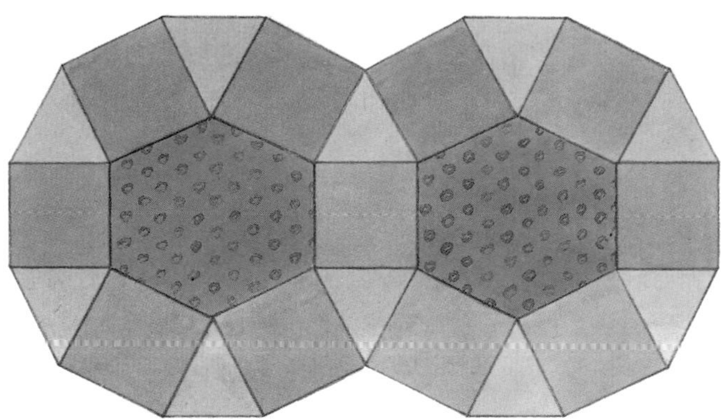

Hexagon Ferris Wheel

Tumbler

Tumbling Blocks

Star variation

Broken Star

Giant Dahlia

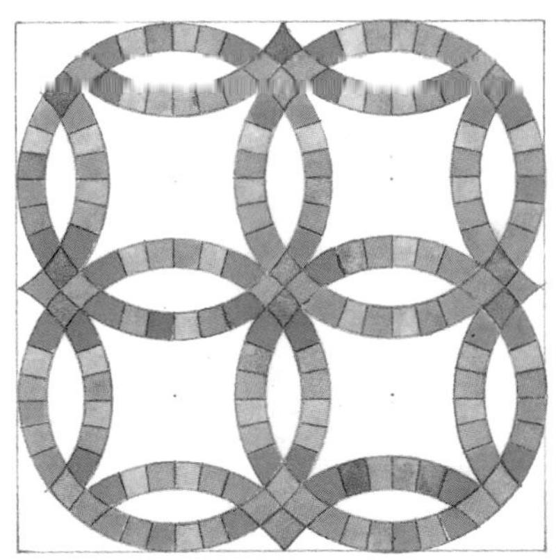

Complex Double Wedding Ring

Flying Geese

Appliqué designs

The shapes in appliqué are stitched onto the fabric and can be as simple or complex as you like. There are an unlimited number of designs that can be used for appliqué; these pages show some of the popular ones. If you are new to appliqué, try simple shapes first, such as leaves, flowers, and birds. Follow the guidelines on page 78 for turning under the raw edges and stitching the shapes to the background. Once you get more confident, you can begin to use more sophisticated designs. Try the Rose of Sharon *patterns,* Crossed Tulip, *or* Radical Rose. *Appliqué shapes can be used on blocks (see Sampler quilt, page 78), or they can be arranged on a much larger background. Appliqué also works well on a background shape, such as a circle, heart, or trefoil.*

Making your own appliqué designs is quite easy. Choose simple shapes or smooth out the lines of more complicated ones; avoid very sharp points and very fine lines. Draw your design full size, then follow the instructions on page 42 for producing templates.

Leaf

Dove

Flower

Shamrock

Rose wreath appliquéd quilt

Tulip detail

Bird

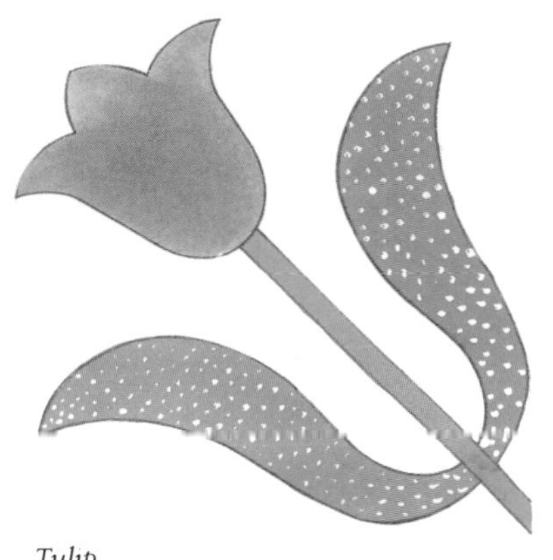

Tulip

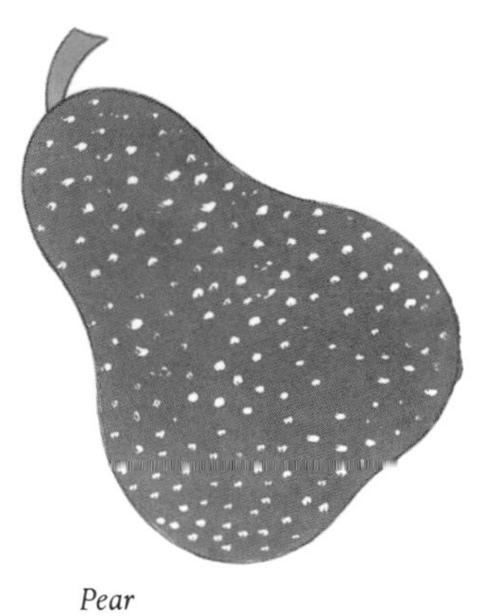

Pear

Radical Rose

Oak Leaf

Ohio Rose

Rose of Sharon

Rose of Sharon variation

Crossed Tulip

Log Cabin blocks

The traditional Log Cabin *block was used in the sampler quilt (**see page 80**), but the technique has many other variations. Two strips of fabric used in each layer produce a chevron design.* Court House Steps *applies the strips of fabric on opposite sides before completing the square with the remaining two strips. This design is often made with light and dark fabrics. The basic design can be varied further: make four smaller blocks to build up into a* Log Cabin *four-patch; make the fabrics different widths to produce an off-center design; stitch the strips at a slant; stitch the strips around a central rectangle rather than a square.*

The Log Cabin *technique can be used to build up blocks of different shapes, too. Work in the same way, but begin with a triangle or a diamond.*

Basic Log Cabin

Log Cabin variation

White House Steps

Log Cabin four-patch

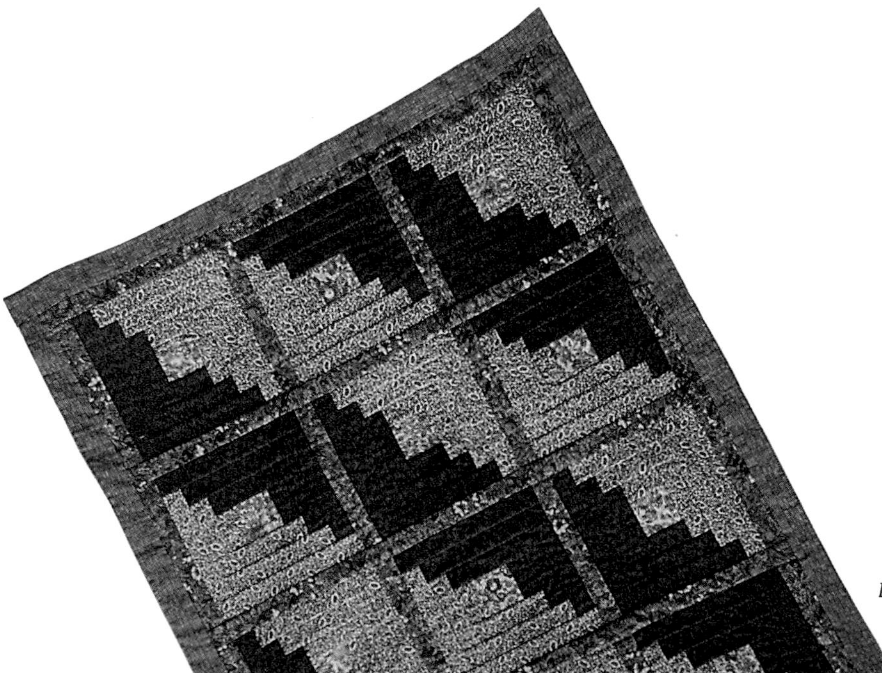

Log Cabin

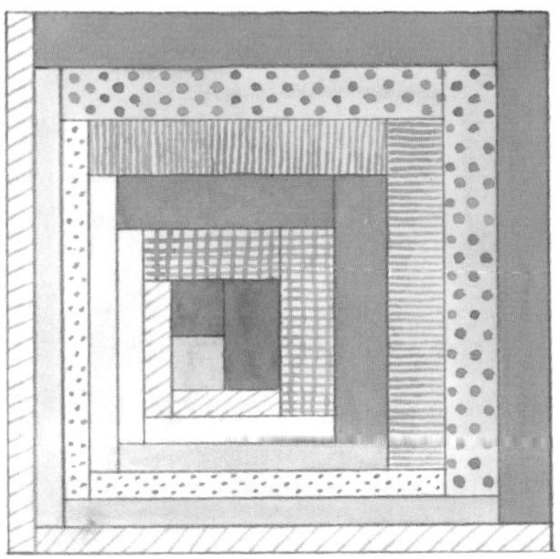

Thick and Thin Log Cabin

Rectangular Log Cabin

Log Cabin corner

Pineapple

Log Cabin Court House Steps

Triangle Log Cabin

Diamond Log Cabin

Crazy Log Cabin

Log Cabin combinations

All of the designs on these pages are made from different types of Log Cabin *blocks. Using the traditional division of light and dark fabrics, several identical* Log Cabin *blocks can be stitched together to make secondary patterns, many of which have their own names, like* Straight Furrows, *and* Barn Raising. *The blocks can be combined so that the light or dark squares form pinwheels, using triangles, squares, rectangles, or parallelograms. Off-center* Log Cabin *blocks combine to make pretty star shapes, while several* Pineapple *blocks together create a design of secondary circles.*

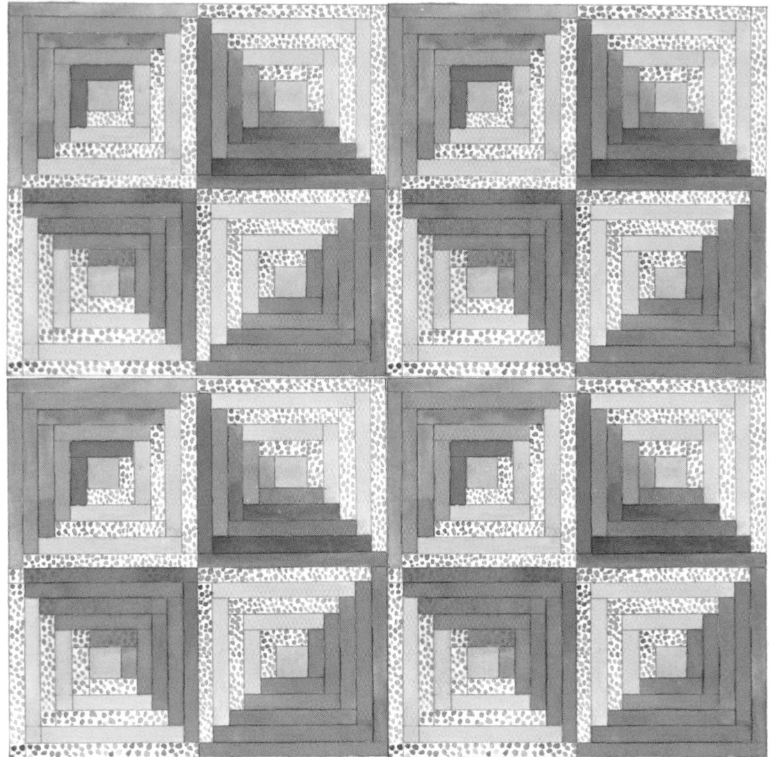

Log Cabin Star

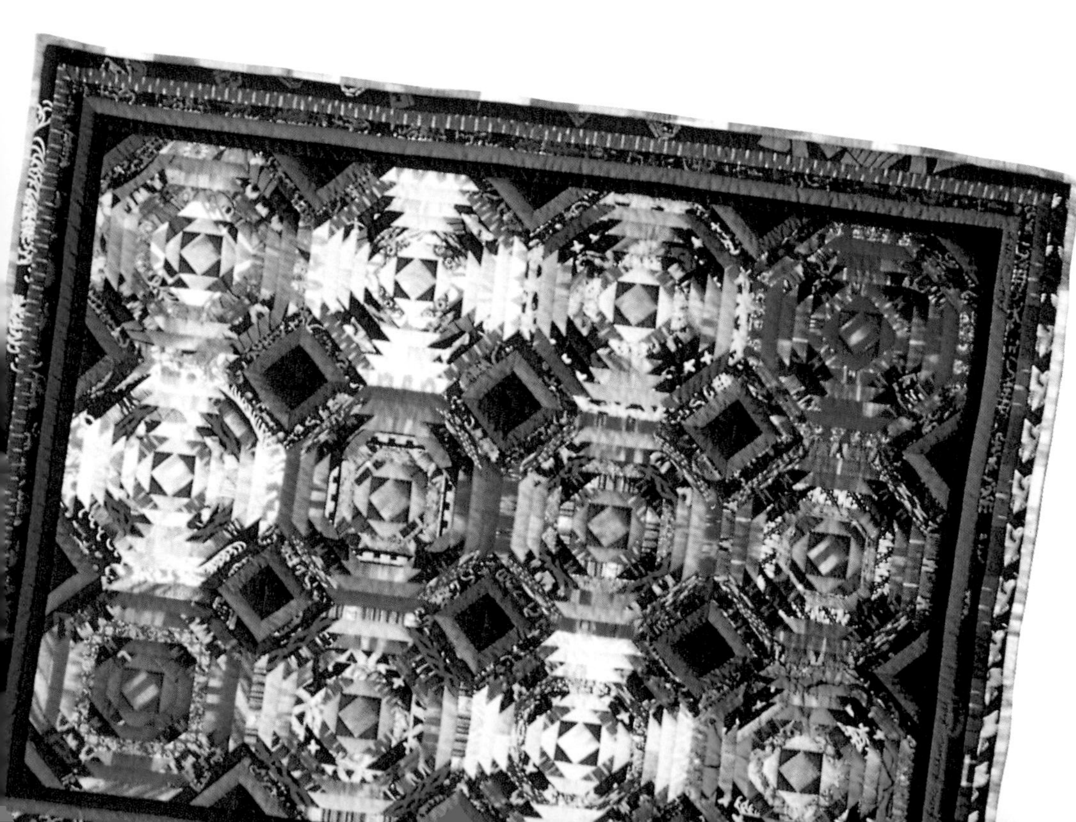

Pineapple Log Cabin design

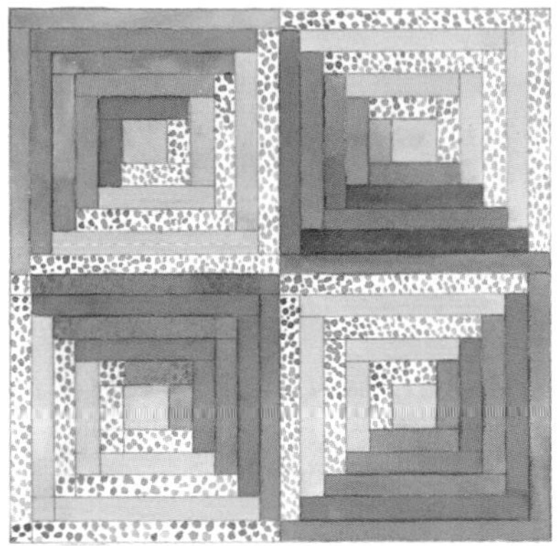

Block for Log Cabin Star

Off-center narrow logs block

Off-center narrow logs combination

Off-center wide logs

Log Cabin Cross

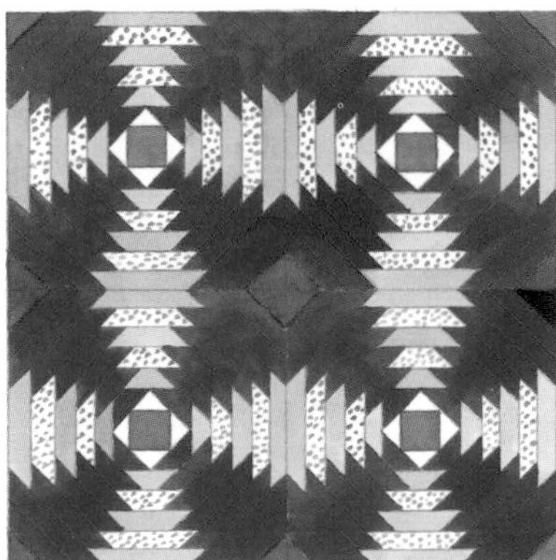

Pineapple

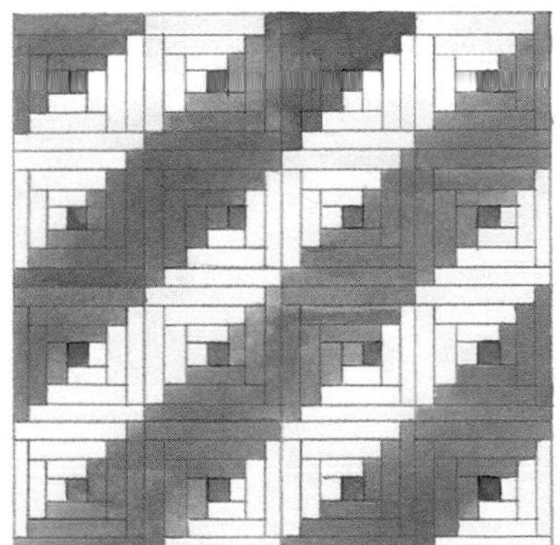

Straight Furrow

Barn Raising

Log Cabin variation

Strip-piecing patterns

The basic principle of strip-piecing involves joining strips of several fabrics, then cutting the new fabric into strips or other shapes and reassembling them to create a secondary pattern. This principle can be applied to create many different patterns, even using a basic combination of two fabric strips. Strips can be cut into diamonds or triangles and reassembled into stars and hexagons, which can in turn be built into larger patterns if you wish.

If you join many strips of fabric, you can create very complex designs like bargello patterns. Irish Chain *consists of strip-pieced blocks (each made up of five strips of five squares in alternating colors) alternated with plain blocks that have been appliquéd or strip-pieced with a contrasting square in each corner.*

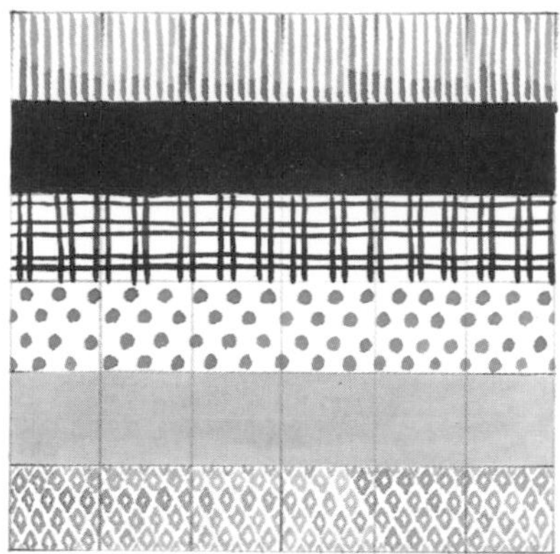

Sew together horizontal strips of even widths. Cut into vertical strips as indicated above.

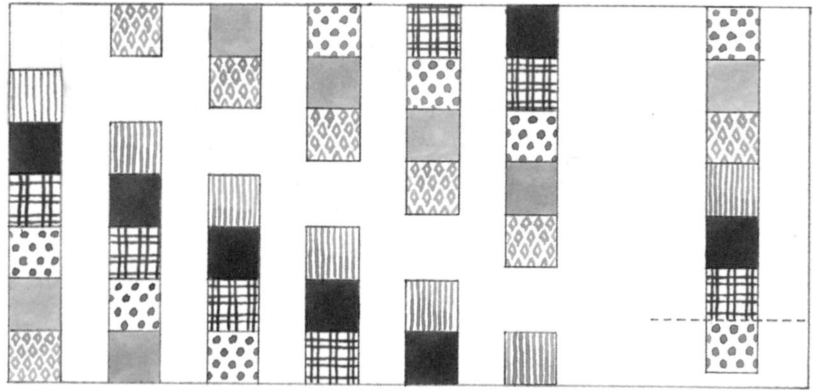

Each new strip will contain several pieces of joined fabric.

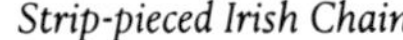

Strip-pieced Irish Chain

Reassemble the new strips so that there are diagonal lines of identical fabrics.

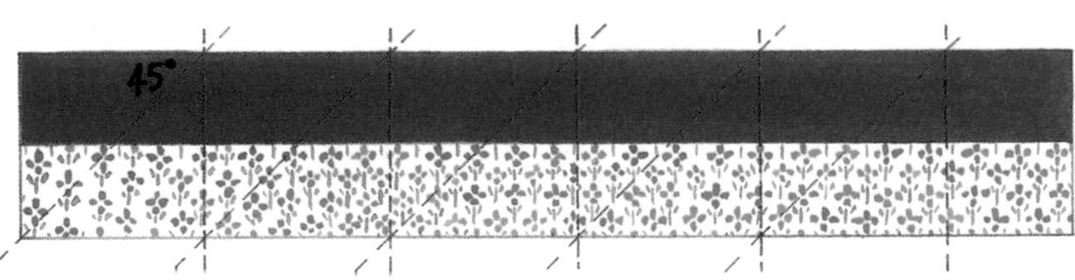

Sew together two strips of equal width. Cut the strip-pieced fabrics into different shapes. A 45° triangle (as shown above) will make patterns 1 and 2: 90° triangles will make pattern 3, and squares will make pattern 4.

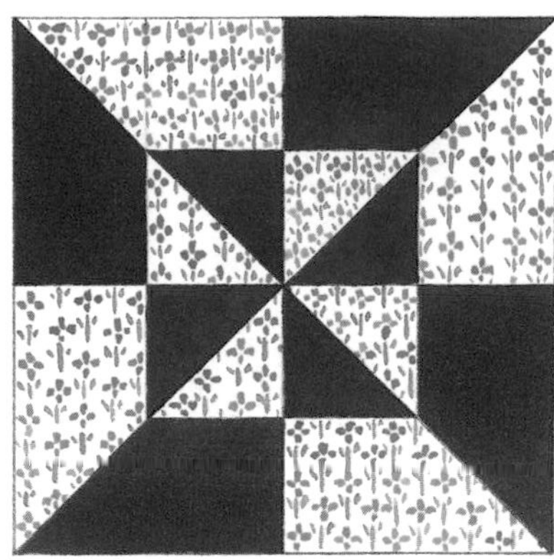

Strip-piecing pattern 1

Strip-piecing pattern 2

Strip-piecing pattern 3

Strip-piecing pattern 4

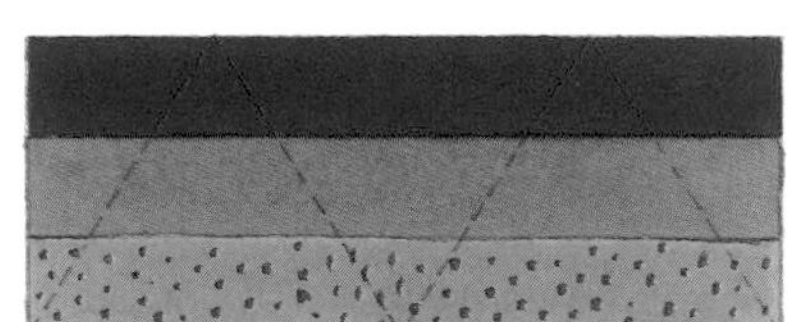

Sew together three strips of even widths and cut into 60° triangles. These triangles can be reassembled to create unusual hexagon designs.

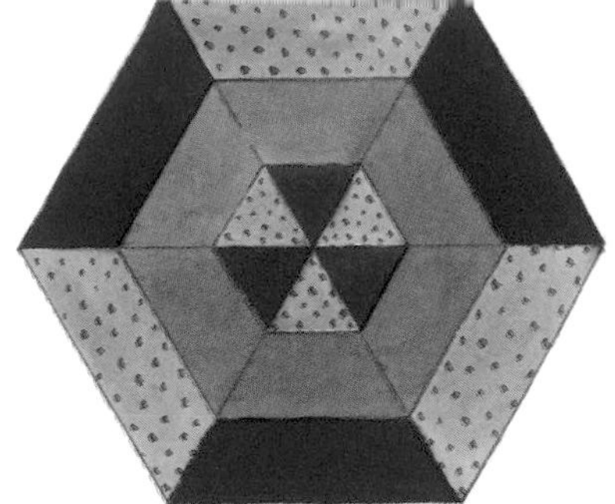

Hexagon

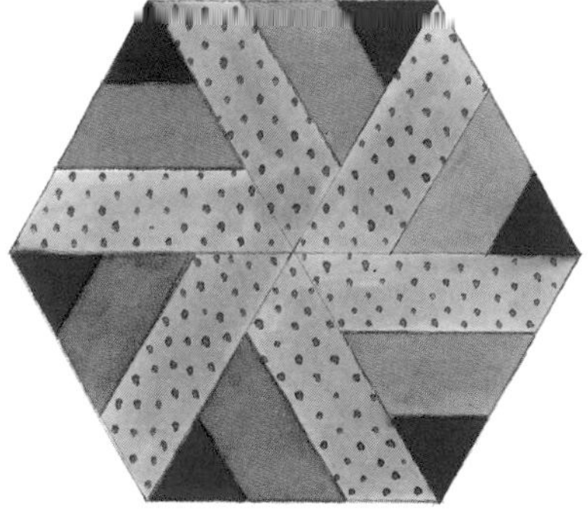

Hexagon variation

Seminole patterns

Seminole work is a variation of strip piecing, but is usually stitched to create long borders to be inserted into garments, purses, quilt borders, and such. Strips of fabric are joined in the normal way, then cut either straight or at an angle to form smaller strips. These smaller strips are then laid at an angle, or offset, or turned top to bottom, and joined once again. Any excess fabric is cut off. Using this method you can create chevrons, zigzags, diamonds, checkerboard designs, and many other variations.

Accuracy is very important in Seminole patchwork. A rotary cutter is excellent for this work. The original strips must be cut and joined accurately; cut any angled strips very carefully so that they are all at exactly the same angle. When rejoined, they need to be positioned against each other carefully so that each part is identical.

Sew together strips of various widths. Cut at an angle.

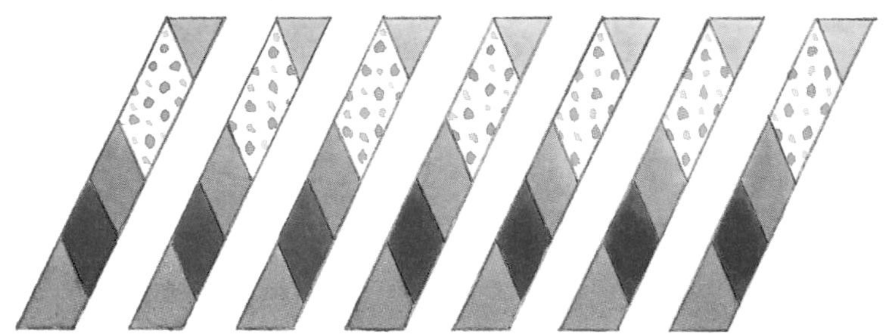

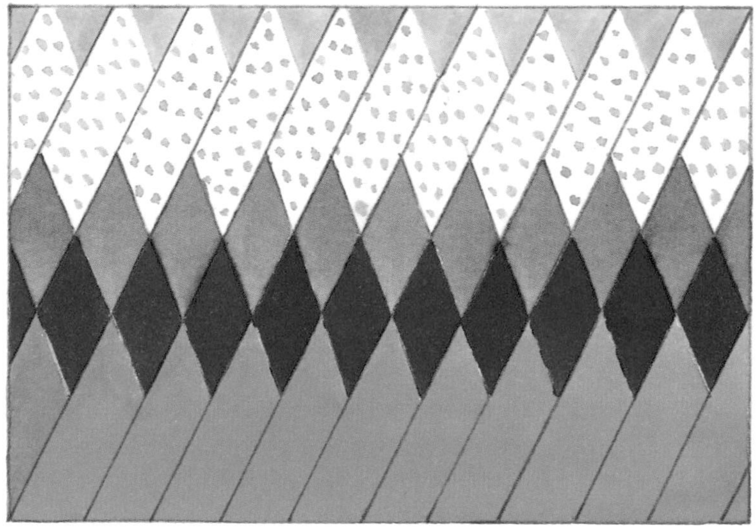

Reposition the cut strips at an opposite slant and reassemble to create different effects.

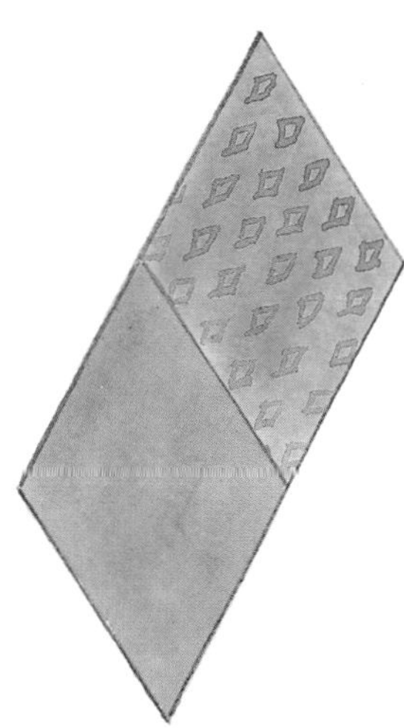

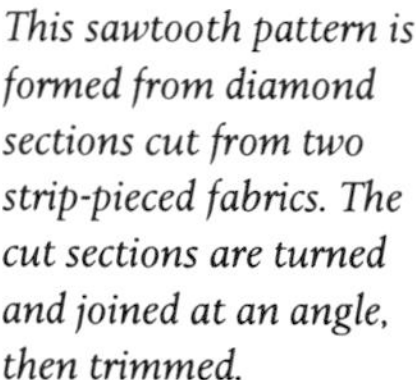

This sawtooth pattern is formed from diamond sections cut from two strip-pieced fabrics. The cut sections are turned and joined at an angle, then trimmed.

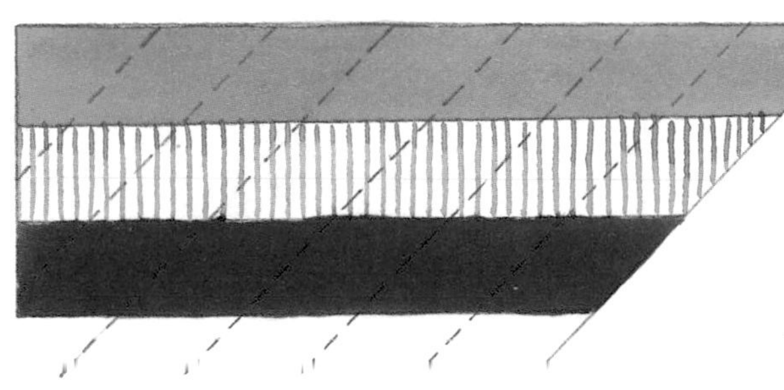

The two strip-pieced sections above and below are cut at opposite angles and joined to form a chevron pattern (right).

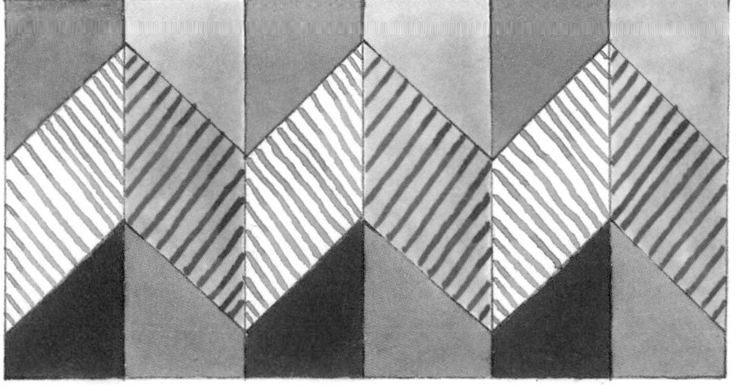

Block and sashing combinations

Blocks are separated with lines of sashing or setting strips (see page 38). These act as frames for the blocks, so that each design can be seen and appreciated in isolation as well as forming part of the whole design.

There are many different ways of setting blocks, and some of the methods are shown here. Blocks can be joined in shapes or in strips of several blocks, with each group then separated from the others by sashing. Amish quilters (see page 104) often set one or more blocks "on point" or as diamonds.

If the blocks are complex, sashing generally looks best in plain or lightly patterned fabrics. Some sashing designs use two different fabrics. Other designs look like criss-cross strips; the square where two strips intersect uses a different fabric, different color, or even a small pieced block.

Diamond blocks

Nine-patch blocks

Star blocks

Maple Leaf blocks

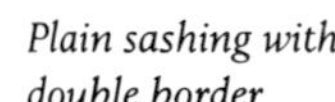

Plain sashing with double border

Nine-patch variation

On point sashing

Churn Dash blocks

Plain sashing

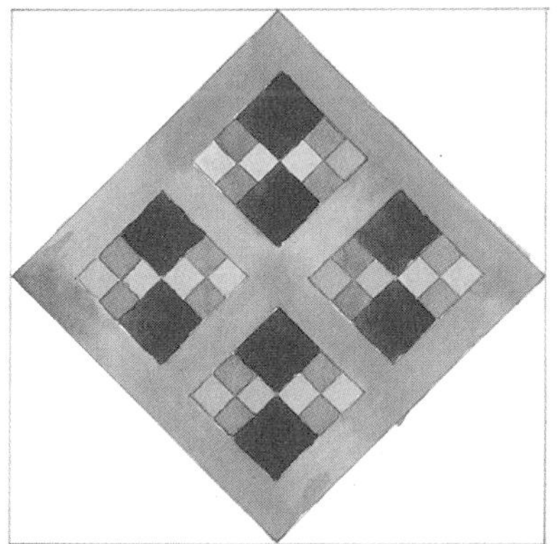

Cross sashing

Pieced-block sashing

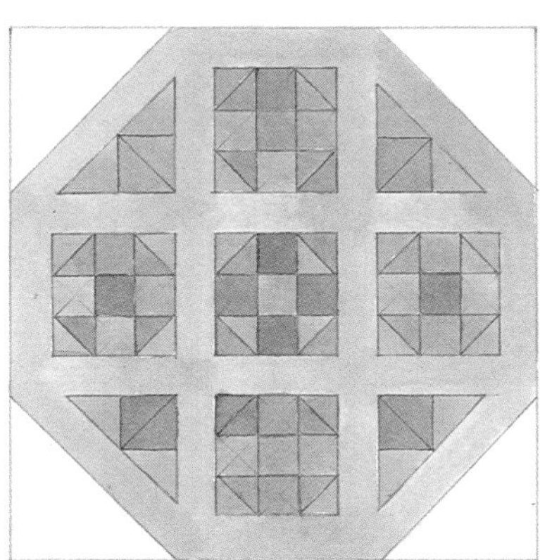

Octagonal design

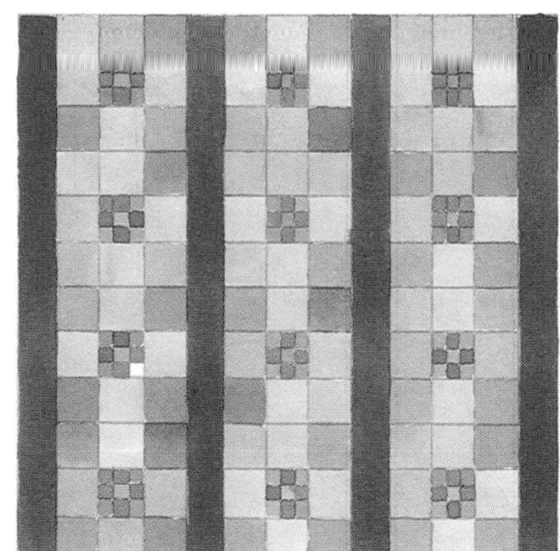

Strip-pieced sashing

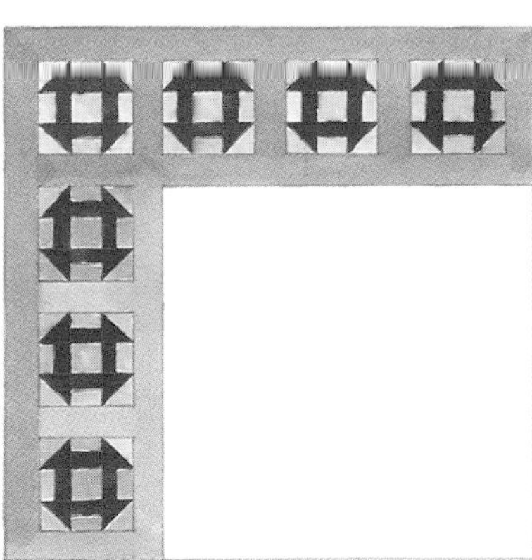

Churn Dash variation in border

Alternate blocks in border

Combining blocks

Quilters like to make use of the secondary patterns formed when blocks are sewn together without sashing. When certain block designs are placed edge to edge, the lines of one block carry visually into the next.

Some blocks can be used to create different patterns: Sugar Bowl *(see page 76) can also make the meandering* Drunkard's Path *and the* Love Ring *flower. New outlines appear from parts of several blocks put together: each leaf of the* Ozark Maple Leaf *pattern is made from a large part of one block and small triangles on adjoining blocks.* *(Continued on page 148)*

Sugar Bowl basic block 1

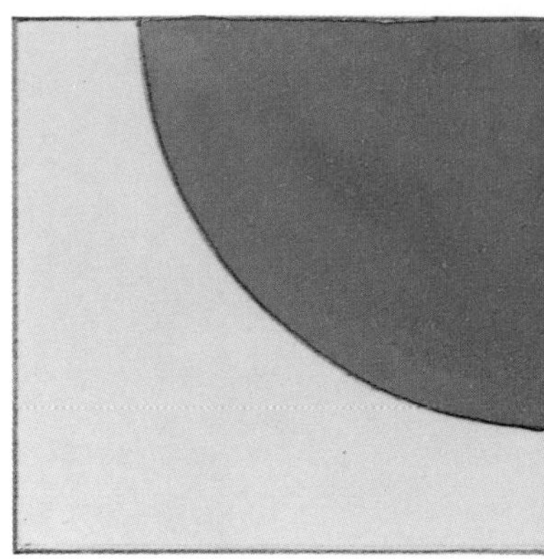

Sugar Bowl basic block 2

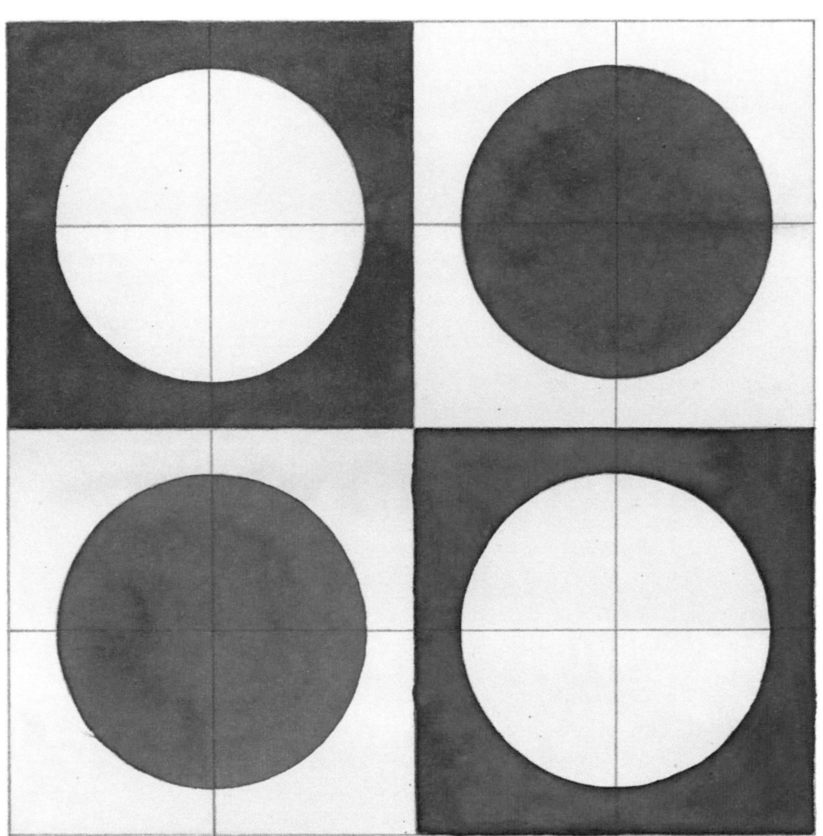

Sugar Bowl basic blocks 1 and 2 combined

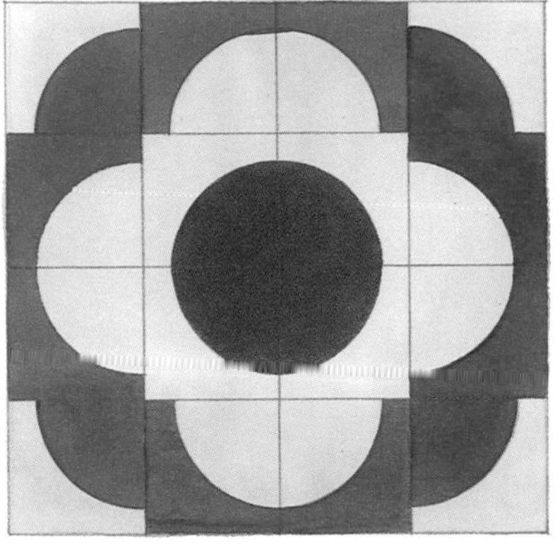

Love Ring

Drunkard's Path

Maple Leaf basic block, light

Ozark Maple Leaf

Maple Leaf basic block, dark

Maple Leaf combined variation

◁ *Familiar block patterns can be adapted to form new patterns. The pattern at bottom right was created by alternating* Rolling Stone *blocks with an adaptation; the result is a new design.*

Snail Trail *makes a continuous pattern across the quilt by alternating pattern blocks of light or dark.*

Snail Trail component block

Snail Trail

Snail Trail component block

Snail Trail combined

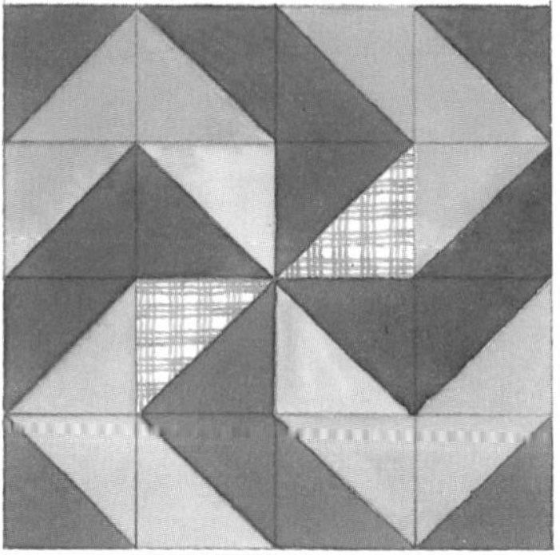

Flyfoot

Flyfoot combined with reverse color blocks

Windmill block

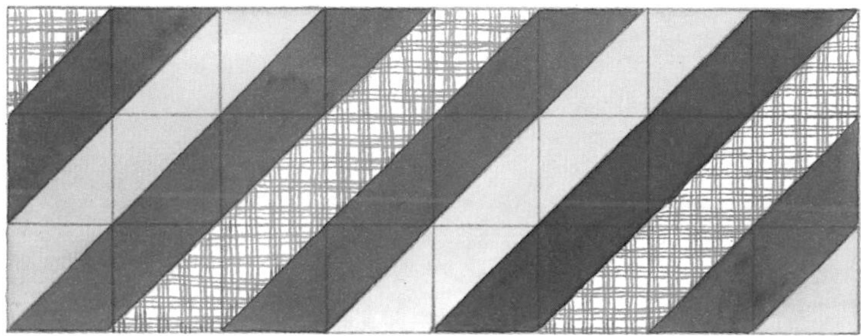

Windmill adapted and combined

Rolling Stone block

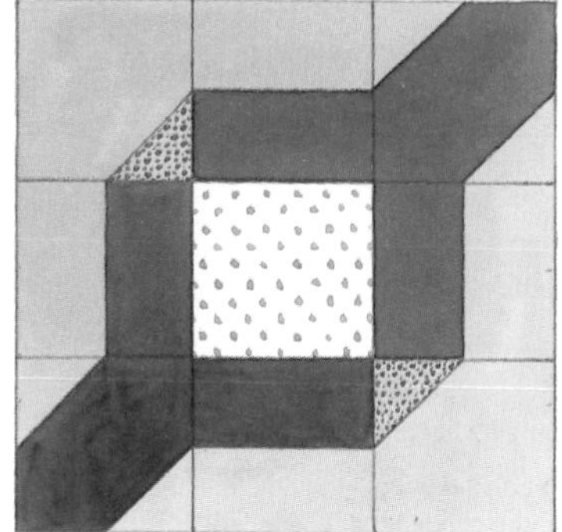

Rolling Stone adapted block

Rolling Stone combined

Pieced border patterns

When planning your border pattern, try to use a motif or an idea from your main quilt. If your central patchwork has a strong pattern of stars or squares, then choose a border pattern based on stars or squares. Sawtooth borders are good for blocks featuring many triangles, such as Bear's Paw, Basket, *and* Tree of Life*; borders using curves are good for edging quilts with curved seams in the blocks, such as* Drunkard's Path. *Strip-pieced borders with quarter-circle corners look just right on* Dresden Plate *or* Grandmother's Fan *quilts while diamond borders make spectacular edgings for complex star designs.*

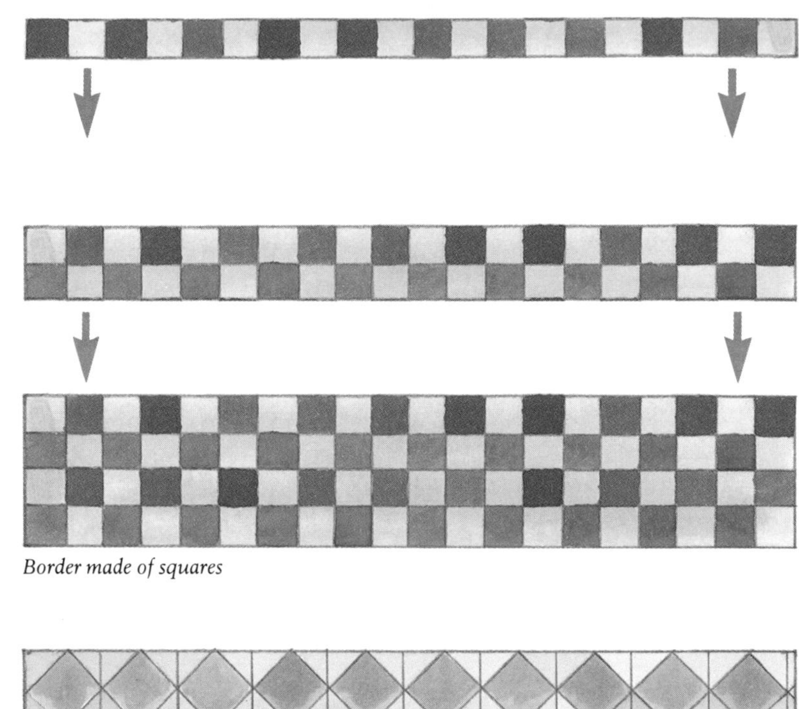

Border made of squares

Diamond border

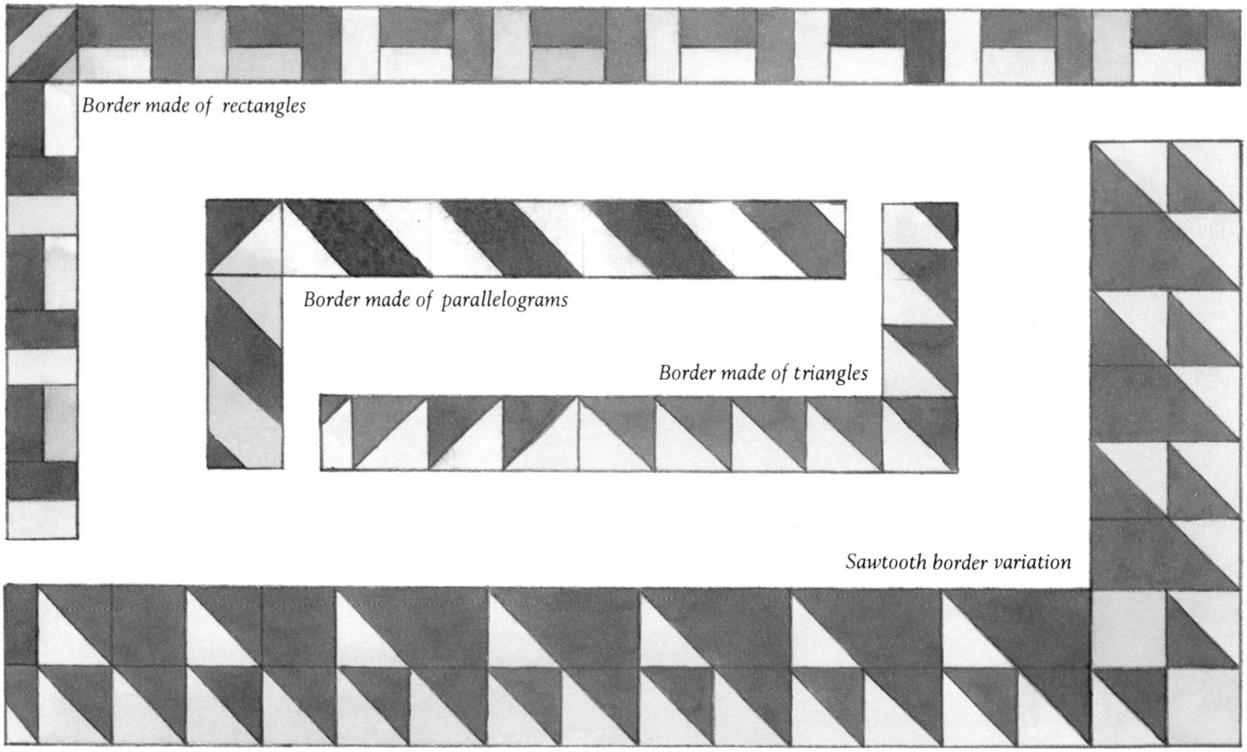

Border made of rectangles

Border made of parallelograms

Border made of triangles

Sawtooth border variation

Twisted Ribbon border
Flying Geese border
Twisted Ribbon variation
Strip-pieced border with quarter-circle corner
Drunkard's Path border
Peaks border
Star border

Quilted border patterns

Border patterns for quilting are numerous and varied. Like the medallions, many of the traditional border patterns use everyday shapes such as flowers, stars, and feathers. Many designs have evolved using variations of braids (three or more strands), twisted cables, and waves. Complex border designs often combine several elements, such as a double cable twist of feathers with flower finials.

Choose your quilted border so that it complements the main design of your quilt. Select some of the same motifs and build a border out of flowers, fans, stars, or feathers, or incorporate a wine glass shape or spiral pattern to match a background texture. You can make an irregular border pattern, such as a waving cable or feather design, fit into a regular shape, such as a rectangle or circle, by filling in the background with one of the traditional textures like checkering or diagonal lines.

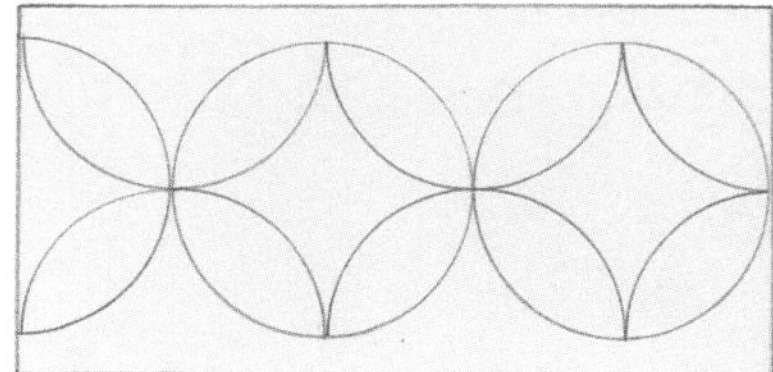

Cathedral Window

Crescent and Heart

Feather and Wave intertwined

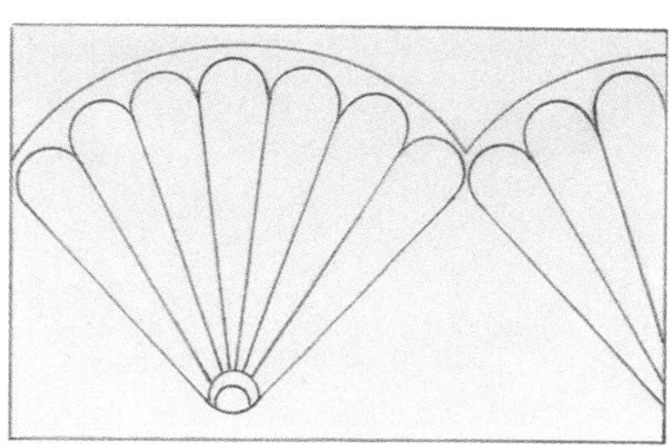

Fan

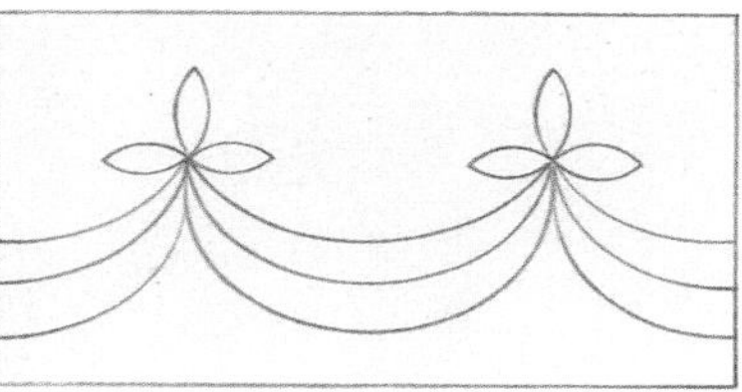

Crescent variation

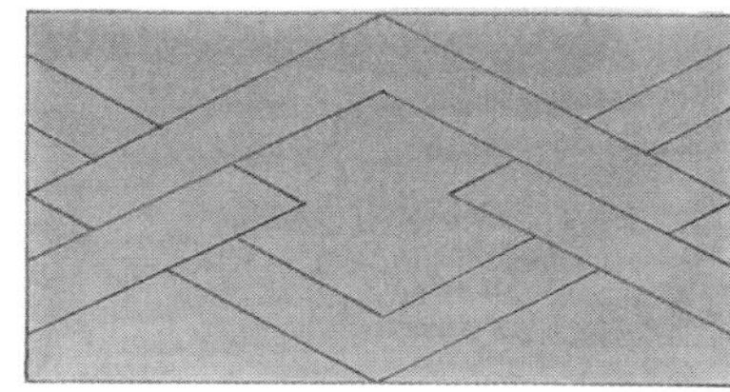

Interlocked Diamonds

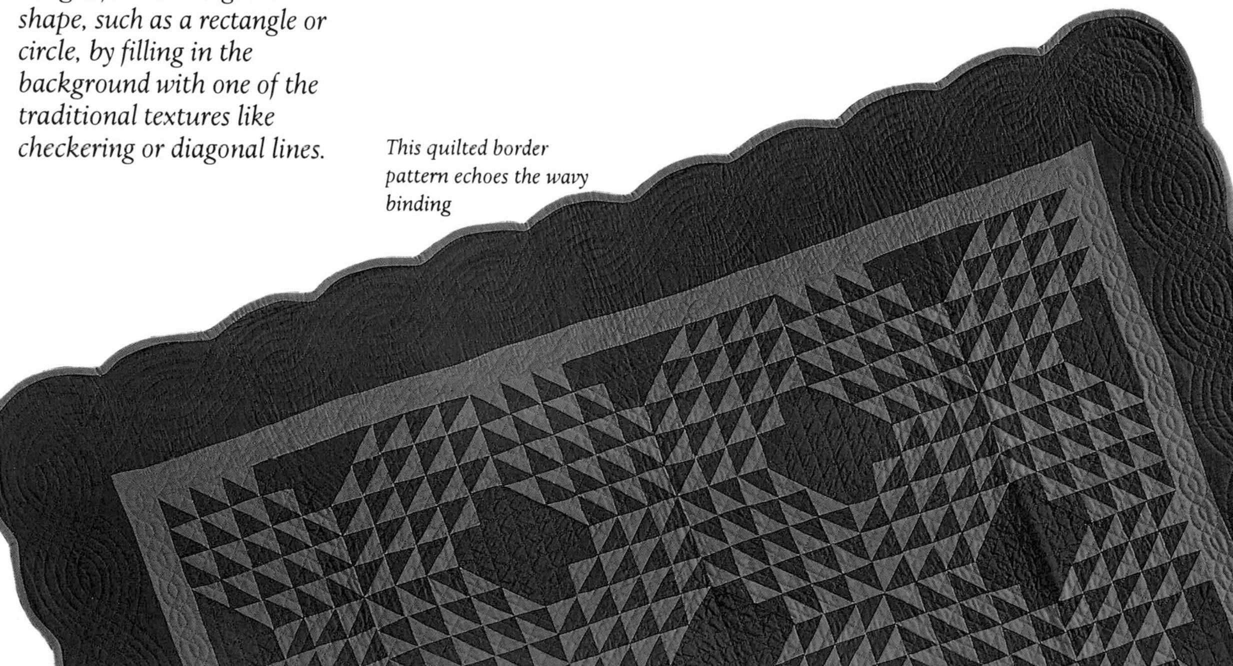

This quilted border pattern echoes the wavy binding

Braid

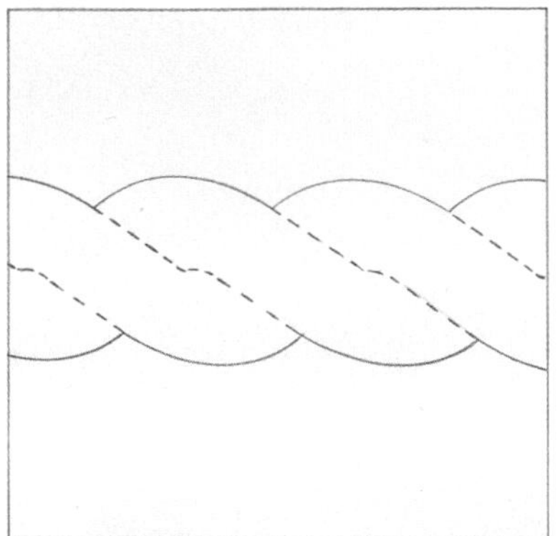

Cable

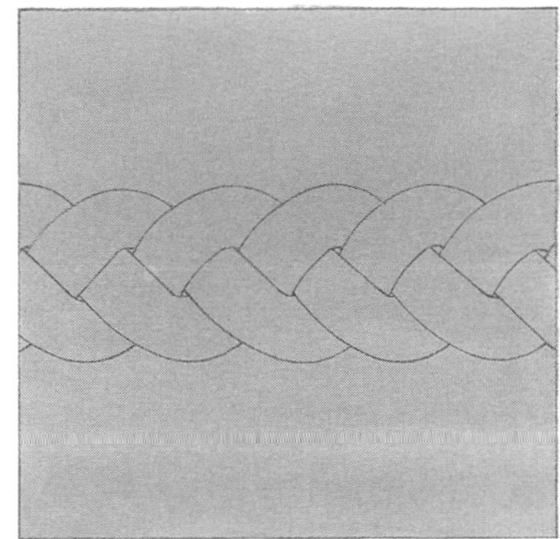

Braid variation

Braid corner

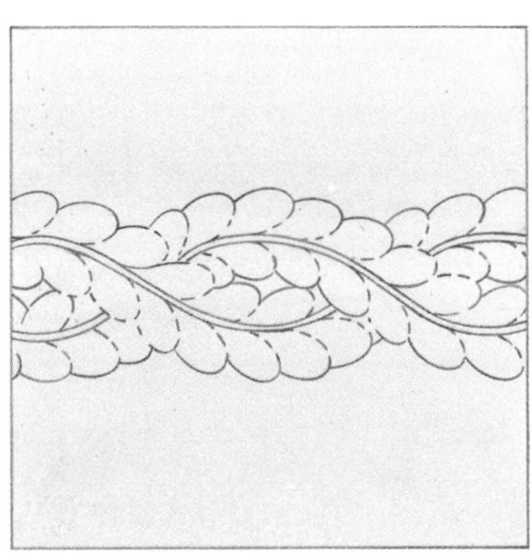

Intertwined Feathers

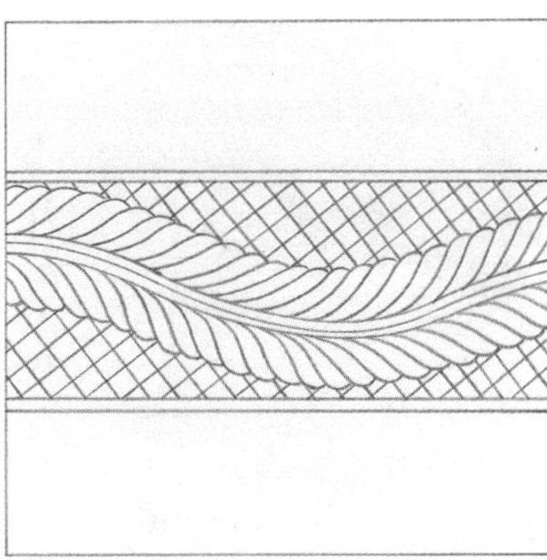

Feather variation

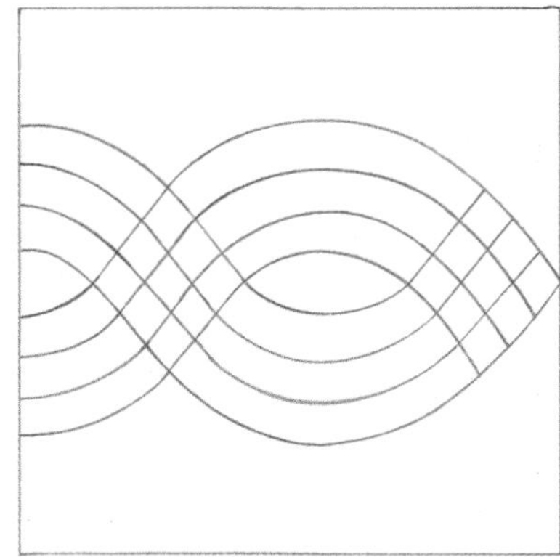

Wave variation

Heart and Flower

Spirals

Background textures

Background textures are used to set off the medallions and borders of quilted designs. Originally these were functional; background textures were added to keep the batting in position and prevent it from bunching. The textures also act as a visual contrast to the main motifs in the quilt.

Choose a pattern in keeping with the style and mood of your main motifs. For instance, if you have a large traditional flower medallion in the center of your quilt, a subtle checkerboard texture or regular diagonal lines will look better than modern asymmetric zigzags. Wineglass, clamshell, rainbow, and spiral designs can easily be marked onto fabric with a circular template if you position it carefully. This is quicker than enlarging a pattern and then tracing it on.

Clamshells

Wineglass

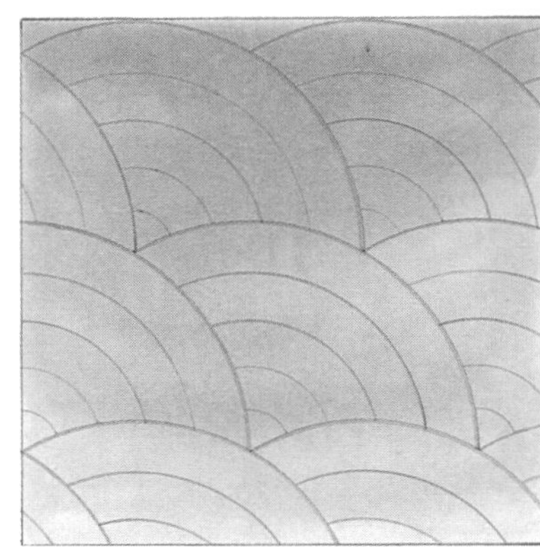

Rainbows

Tartan

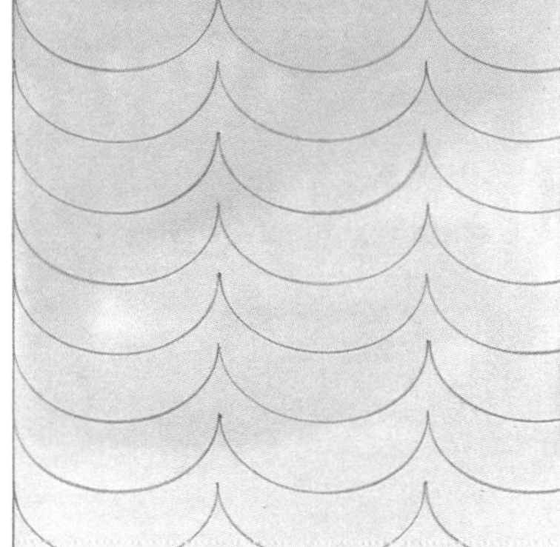

Drapes

Diagonal lines

Diagonal lines variation

Diagonal lines variation

Diagonal lines variation

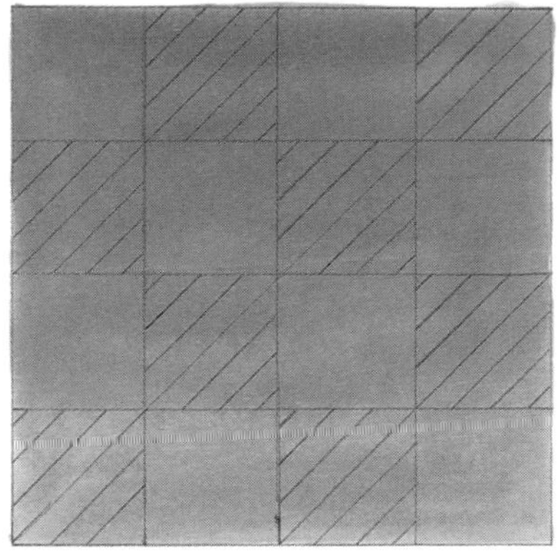

Diagonal lines with Checkerboard

Checkerboard

Checkerboard variation

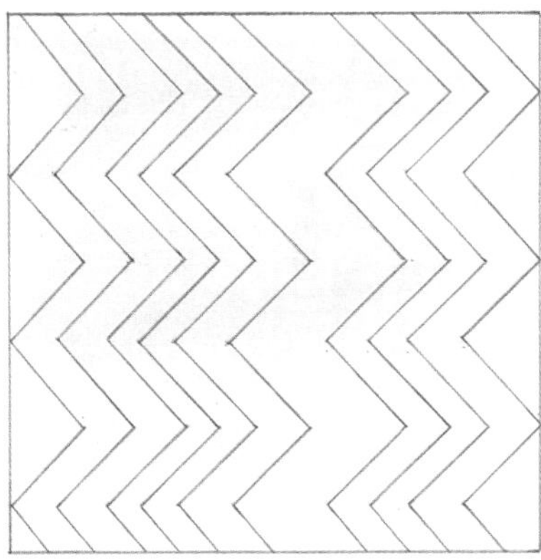

Zigzag variation

Diamonds

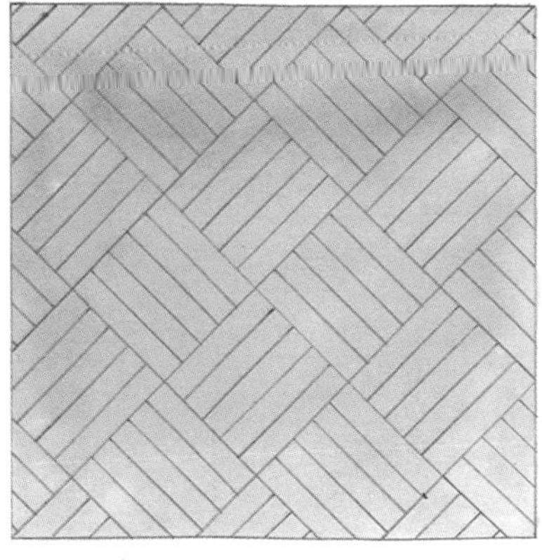

Diamond variation

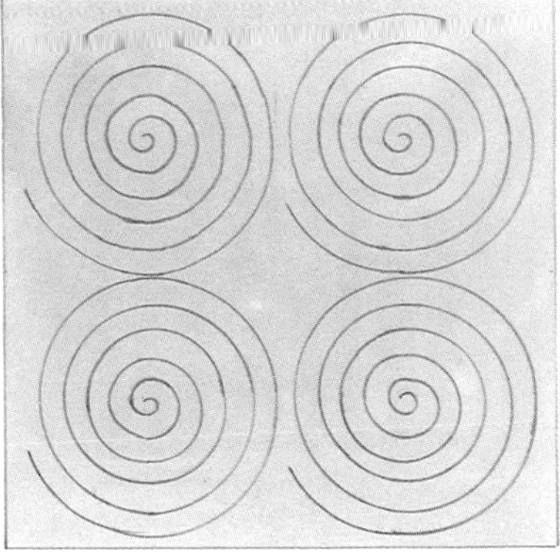

Spirals

Binding and finishing patterns

The binding of your quilt deserves careful planning. Many complex quilts look best with a relatively plain binding. Bias binding (see page 60) can be used to round off corners or edge a scalloped shape; but binding, bias or straight, doesn't have to be plain. For more visual interest, you can bind a quilt with a patterned fabric from the piecing or make your own strip-pieced binding with straight strips (even or uneven), diamonds, or randomly pieced fabrics from the main body of the quilt.

If your project is made from a coarse-weave fabric, fringe the edges, then leave the fringe, or cut it into chevrons or scallops, or knot it. For delicate items like baby quilts, make a pretty ruffle. Finish off fine edges with shaped borders made from two layers of fabric seamed in the normal way or edged with hand or machine cutwork in scallops, waves or chevrons.

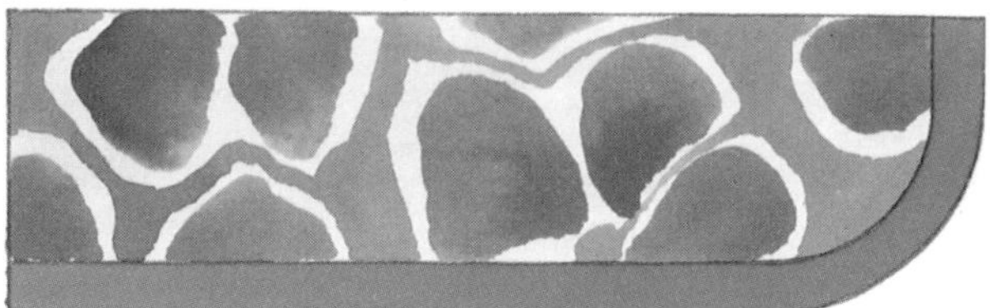
Curved binding

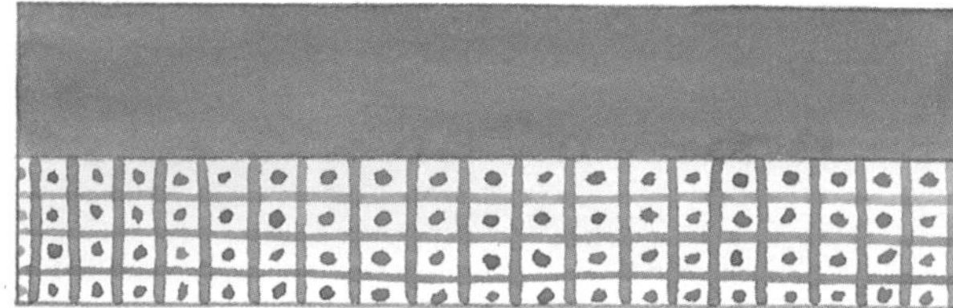
Straight binding with patterned fabric

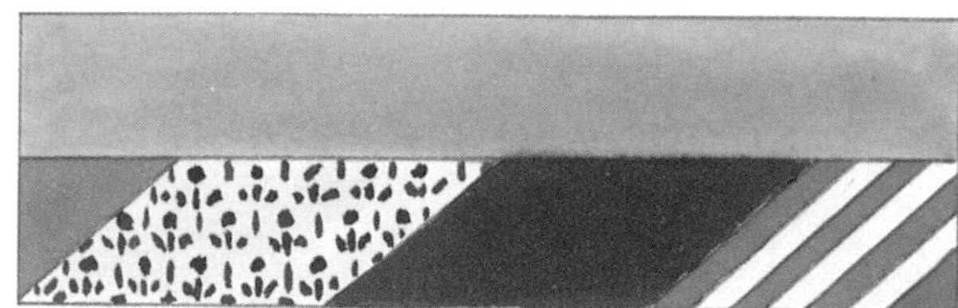
Strip-pieced variation

Strip-pieced variation

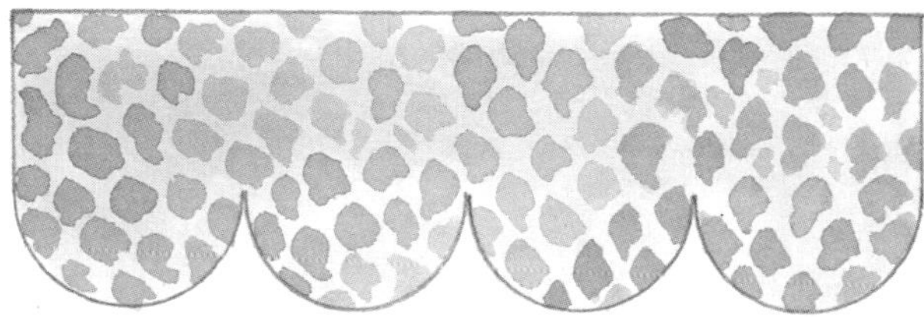
Scalloped edges

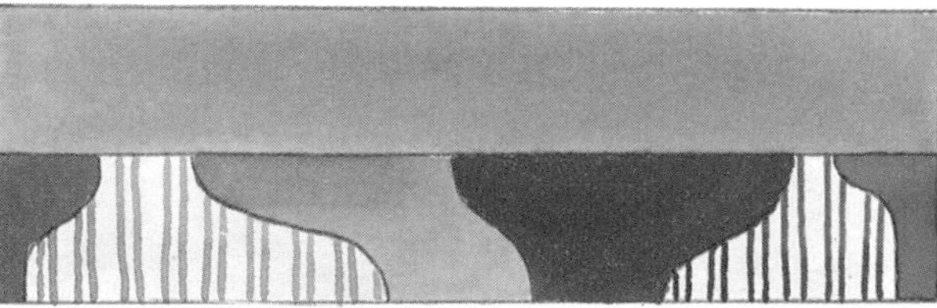
Random pieced binding

Fringed edging

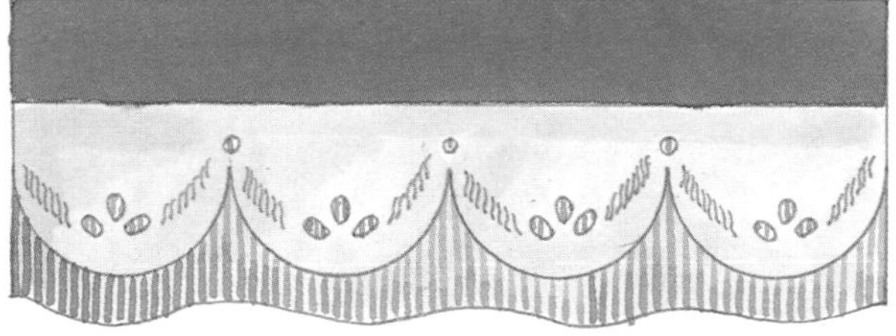

Lace variation

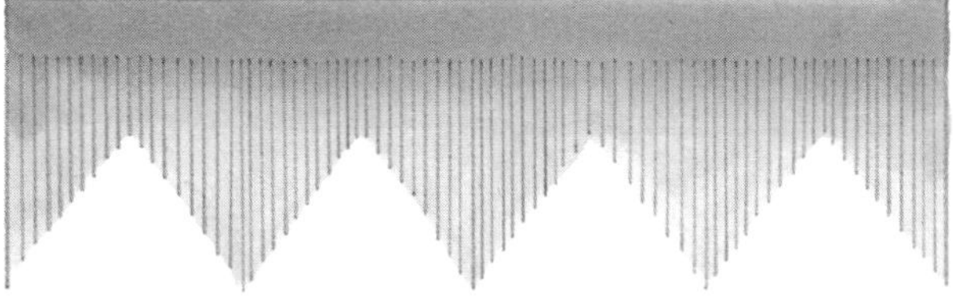

Fringe variation

Lace edging

Knotted edging

Shaped binding

Plain ruffle

Cut-in diamonds

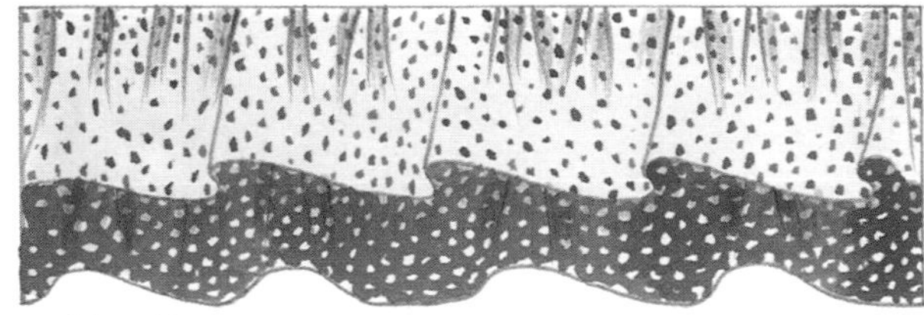

Double ruffles

Shaped variation

Wholecloth motifs

Many of the medallion designs, or wholecloth motifs, shown here are traditional patterns. These, and others, can be combined in an infinite number of patterns and arrangements to fit quilting projects of any size and shape. If you are making a large item, such as a bed quilt or wall hanging, you might want to add a quilted border design (see page 152) or a background texture (see page 154) to set off the main medallions, but the designs are also effective on their own.

Flowers are very common medallion motifs. As these examples show, the petals may be straight, feathered, overlapping, pointed or divided, and similar variations can be used on shell and fan shapes. Feathers are also common in quilting designs, and you can find or draw a feather design to fit virtually any shape. Emphasize the outline of your medallion with a double row of stitching around the main lines or by echo quilting just outside the edge of the design. Some motifs fit into right angles and are often used as corner designs on a rectangular quilt.

Flower with overlapping petals

Star with echo quilting

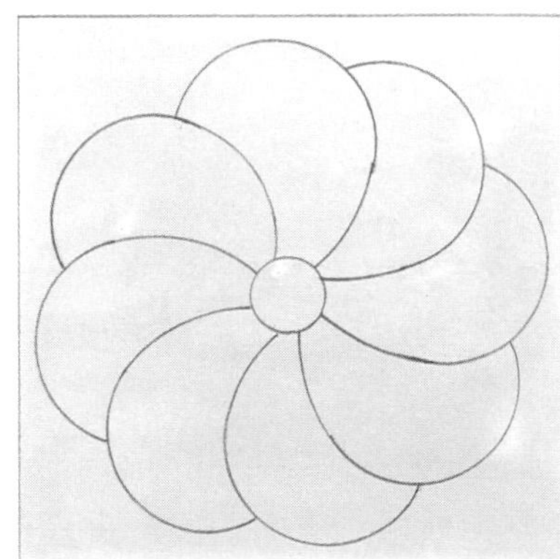

Flower variation

Wholecloth quilt with feather motifs

Feather

Feather in heart shape

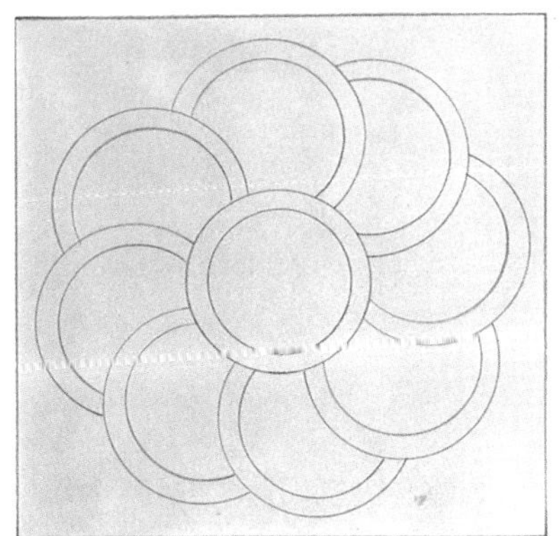

Flower with double stitching line

Ring circles

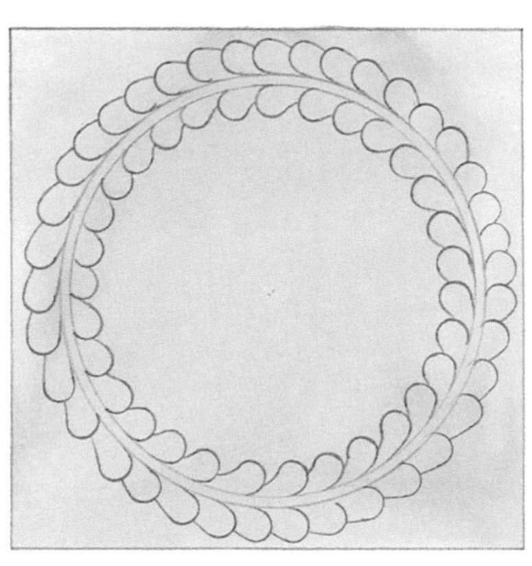

Feather circle

Corner feather

Flower variation

Flower and feather design

Feather circle variation

Amish patterns

Amish quilts are known for their bold use of color and you can give your Amish project extra authenticity by using a traditional design.

Many Amish quilts are built up from a single block set on point often an elaborately quilted diamond, surrounded by a series of colored and black borders, each stitched with its own intricate quilting design. Bars and split bars in vivid colors are favorites, again usually surrounded with single or multiple borders. Many Amish borders use a dark strip at the edge with a light square at the corner, or vice versa; the Garden Maze *design shown here is also popular. Amish block designs include the* Double T, Bear's Paw, Pinwheel, Crown of Thorns, Basket, *and* Tree of Life. Friendship Star *blocks form a pattern of interlocking stars when joined.* Trip Around the World *is a simple design which can be pieced in strips, then cut and reassembled into a stunning quilt top.*

Friendship Star

Water Wheel

Water Wheel variation

Crown of Thorns

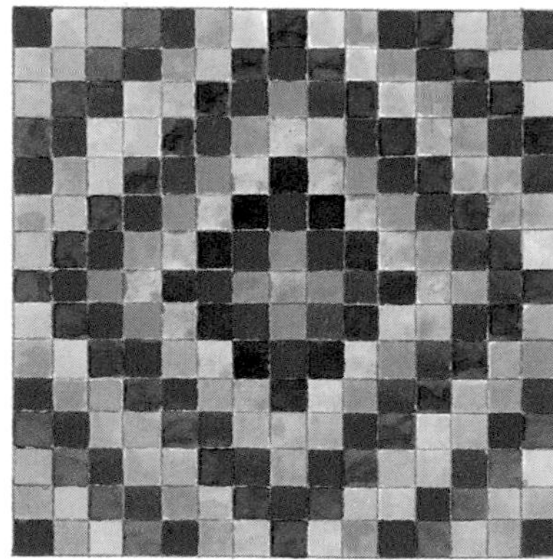

Trip Around The World

Double T

Bear's Paw

Garden Maze

Basket

Basket variation

Tree of Life

Traditional Amish quilt

English patchwork patterns

Because English patchwork is pieced over paper and doesn't require straight machine seams, any mosaic pattern can be used; try and avoid inside angles (Vs) as they make the piecing considerably more difficult. Draw or trace the shapes very accurately, then use them as templates for cutting fabric and papers. Beautiful designs can be built up using simple squares.

To make the Clamshell *design, the outside curves of the fabric shapes are basted over the papers as usual, then pinned or basted in rows. The rows are appliquéd on top of each other, with the curved tops of one row concealing the raw edges of the row beneath.*

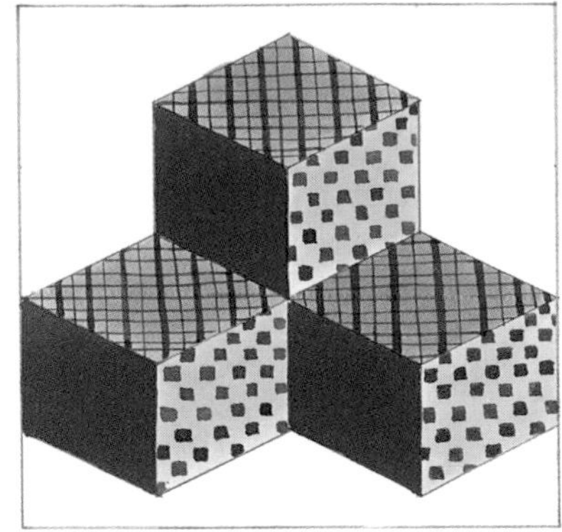

Tumbling Blocks

Mosaics

Mosaics variation

Checkerboard variation

Tumbling Blocks pattern

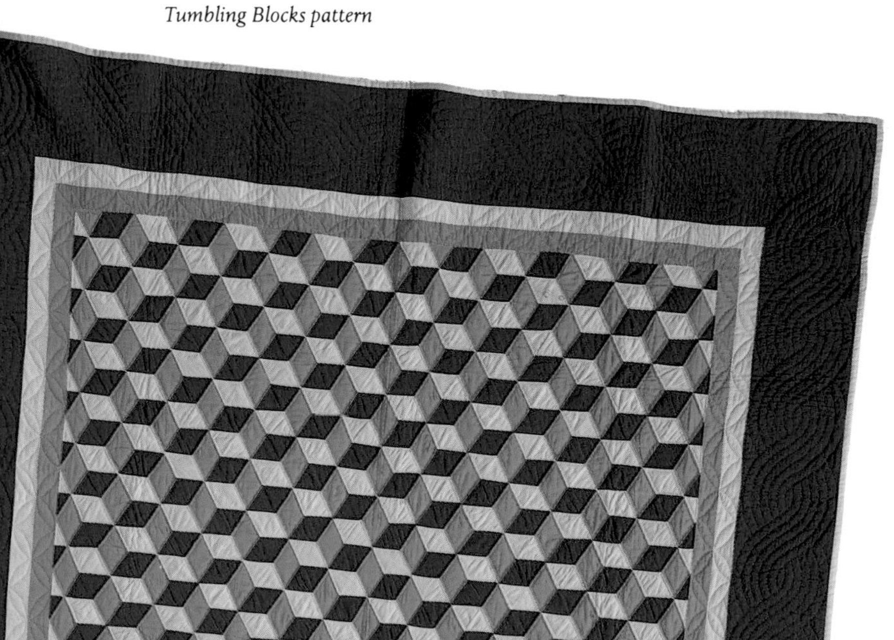

Octagons

Dark and light

Garden Path

Split hexagons

Clamshells

Triangles

Diamond variation

Two-tone Diamonds

3-D Diamonds

Multi-colored Diamonds

Sashiko patterns

Most Sashiko patterns are basic geometric shapes built into simple or complex repeat patterns. On quilted kimonos, Japanese designers often used many different patterns in asymmetric shapes (as we did for the evening bag on page 118). Some of these patterns are very straightforward and can be stitched using long straight or curving lines of stitching; others are more complex and have numerous corners or angles, but once you have marked your fabric clearly, the designs are all easy to stitch. If you use several patterns on a project, choose a variety of curves and straight lines, squares, circles and triangles, zigzags, and wavy lines.

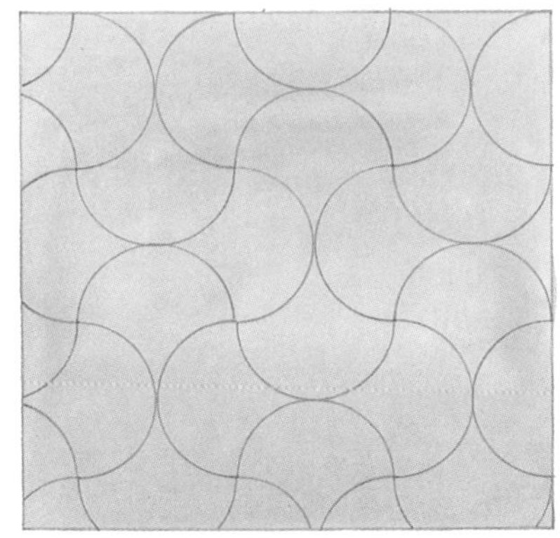

Curved lines

Interlocking lines

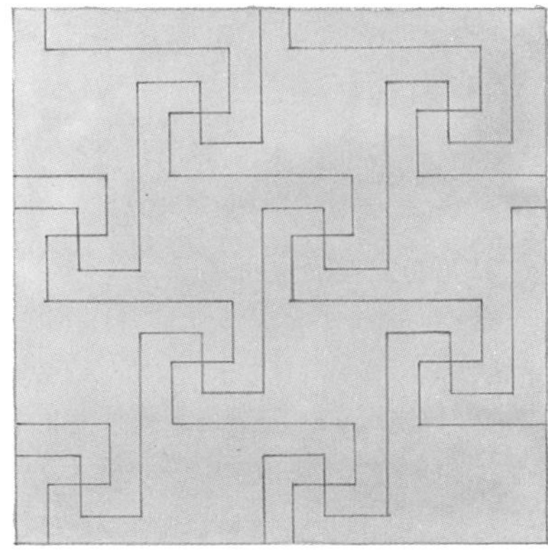

Squares and Corners

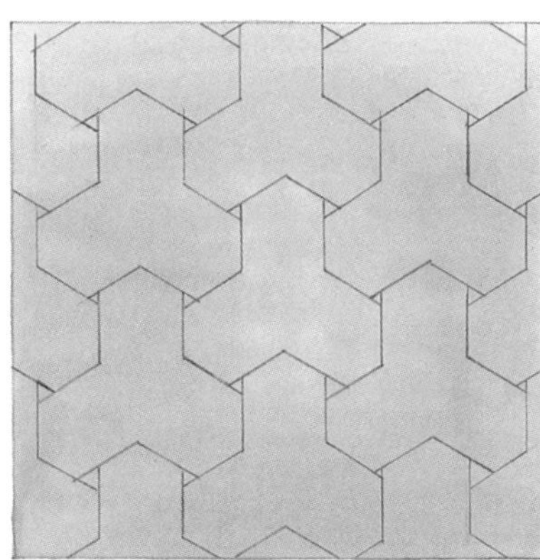

Interlocking shapes

Sashiko jacket quilted with several different patterns

Circles within circles

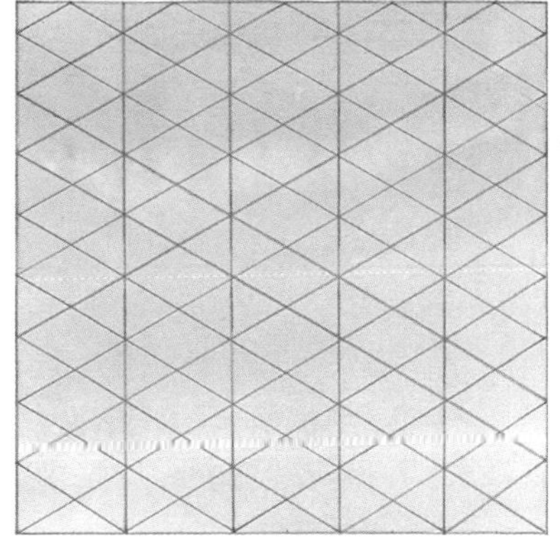

Diamonds

Arches

Peaks

Trellis pattern

Clouds

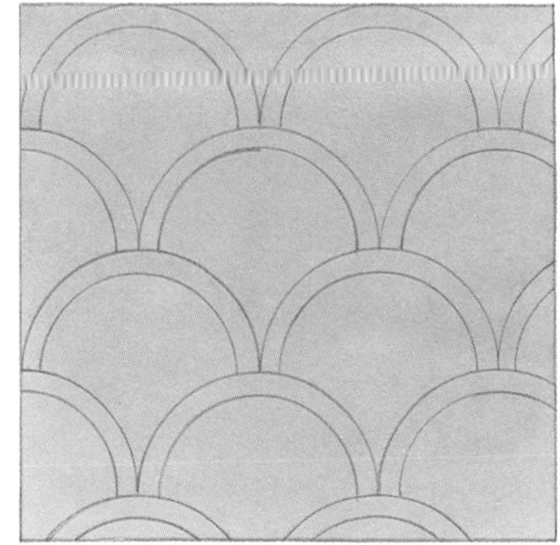

Clamshells

Crosses and Squares

Corners

The two quilts on this page, dating from the late 18th century, show how well quilts retain their color and vibrancy if looked after properly.

Restoring and caring for quilts

Every quilter dreams of browsing through the attic and discovering an immaculately stitched and perfectly preserved quilt. But the days of magical finds are generally over; most people are aware of the intrinsic value of such beautiful pieces and have rescued them from family storage to use or sell. The most likely way to acquire an old quilt today is to buy it.

Quilts in good condition command high prices, especially if they are detailed. Before you begin any restoration efforts, remember that like any valuable antique, your quilt will depreciate in value if you alter it in any significant way, so you need to decide whether you have bought it as an investment or for your own use or pleasure. If you have bought it as an investment, it will be fine to clean it as long as you don't damage it in any way. If you plan to use it, you may want to restore it by repairing or even replacing damaged sections.

Cleaning old quilts is a very delicate matter; the cleaning process may damage them irreparably. The fabrics may not be colorfast or may not have been preshrunk. The battings may not be washable, and in any case, anything but the most gentle handwashing is likely to damage old fabrics. Always test any soap or cleaning substance on a tiny, unnoticeable area of the quilt in case of disasters. Use cold water, as this is less likely to make fabric colors run; always use the minimum amount of water.

If the fabrics are in good condition, you may want to try dry cleaning, though the quilt may not be robust enough to withstand it. If you know what fibers were used in the fabric and batting, the dry cleaner will be able to advise you better. If you aren't bothered about keeping the quilt exactly as it was, you can gently unpick a small area to check the batting and see if an inner backing fabric was used.

If you want to restore a quilt, you may have to replace worn fabrics or stitching. If a

seam has come apart, try to repair it with a ladder stitch so you can work from the right side but still produce an invisible join. If you have to replace pieces of fabric because they have worn through or have been damaged by moths or mold, try to find a fabric as much in keeping with the original as possible. Carefully cut the seams of the damaged pieces of fabric to separate them from the rest of the quilt, and use them as templates for cutting new pieces. Stitch as many of the seams as you can in the conventional way, then use ladder stitch to insert the new sections, requilting if necessary.

Old batting tends to flatten and bunch up. You may be able to fluff it up a little by holding a steam iron just an inch or so away from the quilt surface so the steam can penetrate the quilt. Be careful not to scorch the fabric. If the batting has bunched up beyond remedy but the pieced quilt top is still in good condition, you might consider removing the backing fabric and batting and requilting the quilt over new batting. If parts of the quilt are beyond redemption and the thought of cutting up an old quilt doesn't horrify you, cut out a good section and use it as a baby quilt, a pillow top, to decorate a piece of clothing, or mounted as a picture.

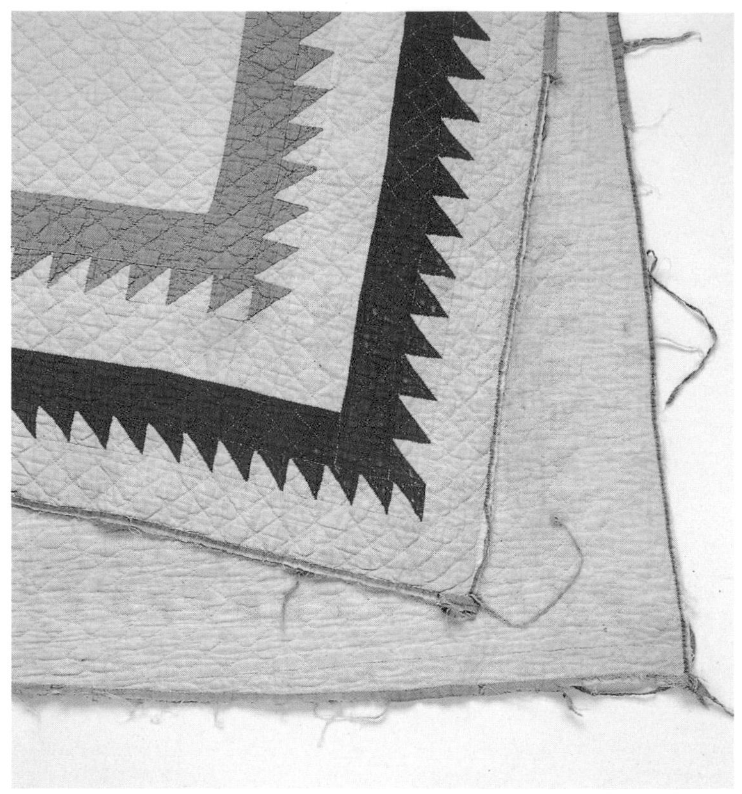

Quilts can become damaged very easily if not handled with care. Edging is particularly vulnerable to fraying through general wear and tear.

There are many ways of displaying quilts. Attach fabric casing or tape loops (see right and middle) to the back of the quilt along one edge. The quilt can now be hung from a rod.

Although many gallery and museum quilts are constantly on display, protective measures are taken to insure they don't fade or gather dirt. When displaying a quilt at home, avoid strong light and excessive moisture, and try to keep it in a constant temperature.

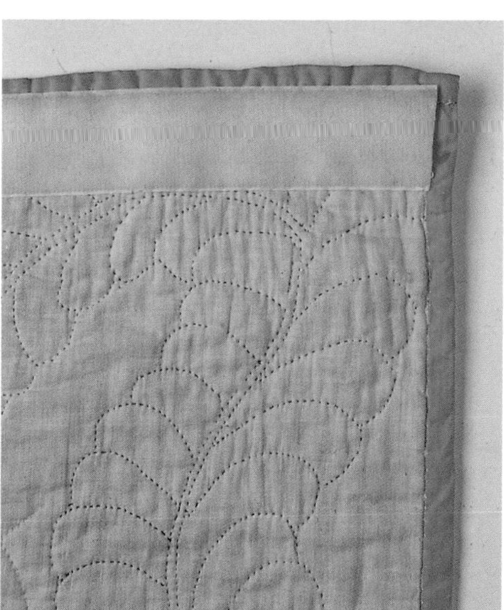

Sew Velcro strips (right) to fabric and attach the fabric to the back of the quilt. Sew the Velcro loops to a fabric-covered frame or other surface. The quilt can now be stretched and hung using the Velcro fastenings.

Glossary

ALBUM QUILT
A quilt made up of different appliqué blocks, sometimes all the same but often with different designs in each block; also called a Baltimore quilt.

AMISH QUILT
A distinctive style of quilting of the Amish, a religious group known for their simple lifestyle.

APPLIQUÉ
A decorative technique which involves stitching one piece of fabric on top of another.

BACKING FABRIC
A piece of fabric, often plain, used to back a quilt or other item.

BACKSTITCH
An embroidery stitch used to create a firm line or outline.

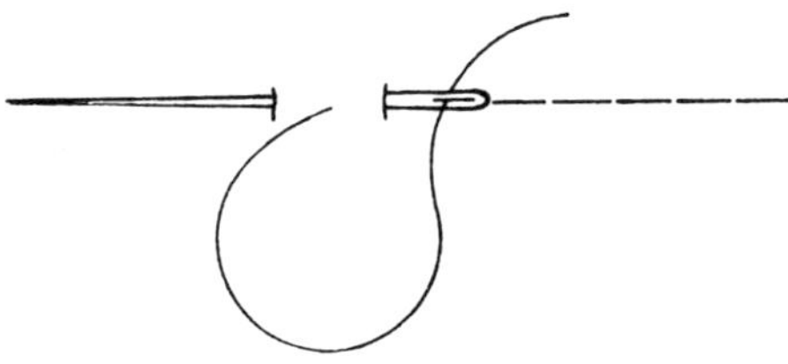

BASTING STITCH
A long, running stitch used to hold fabrics in place temporarily.

BATTING
A layer of padding for quilted work made of natural or synthetic fibers and available in several thicknesses.

BIAS BINDING
A narrow strip of fabric, cut diagonally across the grain; used for binding seams and edges, especially curves.

BINDING
The edging of a quilt which covers and holds all raw edges. Bindings may be plain or decorative.

BLOCK
A small section of patchwork, usually square; most quilts are made from a number of pieced blocks joined together.

BODKIN
A large needle with a large eye used for pulling cord, thick yarn, elastic, etc., through a casing or channel.

BORDER
A decorative pattern which runs around the edges of a quilt top. Borders may be straight, curved, flowing, swagged, and may be pieced or quilted or both.

BRODERIE ANGLAISE
An embroidered lace, white eyelet on white cotton, available as fabric or edging.

BRODERIE PERSE
An appliqué technique using motifs cut from printed fabric.

CASING
A channel of fabric or tape stitched to the back of a quilt through which a rod is inserted.

CATHEDRAL WINDOW PATCHWORK
Patchwork which involves folding squares of fabric into "frames"; the "windows" are filled with contrasting fabric. Sometimes called Mayflower patchwork.

CHARM QUILT
A pieced quilt in which every piece is the same shape, but cut from a different fabric.

CORDED QUILTING
Another name for Italian quilting.

CRAZY QUILT
Quilt made from random sizes and shapes of fancy fabrics such as velvets and silks; the patchwork is embellished with ornate embroidery along seam lines.

CUTTING MAT
A vinyl mat used under a rotary cutter.

DRESSMAKER'S CARBON PAPER
Colored carbon paper used for transferring designs or patterns onto fabric.

ECHO QUILTING
Concentric lines of quilting stitches worked around an outline at regular intervals.

ENGLISH PATCHWORK
A patchwork technique in which the fabric patches are basted over paper templates, then joined before the templates are removed.

FABRIC PAINT
Craft paint formulated for use on fabric; may be specific to particular fibers such as silk. Many fabric paints require heat to be set permanently.

FADING INK PEN
A pen used for marking quilting patterns on fabric; ink fades naturally in light over time.

FOLDED PATCHWORK
Pieced work made from fabric folded into points; typically assembled in star patterns.

FOUR-PATCH BLOCK
A patchwork design made from four rectangular pieces; individual squares can be pieced designs as well.

FRAME
A device used for stretching fabric flat. Quilting frames may be fairly small or large enough for an entire quilt top.

GRAIN
The straight warp or weft of a fabric. The direction of the grain is very important when cutting patchwork pieces or pattern designs.

GRAPH PAPER
Paper marked into small squares and used for drawing templates and patterns; also used to reduce and enlarge designs.

HEM
A finished edge, usually made by folding a raw edge over twice and stitching it down.

HOOP
A circular or oval quilting frame.

ITALIAN QUILTING
A decorative method of threading cord or yarn through channels stitched onto a double layer of fabric.

KAPA LAU
Hawaiian appliqué quilting; large, complex designs are appliquéd onto a background fabric and enhanced with echo quilting.

LADDER STITCH
Used for making an invisible seam from the right side.

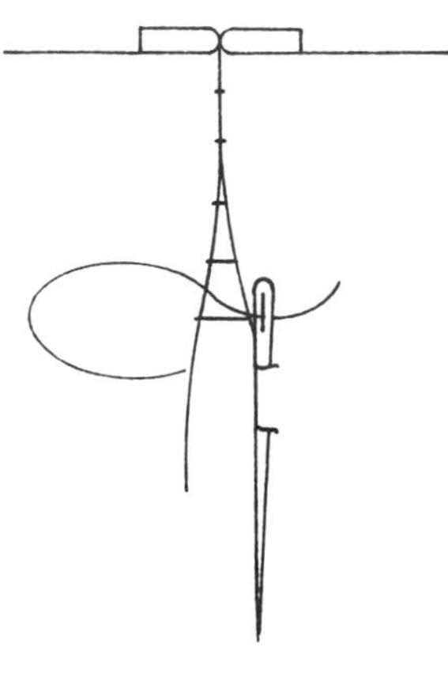

LIGHT BOX
A box with light inside and opaque glass on top; used in quilting for tracing patterns onto fabric or paper.

MEDALLION QUILT
A quilt design featuring one large central pattern or motif.

METALLICS
Fabrics or threads which have a metallic appearance.

MITERED CORNERS
Corners of a binding which are joined with a diagonal (45°) seam rather than with a straight one.

MUSLIN
Inexpensive plain weave cotton fabric often used as a backing fabric or a layer under batting.

NINE-PATCH BLOCK
A square block design made from nine square patches, three across and three down. Individual squares may be pieced designs in themselves.

ON POINT
Mounting a square block at an angle in a quilt top so that it appears as a diamond.

PATCHWORK
Joining one or more fabric shapes to make a pattern.

PIECING
Another name for patchwork.

PRICK AND POUNCE
Transferring designs to fabric by making holes along the main lines of the paper patterns and dusting chalk or other powder through the holes onto the fabric.

QUILTER'S QUARTER
A rectangular plastic rod used for adding $^1/_4$ in seam allowances to straight edges of fabrics or templates.

QUILTING
Stitching a decorative pattern through three layers, usually quilt top, batting, and backing.

QUILTING BEE
A group of people working together on the same quilt.

QUILTING IN THE DITCH
Quilting in which the stitching lines run next to the seam lines.

QUILTING NEEDLE
A short, fine needle helpful for making tiny quilting stitches.

QUILTING THREAD
A strong thread, often waxed, made specifically for quilting; available in many colors.

ROLLING FRAME
A large frame to hold a whole quilt; most of the quilt is scrolled onto the end rollers, leaving one section exposed for quilting.

ROTARY CUTTER
A circular blade used for cutting several layers of fabric simultaneously.

RUFFLE
A gathered edging of fabric or lace.

RUNNING STITCH
A straight stitch, used for most hand quilting.

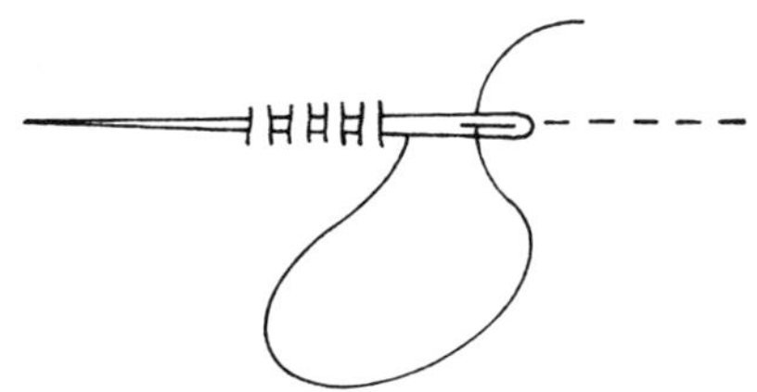

SATIN STITCH
A stitch with a very short length; each stitch touches the next.

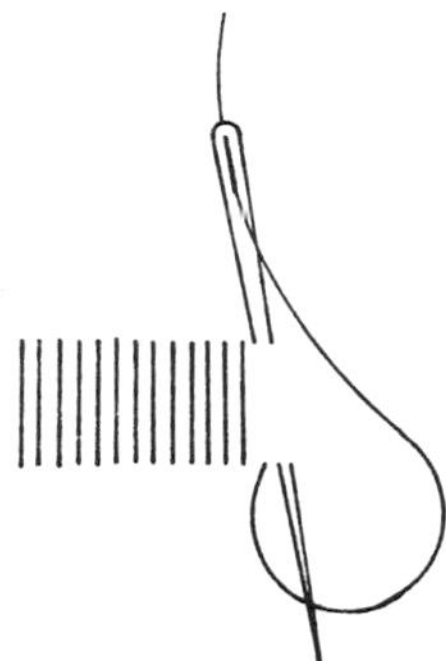

SASHIKO
A Japanese style of quilting, worked with long stitches in repetitive, often geometric, patterns.

SASHING
Strips of fabric used to separate blocks on a quilt top.

SILVERPOINT
Pencil-shaped metal implement used for marking quilting designs onto fabric.

SOMERSET PATCHWORK
One type of folded patchwork.

STAINED GLASS PATCHWORK
Patchwork method where the seams between fabrics are covered with strips of bias to simulate "leading."

STRAIGHT BINDING
A method of binding the edges of a quilt with straight pieces of fabric cut exactly along the grain.

STRAIGHT STITCH
The standard sewing stitch; has length, but no width.

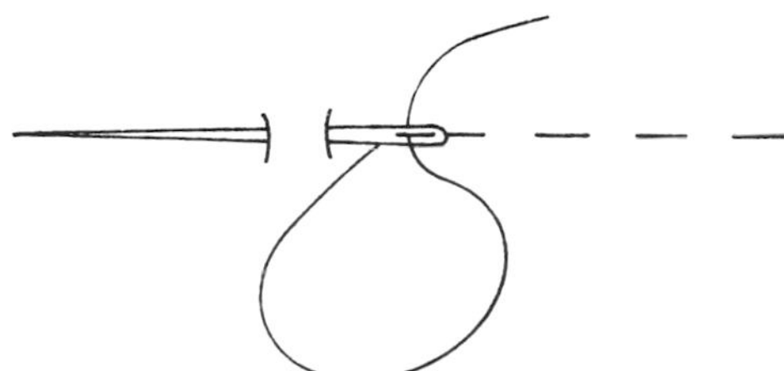

STUFFING
Soft fibers used for filling the pockets in trapunto quilting.

TEMPLATE
An accurate, full-size design used as a tracing and cutting guide; may be made from plastic, metal, paper, or cardboard.

TEMPLATE PLASTIC
A transparent or translucent plastic sheet ideal for making templates.

TONE
The shade of a particular color.

TRAPUNTO
A quilting technique which adds extra stuffing to small pockets stitched into a double layer of fabric.

VALUE
The lightness or darkness of a color.

VELCRO
A fastening material in which one layer of small plastic hooks adheres to another layer of small loops.

WALKING FOOT
A sewing machine foot to enable top and bottom fabric layers to feed at same speed.

WATER-SOLUBLE INK PEN
A pen used for marking quilting patterns on fabric; ink fades when sponged with water.

WHOLECLOTH QUILTING
A quilting method where the top layer is a single large piece of fabric; the design is made with quilting stitches rather than patchwork.

ZIGZAG
A basic machine sewing back-and-forth stitch; has width as well as length.

Index

Page references in *italics* refer to pictures.